In The Names Of God

Sylvia Gunter

Blessings In The Names And Nature
Of Your Father

In The Names Of God

Blessings In The Names And Nature Of Your Father

by Sylvia Gunter

Published by The Father's Business
P. O. Box 380333
Birmingham, AL 35238-0333 USA

www.thefathersbusiness.com
info@thefathersbusiness.com

Fourth printing.

Cover design
by Jan Gannaway

ISBN 978-1-931379-18-2

Table Of Contents

Looking Unto Jesus

Epilogue

Scriptures And Resources

Dedication

To God Our Father Who Blesses

The LORD said to Moses, "Tell Aaron and his sons,
'This is how you are to bless the Israelites. Say to them:
' "The LORD bless you and keep you;
the LORD make his face shine upon you and be gracious to you;
the LORD turn his face toward you and give you peace." '
Numbers 6:22-26

And to all who are blessed in his names and nature

"So they will put my name on the Israelites, and I will bless them."
Numbers 6:27

From the fullness of his grace
we have all received one blessing after another.
John 1:16

Introduction

My life message is who God is and who I am in Christ because of who He is, and blessing the spirit is the single most powerful tool I have used to get this truth from the head to the heart. **There are multitudes of people who don't know who they are**, because their soul, their role as a mother/father/good Christian/you-name-it, has defined who they are, instead of God awakening their spirit to know who they are in Him. **God wants us to discover Him with our spirit**. We can read Scriptures with our minds without having them penetrate as the Living Word into our spirits. **There are names and ways of God** He wants to write on our hearts. **There's more freedom** when Jesus is free to be unhindered in us. If we want to be whole, our spirit and soul must be free.

We all need the ministry of blessing. Very few of us have received blessing throughout our life, and few of us have received the affirmation we need. Our parents didn't know to do that. But God is outside time and is our ever-present Father. Everything is present tense to Him in eternity, so He somehow can re-parent the places that are deficient in our lives. Mark 10:13,16 says, "People were bringing little children to Jesus to have him touch them… And he took the children in his arms, put his hands on them, and blessed them." When I began receiving blessing, I knew I was different inside, as my spirit stirred and reaped the benefits of blessing. I began doing for others what I had received through the ministry of blessing. I began to write blessings for the spirit. These blessings have gone around the world, because they fell on people's spirit like water on thirsty ground.

Thousands of people, all kinds of people in all kinds of life situations, have been blessed. Many have said that they felt like they have come alive all over again. We have hundreds of testimonies… husbands and wives blessing each other, parents blessing children of all ages, including adult children, teachers blessing students in classrooms, parents blessing autistic children, people blessing total strangers on the phone, counselors blessing clients, desperate people who have found a lifeline through the blessings.

Many people have shared with me their experience. Just one story: A lady told me that she said to God one morning "I am in a war zone!" Later that day she read a blessing that said "I bless your spirit as a sanctuary, not a war zone." Imagine all the time and circumstances God engineered for that perfect timing! Nothing surprises me when people begin a glory story with "You will never believe what happened!" Oh, yes, I believe it. God has powerfully and tenderly met His children in sweet fellowship through the blessings many many times in very creative and life-giving ways.

Overview Of Spirit And Soul

What is the human spirit? Our spirit is the essence of who we are. We are a spirit being. God made us a living spirit. We are a living essence from God (spirit), that he gave an expression (soul) in a tangible physical package (the body). We are a living spirit who has a soul housed in an earthly body.

God's pattern is spirit, soul, body in that order, not the other way around, as Paul says in 1 Thessalonians 5:23. "May God himself, the God of peace, sanctify you through and through. May your whole spirit, soul and body be kept blameless at the coming of our Lord Jesus Christ." Yet people most often quote that verse as body, soul, and spirit. That's how we have lived our lives, leading from our bodily appetites and soul satisfactions.

God's design is that we respond to him and life out of our spirits led by his Spirit. Our spirit should lead our soul and body to glorify Jesus. Jesus in his humanity let his Father be seen in all his glory. In our spirit we let him be seen. Every day we have to choose to let Jesus in us respond out of our spirits, instead of reacting out of our souls and bodies.

Years ago I heard Graham Cooke teach, "Take a step back into your spirit, and ask God what he sees, how he wants you to respond." This changes my observations of people and events around me. When God leads my spirit to respond to the spirit of others, I may see that their spirit is trapped in a dysfunctional arrangement of the soul being large and in charge. This allows me to bless the perfect work that the Holy Spirit wants to do in their spirit from his residence in them, even while I may suffer the consequences of the immaturity or carnality of their soul. The spirit of another person is not my enemy. Their spirit is made in the image of God, but their soul has been well-fed and catered to, and he may be dominating from his heavy-weight position.

In blessing the spirit, we acknowledge the spirit and invite it to its place of priority and leadership over the soul and body. When it takes the place that God designed for it, when it listens to the voice of the Father, and when it obeys him in all things, he'll connect the dots and answer with great and mighty things we don't know how to ask for. His purposes for our identity, worth, maturity, and fulfillment will shine forth.

When their spirits are blessed, people have remarkable breakthroughs because something happens in their spirit, and it gives them a fresh breath of life and causes alignment with their heavenly Father. Those whose spirits are open can sense life and growth in the blessing.

The relationship of spirit to soul is somewhat like a marriage. It is a beautiful partnership, but there are times when someone has to lead and someone has to follow. I defer to my husband because he is the head of our household. It's not about whether I matter. Of course, I matter, and I have been chosen by God to bring forth my own contributions of function, beauty, and relationship. But for my good and our good, there are times when he needs to lead. At times he defers to me. That's the beauty of mutual relationship.

The relationship of the spirit, soul, and body is similar. The spirit has the responsibility to lead under the direction of the Father, Son, and Holy Spirit for the benefit of the soul and body. My soul will become healthier and more whole as it takes its proper place in God's design. It is a matter of function. The spirit initiates change and leads in God's transformation, and the soul responds and adds its own unique God-designed contributions. The harmony of the whole is truly beautiful.

Two examples may help illustrate this point. I like the picture of playing follow the leader to explain the relationship of spirit, soul, and body. Children love to play follow the leader. The soul falls in behind the spirit as the leader, and the body joins them, so that they can enjoy the game. The picture of dance partners also speaks to me about how the soul relates to the spirit. It's a beautiful dance when the spirit leads the soul around the dance floor, without the soul trying to lead or stepping on the spirit's toes. It's a magnificent partnership of form and grace.

Janelle Brown tells of a prayer time with her prayer partner of many years. "I surprised myself by praying a prayer that was paradigm-shifting. From deep within, an excitement propelled me to pray in essence, 'Lord, my mind is on the throne of my life, but I am asking You to help me change that. I repent for my mind being in control and letting my spirit rule only occasionally. Lord, forgive me for making it hard for my spirit to guide me under Your rulership. I transfer rulership of me to my human spirit under the authority of Your Holy Spirit. As I do this, I have great confidence that I will be able to live in Your heart and that You actually desire me to live intimately with You while I am still on my earth assignment. I believe You will make it possible for my spirit to be in charge under Your Holy Spirit. I am asking You to do that. In Jesus' Name. Amen.' "[1]

God began to confirm to Janelle the importance of her human spirit being a proactive player in her life. Like all of us, her human spirit had acted principally as a passive conduit of divine life, not the subject of her conscious attention. She says, "Our human spirit is our nexus with the Holy Spirit of God, who is helping us explore the mystery of our original design... A proactive human spirit will offer us a better access to the Father Heart of God and will forever change our ability to live the Christian life... An accurate understanding of the relationship between our spirit and our soul would be key to moving deeper with God."

[1]By permission of Janelle Brown, goodnewsgal@bellsouth.net

Biblical Basis

How have we missed having a theology of the human spirit? This concept stands on biblical ground. Over 100 Scriptures document biblical references to the human spirit. One of the names of God is Father of our spirits (Heb. 12:9). Another name is God of the spirits of all mankind (Num. 16:22).

Let's review some verses from the gospels that mention the human spirit.

Matthew 5:3 "Blessed are the poor in spirit, for theirs is the kingdom of heaven."

Matthew 26:41 "Watch and pray so that you will not fall into temptation. The spirit is willing, but the body is weak."

Mark 2:8 Immediately Jesus knew in his spirit that this was what they were thinking in their hearts, and he said to them, "Why are you thinking these things?"

Mark 8:12 NKJV But He sighed deeply in His spirit…

Luke 1:46-47 Mary said: "My soul glorifies the Lord and my spirit rejoices in God my Savior."

Luke 1:80 And the child grew and became strong in spirit; and he lived in the desert until he appeared publicly to Israel (speaking of John the Baptist).

Luke 2:40 NKJV And the Child grew and became strong in spirit, filled with wisdom; and the grace of God was upon Him (speaking of Jesus).

Luke 23:46 Jesus called out with a loud voice, "Father, into your hands I commit my spirit."

John 4:23-24 "Yet a time is coming and has now come when the true worshipers will worship the Father in spirit and truth, for they are the kind of worshipers the Father seeks. God is spirit, and his worshipers must worship in spirit and in truth."

John 13:21 After he had said this, Jesus was troubled in spirit…

John 19:30 When he had received the drink, Jesus said, "It is finished." With that, he bowed his head and gave up his spirit.

Now read some of the references to the human spirit in the letters.

Romans 1:9 NKJV God is my witness, whom I serve with my spirit in the gospel of His Son…

Romans 8:15 NKJV For you did not receive the spirit of bondage again to fear, but you received the Spirit of adoption by whom we cry out, "Abba, Father."
16 The Spirit Himself bears witness with our spirit that we are children of God,

Romans 12:11 NKJV …not lagging in diligence, fervent in spirit, serving the Lord.

1 Corinthians 2:11 Who among men knows the thoughts of a man except the man's spirit within him? In the same way no one knows the thoughts of God except the Spirit of God.

1 Corinthians 4:21 Shall I come to you with a whip, or in love and with a gentle spirit?

1 Corinthians 6:17 But he who is joined to the Lord is one spirit with Him.

1 Corinthians 6:20 NKJV For you were bought at a price; therefore glorify God in your body and in your spirit, which are God's.

1 Corinthians 7:34 The unmarried woman cares about the things of the Lord, that she may be holy both in body and in spirit.

1 Corinthians 14:2 For anyone who speaks in a tongue does not speak to men but to God. Indeed, no one understands him; he utters mysteries with his spirit.

1 Corinthians 14:15-16 So what shall I do? ... pray with my spirit ... sing with my spirit ... praising God with my spirit...

1 Corinthians 15:45 And so it is written, "The first man Adam became a living being." The last Adam became a life-giving spirit.

1 Corinthians 16:18 They refreshed my spirit and yours also. Such men deserve recognition.

2 Corinthians 2:13 NKJV I had no rest in my spirit, because I did not find Titus my brother.

2 Corinthians 7:1 Therefore, having these promises, beloved, let us cleanse ourselves from all filthiness of the flesh and spirit, perfecting holiness in the fear of God.

2 Corinthians 7:13 His spirit has been refreshed by all of you.

1 Thessalonians 5:23 Now may the God of peace Himself sanctify you completely; and may your whole spirit, soul, and body be preserved blameless at the coming of our Lord Jesus Christ.

2 Timothy 1:7 NKJV For God has not given us a spirit of fear...

Hebrews 4:12 For the word of God is living and powerful, and sharper than any two-edged sword, piercing even to the division of soul and spirit, and of joints and marrow, and is a discerner of the thoughts and intents of the heart.

James 4:5 Or do you think Scripture says without reason that the spirit he caused to live in us envies intensely? (That refers to the human spirit. Greek did not have capital letters. They were inserted by translators. The NIV gives alternate translations at the bottom of the page: "Or that God jealously longs for the spirit that he made to live in us;" or that "the Spirit he caused to live in us longs jealously.") The English Standard Version speaks of the human spirit that dwells in us. James 4:5 ESV "Or do you suppose it is to no purpose that the Scripture says, "He yearns jealously over the spirit that he has made to dwell in us"?

1 Peter 3:4 Rather let it be the hidden person of the heart, with the incorruptible beauty of a gentle and quiet spirit, which is very precious in the sight of God.

There are 14 pages of scriptures about the human spirit and soul in the back of this book, beginning on page 205.

What's The Difference Between The Soul And Spirit?

The spirit and soul are portions of our being that we cannot see. According to Zodhiates,[1] "spirit (*pneuma*) is the element in man which gives him the ability to think of God. It is man's vertical window, while soul (*psuche*) is man's horizontal window making him conscious of his environment." The soul depends on the functioning of our brain, the heart, and the blood circulation to function to express itself. The spirit has a separate existence. Jesus affirmed this as he raised the dead daughter of Jaiarus. "He took [the girl] by the hand and said, "My child, get up!" Her spirit returned, and at once she stood up. Then Jesus told them to give her something to eat. Her parents were astonished" (Luke 8:54-56). Her spirit was separate from her body, and her body needed her spirit to live.

Let's illustrate this in a modern setting: Before surgery, the body and soul of a person are "put to sleep" under general anesthesia. The anesthesia doesn't go into the soul, but when the consciousness of the body is no longer functioning, the soul cannot speak or comment on the people and events in the operating room. It cannot receive information and process it and release it under anesthesia, so the soul depends on the body.

From the stories of people who have died in surgery, we can say that the spirit seems to stand apart from anesthesia. People have died and come back. They report that their spirit left the body and perhaps went to an upper part of the room and watched the commotion. The spirit may go out through a tunnel or vortex of light. It has an encounter with God or a loved one. The person is told that he needs to go back. He doesn't want to come back, but he does. The person often says that he comes back through the same tunnel or portal, he enters the room, he enters the body, and the body starts functioning again. Later the soul can report what the spirit experienced.

We can deduce that the spirit has memory, it can recall the story. It has will— it wanted to stay but came back. It has emotions— it responds to things on the other side being beautiful and emotional. We've been told that the soul is mind, will, and emotion. But our spirit also has mind (it can think), will (it can receive or resist), and emotion (it can feel joy or disappointment, for example). Memory resides in two places in our brain, so there are four components of memory: spirit memory, soul memory, left hemisphere (hippocampus) memory, and right hemisphere (amygdala) memory in the brain.

How Do We Distinguish Between Spirit And Soul?

According to Hebrews 4:12, God distinguishes between soul and spirit. "For the word of God is living and active. Sharper than any double-edged sword, it penetrates even to dividing soul and spirit, joints and marrow; it judges the thoughts and attitudes of the heart." The human spirit is eternal. It functions without being completely controlled by the body. It will be alive after this earthly body ceases to exist.

Vine's Expository Dictionary says this in its discussion of the soul. "The language of Hebrews 3:12 suggest the extreme difficulty of distinguishing between the soul and the spirit, alike in their nature and activities. Generally speaking, the spirit is the higher, the soul the lower element. The spirit may be recognized as the life principle bestowed on man by

God, the soul as the resulting life constituted in the individual, the body being the material organism animated by soul and spirit." [2] We are a living spirit, we have a soul, we live in a body.

We don't begin to understand it all, but we can learn how to engage and bless the spirit distinct from the soul. Psalm 139:14 in the NKJV says, "I will praise You, for I am fearfully and wonderfully made; Marvelous are Your works, and that my soul knows very well." Does that mean that the soul knows the spirit is marvelously made by God? Listen to Mary, the mother of Jesus, giving insight into the cooperation of her soul and spirit in Luke 1:46-47 NKJV. "My soul magnifies the Lord, and my spirit has rejoiced in God my Savior."

How can we tell which is trying to exert itself? The spirit seeks God's highest and greatest and best. The soul usually seeks self's greatest satisfaction, unless the spirit is leading. It is the difference between responding to God in circumstances and reacting to the circumstances. Don't you want people to meet your spirit first thing, so that your spirit makes an impression on them, instead of your soul?

War Between The Soul And The Spirit — Romans 7:22 – 8:11,16

The Bible says that the soul can't receive the things of the Spirit. "As it is written: 'No eye has seen, no ear has heard, no mind has conceived what God has prepared for those who love him'— but God has revealed it to us by his Spirit. The Spirit searches all things, even the deep things of God. For who among men knows the thoughts of a man except the man's spirit within him? In the same way no one knows the thoughts of God except the Spirit of God. We have not received the spirit of the world but the Spirit who is from God, that we may understand what God has freely given us" (1 Cor. 2:9-12).

All of us have experienced an inner wrestling match, a civil war inside. Galatians 5:16 says, "So I say, live by the Spirit, and you will not gratify the desires of the sinful nature. 17 For the sinful nature desires what is contrary to the Spirit, and the Spirit what is contrary to the sinful nature. They are in conflict with each other, so that you do not do what you want. 18 But if you are led by the Spirit, you are not under law. 19 The acts of the sinful nature are obvious: sexual immorality, impurity and debauchery; 20 idolatry and witchcraft; hatred, discord, jealousy, fits of rage, selfish ambition, dissensions, factions, 21 and envy; drunkenness, orgies, and the like. I warn you, as I did before, that those who live like this will not inherit the kingdom of God. 22 But the fruit of the Spirit is love, joy, peace, patience, kindness, goodness, faithfulness, 23 gentleness and self-control. Against such things there is no law. 25 Since we live by the Spirit, let us keep in step with the Spirit."

Our mind is naturally at enmity with God, so we must develop a dynamic of victory within our spirit.

[1] *The Complete Word Study New Testament with Parallel Greek*, Spiros Zodhiates, © 1992, AMG International, Inc. Page 931.

[2] *An Expository Dictionary Of New Testament Words*, W. E. Vine, no copyright in the volume I have. Riverside Book And Bible House, Iowa Falls, IA. Page 1067.

What Does It Mean To Be Filled With The Spirit?

Being filled with the Spirit means being so entirely occupied and controlled with God's Spirit that there is no room for "me." It is not a certain religious experience, but a moment-by-moment relationship with Jesus whereby we are under his gracious control in everything we think, do, and say in our spirit, soul, and body. When our spirit is controlled by his Spirit and is in authority over our soul and body, our whole being is aligned with and conformed to God's truth, his person, and his intention for us. When our spirit is centered in the fruit of his Spirit and is larger than our soul, it takes care of a lot of things, including agreeing with satan's lies, discouragement, and depression. To bless the spirit invites us to freedom from self. We soar above the abuses, rejections, and unforgiveness that the soul nurses. We can in our spirit receive God's river of grace and respond with love and forgiveness and joy.

SPIRIT	**Hebrew Strong's Number:** 7307 **Hebrew Word:** רוּחַ **Transliteration:** rûaḥ **Phonetic Pronunciation:** roo'-akh **English Words used in KJV:** Spirit or spirit 232, wind 92, breath 27, side 6, mind 5, blast 4, vain 2, air 1, anger 1, cool 1, courage 1, misc 6 **Total Count:** 378	**Greek Strong's Number:** 4151 **Greek Word:** πνεῦμα **Transliteration:** pneuma **Phonetic Pronunciation:** pnyoo'-mah **English Words used in KJV:** Spirit 111, (Holy) Ghost 89, Spirit (of God) 13, Spirit (of the Lord) 5, (My) Spirit 3, Spirit (of truth) 3, Spirit (of Christ) 2, human (spirit) 49, (evil) spirit 47, spirit (general) 26, spirit 8, (Jesus') spirit 6, (Jesus') ghost 2, misc 21 **Total Count:** 385
SOUL	**Hebrew Strong's Number:** 5315 **Hebrew Word:** נֶפֶשׁ **Transliteration:** nepesh **Phonetic Pronunciation:** neh'-fesh **English Words used in KJV:** soul 475, life 117, person 29, mind 15, heart 15, creature 9, body 8, himself 8, yourselves 6, dead 5, will 4, desire 4, man 3, themselves 3, any 3, appetite 2, misc 47 **Total Count:** 753	**Greek Strong's Number:** 5590 **Greek Word:** ψυχή **Transliteration:** psychē **Phonetic Pronunciation:** psoo-khay' **English Words used in KJV:** soul 58, life 40, mind 3, heart 1, heartily 1, not tr 2, **Total Count:** 105
BODY	**Hebrew Strong's Number:** 1320 **Hebrew Word:** בָּשָׂר **Transliteration:** bāśār **Phonetic Pronunciation:** baw-sawr' **English Words used in KJV:** flesh 256 , body 2, fat-fleshed 2, lean-fleshed 3, kin 2, mankind 1, myself 1, nakedness 1, skin 1 **Total Count:** 269	**Greek Strong's Number:** 4983 **Greek Word:** σῶμα **Transliteration:** sōma **Phonetic Pronunciation:** so'-mah **English Words used in KJV:** body 144, bodily 1, slave 1 **Total Count:** 146

What Does It Mean To Bless?

Why bless? What does it mean to bless and receive a blessing? What is our authority to bless? What is the priestly function of that? The Bible was written in and to a culture that was steeped in blessing — the blessing of shalom, blessing the child with his name, the patriarchal blessing to the sons, the blessing of God for his people, the blessing of Jesus, of the disciples, of the early church, of Peter, Paul, and James in the New Testament, and the new kingdom of priests that we are since the cross.

Our culture doesn't understand blessing as it was practiced in the Bible. All we have known about blessing is very shallow vague good wishes or a liturgical way to end a church service ("Please stand for the benediction"). In fact, many people think benediction means "the end, good bye." Benediction means well-speaking or blessing. In the Bible, blessing flows three ways: from God to people, from people to God, and from person to person. You may have wondered if you can bless others. Can we do that? Here are some Scriptures that speak to that.

Blessing was one of the duties of the priests.
Deuteronomy 10:8 At that time the LORD set apart the tribe of Levi to carry the ark of the covenant of the LORD, to stand before the LORD to minister, and to pronounce blessings in his name, as they still do today.
1 Chronicles 30:27 The priests and the Levites stood to bless the people, and God heard them, for their prayer reached heaven, his holy dwelling place.
Leviticus 9:22 Then Aaron lifted his hands toward the people and blessed them.
Numbers 6:22-27 The LORD said to Moses, "Tell Aaron and his sons, 'This is how you are to bless the Israelites. Say to them:
' "The LORD bless you and keep you;
the LORD make his face shine upon you and be gracious to you;
the LORD turn his face toward you and give you peace." '
"So they will put my name on the Israelites, and I will bless them."

God said his people will be a blessing.
Genesis 12:2-3 "I will make your name great, and you will be a blessing...and all peoples on earth will be blessed through you."

The people of God understood it in the Old Testament.
Genesis 24:60 And they blessed Rebekah and said to her, "Our sister, may you increase to thousands upon thousands; may your offspring possess the gates of their enemies."
Genesis 49:28 All these are the twelve tribes of Israel, and this is what their father said to them when he blessed them, giving each the blessing appropriate to him.

Moses blessed.
Deuteronomy 33:1 This is the blessing that Moses the man of God pronounced on the Israelites before his death.

Even Balaam blessed.
Numbers 22:6 For I know that those you bless are blessed, and those you curse are cursed.

Joshua blessed the people.
Joshua 22:6 Then Joshua blessed them and sent them away.

Eli blessed Hannah and Elkanah.
1 Samuel 2:20 Eli would bless Elkanah and his wife, saying, "May the LORD give you children by this woman to take the place of the one she prayed for and gave to the LORD."

King David blessed the people.
1 Kings 8:14 While the whole assembly of Israel was standing there, the king turned around and blessed them.
1 Kings 8:55 He stood and blessed the whole assembly of Israel in a loud voice, saying…
1 Chronicles 16:2 After David had finished sacrificing the burnt offerings and fellowship offerings, he blessed the people in the name of the LORD.

The people blessed David.
I Kings 8:66 On the following day he sent the people away. They blessed the king and then went home, joyful and glad in heart for all the good things the LORD had done for his servant David and his people Israel.

Joab blessed the king.
2 Samuel 14:22 Joab … blessed the king.

David blessed his family.
1 Chronicles 16:43 David returned home to bless his family.

Blessing was understood in the Psalms.
Psalm 10:3 He blesses the greedy and reviles the LORD.
Psalm 109:17 He loved to pronounce a curse—may it come on him; he found no pleasure in blessing—may it be far from him. 28 They may curse, but you will bless…
Psalm 129:8 "The blessing of the LORD be upon you; we bless you in the name of the LORD."

Solomon blessed.
1 Kings 8:55 [Solomon] stood and blessed the whole assembly of Israel in a loud voice.

Blessing was commended in Proverbs.
Proverbs 30:11 There are those who curse their fathers and do not bless their mothers.
Proverbs 31:28 Her children arise and call her blessed; her husband also, and he praises her.
Song of Solomon 6:9 The maidens saw her and called her blessed.

The priest Simeon blessed Mary and the baby Jesus.
Luke 2:34 Then Simeon blessed them and said to Mary, his mother…

Jesus commanded his disciples to do it.
Luke 6:28 Bless those who curse you, pray for those who mistreat you.
Luke 10:5 When you enter a house, first say, 'Peace to this house.'

Jesus blessed.
Mark 10:16 [Jesus] took the children in his arms, put his hands on them and blessed them.
Luke 24:36 While they were still talking about this, Jesus himself stood among them and said to them, "Peace be with you."
John 20:21 Jesus said, "Peace be with you! As the Father has sent me, I am sending you."
Luke 24:50 When he had led them out to the vicinity of Bethany, he lifted up his hands and blessed them.

The early church blessed.
Acts 15:33 After spending some time there, they were sent off by the brothers with the blessing of peace to return to those who had sent them.

Paul commanded blessing.
Romans 12:14 Bless those who persecute you; bless and do not curse.

Paul blessed.
1 Corinthians 4:12 When we are cursed, we bless…
2 Corinthians 13:14 May the grace of the Lord Jesus Christ, and the love of God, and the fellowship of the Holy Spirit be with you all.
Romans 16:20b The grace of our Lord Jesus be with you.
Galatians 6:16 Peace and mercy to all who follow this rule, even to the Israel of God.
Galatians 6:18 The grace of our Lord Jesus Christ be with your spirit, brothers. Amen.
Philippians 4:23 The grace of the Lord Jesus Christ be with your spirit. Amen.
1 Thessalonians 5:23 May God himself, the God of peace, sanctify you through and through. May your whole spirit, soul and body be kept blameless at the coming of our Lord Jesus Christ.
2 Thessalonians 3:18 The grace of our Lord Jesus Christ be with you all.
2 Timothy 4:22 The Lord be with your spirit. Grace be with you.
Philemon 25 The grace of the Lord Jesus Christ be with your spirit.

Hebrews gives two examples of blessing in the faith hall of fame.
Hebrews 11:20 By faith Isaac blessed Jacob and Esau in regard to their future.
Hebrews 11:21 By faith Jacob, when he was dying, blessed each of Joseph's sons, and worshiped as he leaned on the top of his staff.

Peter commanded it.
1 Peter 3:9 Do not repay evil with evil or insult with insult, but with blessing, because to this you were called so that you may inherit a blessing.

Read a few more scriptural examples of blessing in the New Testament.

Acts 3:25-26 And you are heirs of the prophets and of the covenant God made with your fathers. He said to Abraham, 'Through your offspring all peoples on earth will be blessed.' When God raised up his servant, he sent him first to you to bless you by turning each of you from your wicked ways.

Hebrews 13:20 May the God of peace … 21 equip you with everything good for doing his will, and may he work in us what is pleasing to him, through Jesus Christ, to whom be glory for ever and ever. Amen.

1 Peter 5:14 Peace to all of you who are in Christ.

Revelation 22:21 The grace of the Lord Jesus be with God's people. Amen.

The blessings from the heart of God in this book echo the truth and practice of the Bible. Through them God brings forth our birthright to be all he wants us to be and from that place of wholeness to do all that he designed us to do.

Godly Boundaries Or Guidelines For Blessing The Spirit

Be careful to only bless with words that God wants you to use. Ask him and listen for his direction. It is best to invite the spirit to look into the face of God and get its specific instruction from him. Be careful not to mix in your own agenda. Don't use this as a manipulative or corrective tool to try to persuade people to do a certain thing. That is God's prerogative, not ours. We can use Bible promises and the commands in the Bible. We can safely use anything that Paul instructs us to be or do. For example,

- Be filled with the Spirit. Ephesians 5:18
- Live by the spirit and do not gratify the desires of the sinful nature. Galatians 5:16-17
- Against the fruit of the Spirit there is no law. Galatians 5:23
- Since we live by the spirit, keep in step with the spirit. Galatians 5:25
- Let us be alert and self-controlled. 1 Thessalonaians 5:6
- Put on faith and love as a breastplate, and the hope of salvation as a helmet. 1 Thessalonians 5:8
- The articles of the armor. Ephesians 6
- Grow up into Christ, who is the head. Ephesians 4:15

There are many more verses that could be cited.

Using Scripture For Blessing

Blessing the human spirit doesn't depend on any written blessing. The Bible is the blessing book that God wrote. Become a student of the Bible promises. We can listen for God to point out to us a verse or verses that he wants to turn into a blessing for ourselves or for others. He will take any passage of his Word and turn it into a blessing, and we know we are blessing according to his will.

My favorite and strongest blessings are using the names of God in blessing. Every name of God can be turned into a blessing, because he is who he is, and he is all that to his children all the time. In the words of a wonderful worship song, "His name is holy… his name is Savior… his name is awesome… his name is all that." He wants to be free to be all that in us unhindered.

How Is Blessing The Spirit Different From Praying For People?

Is there extra authority in blessing more than in prayer? Is there a difference? Does it matter which form we use? Jesus tells us to do both in Luke 6:28. "Bless those who curse you, pray for those who mistreat you." In all his letters, the apostle Paul blessed people and prayed for people.

Prayer: Lord, cause them to love you with all their heart.
Blessing: Be blessed with loving God with all your heart.

Prayer: Lord, let them know the voice of their Shepherd.
Blessing: Be blessed with knowing the voice of your Shepherd.

Can We Bless Our Own Spirit?

These blessings are designed for one person to read to another or for a person to read to himself. Most people can read the blessings to themselves, bless their own spirit, and experience significant transformation. Others cannot. We don't know what makes the difference, except that every person is fearfully and wonderfully made. If you cannot bless yourself, get a partner to bless you. One way or the other, just do it, because these blessings are transformational.

Do We Have To Be With A Person To Bless Their Spirit?

Can we bless someone at a distance? Of course, we can bless someone who is not present, the same way prayer works without the person being present. Their life will be impacted, even if they don't know we are doing it. Be careful to bless with the blessing that God wants you to give. Don't use this in a manipulative or corrective or directive way. That is not God. Bless the spirit, bottom line, to look into the face of God and get its specific instruction from him.

Can We Bless The Spirit Of A Pre-Christian?

The Bible says that the spirit will live eternally in heaven or hell, so everybody has a spirit. The pre-Christian's spirit is limited in what it can comprehend (1 Cor. 2:11-14), but the Holy Spirit is at work to draw the person to Jesus. Blessing seems to be a common language. Ask permission. Say, "May I bless you?" Generally people welcome it. If they say "no," then don't do it. Keep your blessing short and immediate, led of God to speak into their need, and use simple language. People are dying for a drink of the water of life. You can be that refreshment in the power of Jesus.

Can We Bless People's Spirits In A Group?

Certainly. Pastors and teachers are doing it every week. One pastor nearby is blessing the spirits of his congregation every Sunday with dynamic results. Not only can we do it, but we should do it. People who are large in spirit will more quickly respond to instruction in God's Word and by his Spirit. People whose spirits need to be awakened and nurtured will begin to engage with his Spirit in the truth of his Word.

How Do We Know If The Human Spirit Is Responding?

People will know when their spirit has responded. Many times, the spirit responds to the first blessing, but it may not. We may not know, except for what the person tells us. Engage their spirit, allow time, and in time the spirit will respond. Speak confidently in the direction of the spirit, because they have a spirit, and it needs blessing. If we speak the truth of God in the direction of somebody's inner being, even if their spirit doesn't seem to respond to us, we have spoken truth, and God promises it will not return to him void. Begin and keep doing it. It's not about us anyway; it's about him.

More About The Human Spirit

Working With The Human Spirit Does Not Replace What We Have Been Doing.

Blessing the spirit does not replace the prayer or counseling methods we have been using. Working with the human spirit adds another dimension to what we have been doing. It addresses an empty spot in our understanding. The majority of our methods have focused on three areas—the human soul (inner healing), the Holy Spirit (his role in healing), and unclean spirits (to be evicted by deliverance). Now we can deal with the soul, the Holy Spirit, unholy spirits, and the human spirit.

Some people have said, "I got deliverance, but it didn't work." The ministry was no doubt effective, but the spirit was not strong enough to occupy the ground that was taken. God repeatedly told the Israelites to go in and possess the land, which means to subdue it, occupy it, and control it. One battle may be a victory, but it is not the whole war. Our spirit must subdue and occupy the entire person with the truth of what God says, instead of the lies it has believed. Lies are the stock-in-trade of the father of lies. Knowing who we are in Christ takes away ground he seeks to control in us, and one of the best ways to know who we are in Christ is to receive it as blessing for our spirit.

John Wimber used to say that it is important that we approach every ministry time with an empty tool box. No matter how long or how often our ministry methods have worked in the past, there is no guarantee that that is how the Holy Spirit wants to work today. We must depend on the Holy Spirit. We ask him what he wants to do, and do it. We seek him for wisdom how to take from the old and the new, weave them together to synchronize with him, and go where he wants to go to do for this person what he wants to do at this time.

What Are The Seven Portions Of Our Spirit?

The seven-fold nature of the Spirit of God is seen in Isaiah 11:2. "And the spirit of the LORD shall rest upon him, the spirit of wisdom and understanding, the spirit of counsel and might, the spirit of knowledge and of the fear of the LORD." We see this in Revelation. "These are the words of him who holds the seven spirits of God and the seven stars" (Rev. 3:1). "Before the throne, seven lamps were blazing. These are the seven spirits of God" (Rev. 4:5). We might call that the seven-fold nature of the Spirit of God. Seven is the number of completion or perfection.

God is light, and we are made of his light. As a light goes through a prism, the light rays are bent in such a way that the component parts of light are seen: red, orange, yellow, green, blue, indigo, and violet. All those colors are present in light, but our naked eye cannot see them. The raindrops in a cloud do the same thing, and then we see a rainbow with these seven colors. Our spirits are like that, because God is like that. The psalmist said, "My frame was not hidden from You, when I was being formed in secret and intricately and curiously wrought (as if embroidered with various colors)..." (Ps. 139:15 The Amplified Bible).

The seven portions of our spirit correspond with the seven gifts in Romans 12:6-8—prophet, servant, teacher, exhorter, giver, ruler, and mercy. Blessing our spirit is not just Christ in us as a total entity, although he is. It is also about his residence in all portions of our spirit. He calling to life all aspects of our spirit, awakening it, enlarging it, and strengthening it as a process of our responding to him more fully with our whole being dedicated to him. Blessing gets past the soul to our spirit, where the Holy Spirit penetrates for greater understanding and freedom.

A local pastor blessed his congregation with the covenant names of God straight from *Blessing Your Spirit*. I was one of hundreds whom he blessed in that service. He used the seven names in turn (Jehovah-Jireh, Jehovah-Rophe, Jehovah-Shalom, Jehovah-Nissi, Jehovah-Shalom, Jehovah-T'sidkenu, and Jehovah-Shammah) as he blessed the seven portions of our spirits. My spirit responded, and God did something to me in my inner being. It made the fact that "I am a covenant daughter" come more alive in me, as seven covenant names of God settled deeply into my spirit. My place in God's covenant means more to me than ever before, because my spirit responded specifically to each of the covenant names of God, instead of responding in general.

There Is A Process Of Growth In The Spirit.

There is a process of being made complete in our spirit by the Holy Spirit in us. Paul said, "Now may the God of peace Himself sanctify you entirely; and may your spirit and soul and body be preserved complete, without blame at the coming of our Lord Jesus Christ" (1 Thess. 5:23 NASB). Philippians 1:6 says "being confident of this, that he who began a good work in you will carry it on to completion until the day of Christ Jesus."

We don't take a baby through weight training to enlarge it. We nourish it and nurture it, and it matures and strengthens over time. We are tempted to read a blessing book looking for the answer to our immediate need or what's bothering us, and we try to apply a quick fix. As we take *Blessing Your Spirit* and this blessing book and work through them as a process, we will be awakened, strengthened, and enlarged in our spirit. Then the whole need of our spirit will be addressed, and we will be coming to completion in Jesus. Paul told the Colossians that he labored among them in the energy of God to make known to them the glorious riches of Christ in them, their hope of glory. Then he said, "And we proclaim Him, admonishing every man and teaching every man with all wisdom, that we may present every man complete in Christ" (Col. 1:28 NKJV). Our spirit can minister to our own healing, but it can't do that if it is not awake and large and strong enough to assert its God-given leadership.

This process in the spirit means awakening to what God already put in us, as Peter tells us in 2 Peter 1:2-8. Listen to verse 2. "Grace and peace be yours in abundance through the knowledge of God and of Jesus our Lord." Before we receive the knowledge of who we are in him, we have to know God and Jesus our Lord. That means more than a casual nod or merely "Thank you for my salvation." It means *yadha*, to know him deeply and intimately by experience. Before we can take our stand in the grace and peace that is ours in abundance in Christ, we have to know the truth of who he is. Then we are ready for the next step.

Listen to 2 Peter 1:3. "His divine power has given us everything we need for life and godliness through our knowledge of him who called us by his own glory and goodness." The verb is past tense, *has given*. We already have in us as a gift from God everything we need, and Jesus is the gift. Blessing the spirit is the process of realizing this, growing up in it, and strengthening it in all its fullness. When we bless the spirit, we are affirming and adding an "amen" of agreement to what God is already doing, and perhaps we are hearing it and realizing it for the first time or in a new way.

Listen to 2 Peter 1:4. "Through these he has given us his very great and precious promises, so that through them you may participate in the divine nature and escape the corruption in the world caused by evil desires." When we know God experientially, our spirit is already being enlarged. God is spirit, and our spirit relates more fully and truly to him than our soul does. To know God with only head knowledge is the specialty of our soul.

We have heard 2 Peter 1:5-8 preached without the context and in such a way that the soul is badgered or guilted into "doing better" in an effort to achieve faith, goodness, knowledge, self-control, perseverance, godliness, brotherly kindness, and love. This is no more than behavior modification. This passage tells us that God by his own glory, goodness, power, and precious promises has given us everything we need for these virtues in himself, in his divine nature which lives in our spirits. That's where the Holy Spirit indwells us, and from him we will possess the qualities of faith, goodness, knowledge, self-control, perseverance, godliness, brotherly kindness, and love. This list sounds a lot like the fruit of the Spirit, doesn't it? And in him we can possess these qualities in increasing measure, guaranteeing effectiveness and fruitfulness in Jesus (2 Pet. 1:8).

Scattering Benedictions

Jill Carattini

The prolific author F.W. Boreham was once described as a man who went about his life "scattering benedictions." I have never seen a picture of this much-loved minister, but that description colorfully puts an image in my mind.

For many the word "benediction" signals the end of a church service, the parting words of a pastor with lifted hands sending forth the congregation in the grace and love of Jesus Christ. The word comes from two Latin words meaning literally "good speaking" and is most often translated "blessing." Benediction is the act or pronouncement of divine blessing upon another person.

To pronounce a person or group of people blessed was given as a commandment to Aaron and his sons, the tribe chosen to serve as priests among the Israelites. The book of Numbers recounts that the Lord spoke to Moses, saying, "Speak to Aaron and his sons, saying, 'Thus you shall bless the people of Israel: you shall say to them, The LORD bless you and keep you; the LORD make his face to shine upon you and be gracious to you; the LORD lift up his countenance upon you and give you peace' " (6:22-26).

It is a sublime utterance, blessing as much as it teaches. The hearer is lifted in the name of the Lord, the keeper of creation, the giver of peace, the one who so longs to bless us that it is given as a command. As a father looks at his son and delights to find his own smile, so the Lord lifts his face to those made in his own image, shining upon those called the "apple of his eye." The name of the LORD is exalted, for it to be upon us is a great blessing, and in it, God is glorified.

Herein lies the potency of benediction. At the end of his instructions for the Aaronic blessing, God adds distinctly, "So shall they put my name upon the people of Israel, and I will bless them" (v. 27). Whereas doxology is ascribing praise to God, and prayer is expressing oneself to God, a benediction is a word of blessing on *behalf* of God. The former rise from the heart of the saint, the other overflows from the heart of God. As author and theologian Samuel Chadwick notes, "[T]he benediction does not approach the subject from the standpoint of theology but of *experience*. It is not concerned with definition, nor does it contemplate the glory of God in the absoluteness of his deity; but it sets Him forth as He is realized in the soul."

Scattering benedictions, it seems, is a high calling, and I would add, a precious gift given to each of us made in the image of God. The putting of God's name upon one another as we go about life is the tongue's greatest utterance. It is a hopeful command, and our most uplifted effort. As God's name is set forth, not only is it God who does the blessing, it is God who is the very fulfillment of the words we offer. God is Himself the blessing.

Therefore, may the blessing of the LORD be upon you, and may you know the joy of putting his name upon others. For indeed, blessed are those who walk in the light of God's face.

Jill Carattini is senior associate writer at Ravi Zacharias International Ministries in Atlanta, GA.

Identity And Legitimacy

1 Wake Up — Ephesians 5:14

Spirit, be blessed from the Word of God in 1 John 1:5. “God is light; in him there is no darkness at all.” And in Ephesians 5:14. “Wake up, O sleeper, rise from the dead, and Christ will shine on you.”

Beloved child of God, invite your spirit to the front to receive the ministry of the Holy Spirit, to receive this blessing. Take authority over anything that would try to keep you from receiving this truth from the Spirit of truth.

Wake up, slumbering spirit, and receive from the Light who created you and formed you and lives in you. Be blessed to become fully alive and responsive to God’s light. Be blessed with God’s richest blessings which he stored up for you before he said, “Let there be light” in the world. The resurrection power of the Son is actively working in you and for you. Jesus said that this is the “day when salvation and the favor of God profusely abound” (Luke 4:19, Amplified). Be blessed with meeting God deeply.

Spirit, be blessed to see who God made you to be. Be blessed to discover the wonder of who you are, a person after God’s own heart, a unique spirit. When you are fulfilling his design of you, you will find marvelous freedom. Be blessed as you resonate with your Father’s love that you were born to enjoy. He wants you to say “Yes and Amen” to the sparks of life he has placed inside you. Be blessed with being centered in his joy and peace, larger than soul joy and soul peace.

God is reviving you, spirit. No longer live as if you are sleep-walking. Be blessed and encouraged as you live with God. Your Father’s light is rising like the dawn in you. His heart for your identity, legitimacy, and birthright is being revealed in you. Receive from him everything you need for living in covenant with him and others as a life-giver. The Holy Spirit is permeating into you his truth and instruction.

Be blessed with daily spirit renewal and revival. Be blessed to receive the ministry of the Spirit of grace and supplication to train and transform you. You have victory, so don’t let anything rob you of your peace and joy in Jesus. Be blessed with healing and revelation from God day by day. Be blessed with peace and contentment that you know have come from his Spirit. If you want to be whole, you have to be free! Receive from him and see how good it feels to be free.

Spirit, you are complex and wonderfully designed by God to do what your soul can’t do. Be blessed in your spiritual DNA. Your Father of lights knows your strengths and potential and delights in your unique design. He knows the “much more” he has for you. Your Creator is totally investing in nurturing you and healing your soul like you have never experienced. He blesses you with life-changing truth and revelation from his Spirit and from his Word. Be blessed with being filled with the Spirit of your Father, controlling you spirit, soul, and body. Be blessed to lead your soul in the ways of his Spirit, so that your whole person is conformed to God’s intention for you.

Be blessed to get in tune with your Father’s heart for your identity, legitimacy, and birthright. Be blessed to be awake, enlarged, strengthened, and empowered in new ways in him.

Be blessed in the name of Christ who is your light (1 John 1:5).

2 You're Alive, Be Strong — Romans 8:10-11

Spirit, listen to the Word of God for you in Romans 8:10-11. "If Christ is in you, your body is dead because of sin, yet your spirit is alive because of righteousness. And if the Spirit of him who raised Jesus from the dead is living in you, he … will also give life to your mortal bodies through his Spirit, who lives in you."

Spirit, you are alive in the Spirit of God, and your Father intends for you to be awake, nurtured, strong, and enlarged in him. The Holy Spirit is present in you, igniting revelation in you of who you really are. You are meant to live life rejoicing in God with ears to hear from him. Be blessed as the Spirit of the Lord in you activates your full spiritual DNA. Exchange slumber and passivity for the rising glory of being perfectly awakened and enlarged in him. Be blessed to live from who you are, feeling completely alive. Receive who your Father says you are, not who others say you are. Be blessed to embrace life as you connect with his Spirit in a life-giving way. Be blessed with fresh manna of truth that wipes out deception and refutes the constant bombardment of the world, the flesh, and the devil.

Spirit, listen to the heart cry of Paul for his Ephesian disciples and friends. "I pray that out of his glorious riches he may strengthen you with power through his Spirit in your inner being" (Eph. 3:16). Be blessed to know and live from the strength of the Spirit in you. You are active and strong, not passive. Be blessed, spirit, to lead your soul, directing and instructing it in the ways and will of God's intention for you. Be blessed with healthy conversation between your spirit and your soul like David in Psalm 42:5. "Why are you downcast, O my soul? Why so disturbed within me? Put your hope in God, for I will yet praise him, my Savior and my God." Be blessed to welcome your soul and converse with your soul from strength, and tell it to line up behind you and let you lead. Be blessed to strengthen your vertical connection with God's Spirit, with the soul following in God's order.

Spirit, there is pain when you use physical muscles in ways that are out of your comfort zone or have not been used in a long time. In the spirit, there's stretching as you learn new skills, but it will be redemptive pain. The key to many sports is muscle memory. Athletes spend hours practicing what they want their muscles to do in the game. Spiritual muscle memory is the same. So faithfully exercise your God-given identity and legitimacy. God is up to something significant and eternal in enlarging you and strengthening you. Be blessed with being active and strong, so that you will be complete spirit, soul, and body (1 Thes. 5:23).

Be blessed in the name of One who gives you life through his Spirit (Rom. 8:11).

3 God's Image-bearer — Genesis 1:27

Spirit, listen to the Word of God in Genesis 1:27. "So God created man in his own image, in the image of God he created him."

Spirit, God made you in his own image. You are made of his light. In your essence, you are good, and the light in you is loaded with the richness, magnificence, and knowledge of God. David said, "Let the light of your face shine on us" (Ps. 4:6). Your Father's light shines from his face into your eyes. Lift your face up to his face. He wants you to receive an eye-to-eye transfer directly from him.

Spirit, be blessed in the godly desires that he programmed into you, the godly DNA that he put in you when he made you in his image. You participate in his divine nature as he unpacks his deposit in you (2 Peter 1:4). He delights in enlarging you. He is enjoying the process of your growth.

Spirit, God intends for you to lead the soul. You are made to heal the soul. You can do it. When you are strong and full of light, you reflect the nature and character of God, but you have not been in control. At many points you have been captive to the soul: stuck in the past, wounded, undernourished, in bondage, in fear, shame, and control. You have been run over by others through manipulation. You have been controlled by your own wounded or fearful reactions. You have been trapped, you have been a victim. You are not a victim! That is not the real you, made of the essence of the light of God. You have the best intentions, but the wounded soul keeps you from being seen as you really are. Be blessed to heal the soul by speaking truth to it. Be blessed with growth and tenacity and strength to overcome and to lead. God designed you to lead the soul and your soul to submit to you. God wants to be in control in you.

Spirit, be blessed with God's life in you where you have been wounded. You are meant to manifest the good things that God wants. Be blessed to be large and strong to implement the will of God in your life. Let him make you who he wants you to be in his time and by the path that he takes you. You are a wonderful child of God. Be blessed with becoming everything God knows you can be. Be blessed to live in dignity and honor, in your true authority and birthright.

**Be blessed in the name of the Image of the invisible God,
the firstborn over all creation (Col. 1:15).**

4 The Word Of God Separates Between Soul And Spirit — Hebrews 4:12

Spirit, listen to God's Word for you in Hebrews 4:12 "The word of God is living and active. Sharper than any double-edged sword, it penetrates even to dividing soul and spirit, joints and marrow; it judges the thoughts and attitudes of the heart."

Spirit, God wants you to differentiate between you and the soul, so that each part can operate in its designed position. Listen to Hebrews 4:12 in The Amplified Bible. "The word that God speaks is alive and full of power — making it active, operative, energizing, and effective; it is sharper than any double-edged sword, penetrating to the dividing line of the breath of life (soul) and [the immortal] spirit, and of joints and marrow [that is, the deepest parts of our nature] exposing and sifting and analyzing and judging the thoughts, and attitudes, and purposes of the heart."

Spirit, let God take the sword of his Spirit and cut between soul and spirit, to judge what comes from the spirit and those thoughts and intents that come from the soul. God divides spirit and soul as he exposes your innermost thoughts and desires. You don't do it; that makes a difference. God will separate and strengthen the godly intents of the Spirit of the Lord who is resident in you. When the soul is in turmoil from double-mindedness, or obsessions, or bondages, you, spirit, cannot be who you are capable of being or do what you are capable of doing. When the soul reacts with unforgiveness or fear or anger or judgment, you get shut down and overruled.

Spirit, Galatians 5:16-17 admonishes you to "live by the Spirit, and you will not gratify the desires of the sinful nature. For the sinful nature desires what is contrary to the Spirit, and the Spirit what is contrary to the sinful nature. They are in conflict with each other, so that you do not do what you want." Paul then lists the acts of the sinful nature, which are the specialty of the soul. He contrasts those with the fruit of the Spirit, which are your best characteristics when you are led by God's spirit: love, joy, peace, patience, kindness, goodness, faithfulness, gentleness, and self-control (Gal. 5:22-23).

The Spirit and the Word of God divide between the spirit and the soul. The soul is not evil, but it is prone to choose its own way. Choose to let the Holy Spirit in you correct the imbalance between you and a strong soul, so that the soul does not push you around with its agenda.

Spirit, stand up for Jesus living in you. The essence of God dwells in you. His Word says that you are his home. God will work in you so the soul doesn't overrule you. He imprinted you with his eternal image. He designed you to know the truth and to reflect his holiness and character. He purposed that his Son the Prince of peace will have dominion in you, supplying you with peace in God, peace with God, peace with yourself, and peace with others.

Be blessed today in the name of Jesus the Word in whom is life (John 1:1,4).

5 Spirit, Soul, And Body — 1 Thessalonians 5:23-24

Spirit, listen to the Word of God for you in 1 Thessalonians 5:23-24. "May God himself, the God of peace, sanctify you through and through. May your whole spirit, soul and body be kept blameless at the coming of our Lord Jesus Christ. The one who calls you is faithful and he will do it."

Spirit, the God of peace is at work in you to make you like his Son, blameless and spotless before him in every aspect of spirit, soul, and body. Jesus endured and overcame all the hosts of hell to purchase you. In Christ you are blessed; you possess the favor of your Father. You possess the fullness of God. He set his Holy Spirit as a seal on you. He set his kingdom in you. You are a covenant son/daughter in whom he was well-pleased to place his Spirit. You live in a state of blessedness because of Christ.

The great heart of God willed your spirit, soul, and body into existence for honor and dignity. He designed you with special gifts to give to you first, then your family, and then the world. God knows who you are and what you can do through his light in you.

Regardless of what has happened in your life, the light of God lives in you...
… under the wounding that produces fragmentation and other negative things in the soul…
… under demonic assignments of death, darkness, and destruction that produce bondage to fear and control and anger (which is murder in your heart)…
… under unforgiveness, curses, sin, and a victim mindset …
… under the idolatry of self, family, the past, land, or religious tradition…
… under all of this, his covenant of life is in your being.

In the Old Testament he told his people he wanted them to clean out the temple, as Josiah did. Jesus himself cleansed the temple, and you are his temple. He cleanses you as a place of his habitation. Spirit, God is pleased to have his Son abide in you. His covenant of lovingkindness is your identity and will be all the days of your life. The unfailing goodness and mercy of God is your inheritance — surer, deeper, richer, and holier than your physical inheritance. Be blessed to tap all the potential that God wrote in his book for you and all the possibilities that he planted in your DNA, both naturally and spiritually. The gifts and callings of God are irrevocable. They are the foundation for a treasure of generational blessing for you to draw from.

Be blessed as you live, spirit, leading your soul and body as God intends. Be blessed to be centered in spirit joy and peace that transcends soul joy and peace. God promises that he is powerful and faithful in you to do it, so stand up and take your rightful place in Jesus your Lord and Savior.

Be blessed in the name of the God of peace who sees you as holy and blameless in Christ (1 Thess. 5:23).

6 God's Masterpiece — Ephesians 2:10

Spirit, receive God's Word for you from Proverbs 8:30-31. "Then I was the craftsman at his side. I was filled with delight day after day, rejoicing always in his presence, rejoicing in his whole world and delighting in mankind." And in Ephesians 2:10 NLT. "For we are God's masterpiece..."

Spirit, God delights in how he made you. You are one of his masterpieces. You are his song to be sung in a key of music that is unique to you, in a rhythm, a harmony, and an orchestration that God rejoices to sing inside of you. The music of heaven graces your life as others see and hear and touch who you are, so that they receive from him the awesome display of his delight in you.

For years, we have hurried over the first part of Ephesians 2:10 to concentrate on the works we are supposed to do, without appreciating the delightful work of God's hands that we are. God designed what you do to be built on the foundation of who you are in him. Ecclesiastes 3:11 says, "He has made everything beautiful in its time. He has also set eternity in the hearts of men; yet they cannot fathom what God has done from beginning to end."

Spirit, you are not just a tool designed to function to do a set of good works because the world needs them done. God has given you the authority and compassion to be a part of meeting those needs, but higher than that, you are beautiful and complete like the portrait that God painted in 1 Samuel 16:18. You are a worshiper who sings back to him the songs of heaven you hear. You are brave with holy boldness, kept by the One who stands strong in you. You are a warrior who fights the right battles because you listen to your Commander. You have wise and gracious words on your lips that come from the wellspring of a righteous heart. You are fine-looking with the reflected image of Jesus. You possess the signature that the Lord is with you. He "signed off on you." Receive the seal of his signature on you.

Spirit, be blessed to live in the beauty of being well-pleasing to your Father. You are beautiful, dressed in royal robes designed to express the position and privilege of the King's heir and to signify your inheritance of authority and privilege. You are a display of the many facets of his splendor from his throneroom. Be blessed with fulfillment in the grace and beauty of heaven seen in you. Be blessed with the peace and joy of heaven about you. People are attracted to you because the perfume of heaven is about you. Be blessed with the color and light of heaven reflected upon you.

Spirit, God is investing in you, caring for you, nurturing you, blessing you, so that you can be a treasure and a blessing to the world. Be blessed with becoming everything he has called you to be and being all he has designed you to become in the way that makes all of heaven rejoice. Spirit, receive the delight of Jesus in his creation — you!

Be blessed in the name of the One who rejoices in his works (Ps. 104:31).

7 You Are God's Design — Ephesians 2:10

Spirit, listen to God's Word in Ephesians 2:10. "We are God's workmanship, created in Christ Jesus…"

Spirit, come to the front to accept and receive this truth deeply in your sense of being. Your Father had his eye on you long before you loved him. He intended you and wanted you. He planned you; you were not an accident. You are a product of his love. You were not mass-produced. We live in a disposable age, but you are not throw-away. You are one of his best ideas, the result of his fine craftsmanship. His wisdom creatively designed you for himself. You are "a keeper," a treasure, valuable and valued. You are carrying a huge reservoir of treasure of generational blessings, because he is generous. He is a just and extravagant God. He celebrates everything that he planned and deposited in the gold mine that is you, everything that he intended for you and pledged to you, and he cannot lie. In him you know who you are and what you are living for. Be blessed to live in the freedom of maximum fulfillment as you accept and approve and receive your design, how God made you to be.

Spirit, listen to the Word of God for you in Matthew 15:13. Jesus said, "Every plant that my heavenly Father has not planted will be pulled up by the roots." Be blessed to receive the restoration of God's original intent for you. Receive the hand of your Father removing everything that he didn't install in you, everything you got from ungodly generations, in the womb, and since then from unholy sources. Be blessed with seeing the hand of your Father plucking up by the roots what he did not plant in you. Receive God's restoration of what needs to be restored to its rightful formation and place. He put some special things in you when he created you, and you may have tried to remove them, hide them, or change them. Others may have tried to squelch you or change you all your life. Be released from the soulish plans, prayers, and manipulations of others to make you other than who God intended you to be.

Spirit, hear God's Word for you in Romans 12:2 NLT. "Let God transform you into a new person by changing the way you think, and you will know how pleased God is with his will for you and what God wants you to do." He has designs on you for glorious living in his purposes, to set you in the fullness of Christ in everything in every way. He is actively working out his purposes that are beyond your comprehension. Paul said that no mere man has heard, seen, or even imagined what wonderful things God has for those who love him. The power of the Holy Spirit in you is renewing your mind and soul, to give you a new attitude of heart. Jesus, the author and finisher of your faith, is helping you to trust God completely and believe that he knows what is best for your life.

Spirit, let God confirm to you those facets of yourself that he designed to be revealed. Jesus lives in you to shine out of you. Be blessed to grow in all the character, skills, potential, and magnificence that is in your true spiritual DNA. Be blessed to be you.

Be blessed in the name of the Spirit of God who made you,
the breath of the Almighty who gives you life (Job 33:4).

8 Legitimacy — Ephesians 1:3-6

Spirit, listen to the Word of God for you in Ephesians 1:3-6. "Praise be to the God and Father of our Lord Jesus Christ, who has blessed us in the heavenly realms with every spiritual blessing in Christ. For he chose us in him before the creation of the world to be holy and blameless in his sight. In love he predestined us to be adopted as his sons through Jesus Christ, in accordance with his pleasure and will — to the praise of his glorious grace, which he has freely given us in the One he loves."

Precious spirit, receive the defining love and grace of your God and Father of your Lord Jesus Christ. You existed in God's heart from eternity as a precious being before time was. You abide in his everlasting love that adopted you as his son through Jesus Christ.

Spirit, be blessed to hear your Father speak his blessings to you. Be blessed to be enlarged and strengthened as you discover many deposits of his blessings in your inner being. Let them trickle down to soul, heart, emotions, will, identity and legitimacy. Be blessed to live and move in tune with your Father's heart for your identity, legitimacy, and birthright. Jesus living in you is the unique glory of your life. He created you for the praise of the glorious grace of Jesus. This is God's final word on who you are. Be blessed as you receive all the good gifts of life-giving incarnation from the Spirit of the Life-giver in you. Receive his faith, hope, and love.

Your life is like a treasure map, and you are on a journey of discovery of your true identity, legitimacy, and confident freedom. Feel God's light shining upon you, revealing the seven colors of the rainbow of his covenant to you. Be blessed as your God and Father creates new pathways of significance where none has consciously existed. Be blessed as you discover how the seven colors of God's covenant are displayed in you. Be blessed with deepening significance that you can sense should be there. Receive the gentle voice of your Father speaking in the core of your essence, "You are my beloved."

Receive the different voices that affirm you, but don't find your identity and legitimacy from any person, thing, or accomplishment. Only your spirit connection with your Father is significant to your identity and legitimacy. That's the truth of your life. Claim it, and live it.

Spirit, be blessed as you live your life as a redeemed eternal son or daughter of your eternal Father. His will for you is that you know that you are beautiful, his own special creation. Be blessed to know that he determined for you an appointed place and time and purpose and that in him you live and move and have your being (Acts 17:26,28). Be blessed to live and move in tune with your Father's heart for your identity, legitimacy, calling, authority, and birthright. You can trust that today is the day of his favor for you. Be blessed as you stand tall in all your legitimacy as a covenant right from your Father the King. Be blessed as you choose to live from his heart and in your authority in him. Be blessed in Jesus' name as a son or daughter of his God and Father (Eph. 1:3).

Be blessed in the name of the Spirit of adoption
(Rom. 8:15 NKJV, Spirit of sonship in NIV).

9 Belonging And Worth — Psalm 139:13-16

Spirit, listen to what your Father says about you, how he made you, how he sees you. David was talking to God about his life, when he said in Psalm 139:13-16. "You created my inmost being; you knit me together in my mother's womb. I praise you because I am fearfully and wonderfully made; your works are wonderful, I know that full well. My frame was not hidden from you when I was made in the secret place. When I was woven together in the depths of the earth, your eyes saw my unformed body."

Spirit, come to be blessed by your Father and Creator. According to God's Word, you are very special — created, crafted and designed by God your Father. He planned for you before he said, "Let there be light." You are no accident, not conceived of the will of man. He reached down and chose a family to place you in. You did not have to exist — he wanted you to be. He willed you into existence.

You are welcome in his world. God had been waiting for millennia for the particular point in time when you were conceived. He smiled that day. You are one of his best ideas! He chose every pair of your 23 pairs of chromosomes and every one of your more than 10,000 genes. He was pleased when his plans came together as he wove you together in your mother's womb. He chose the day and the time you would come into the world. You are unique, one of a kind. There is nobody else like you.

Spirit, know that God celebrates his marvelous design of you. He made your inmost being. The essence of who you are is worthy of praising him, because you are fearfully and wonderfully made. Every detail of how your body is shaped and formed, how every organ and every cell fits together is the result of God's thoughts. Every facet of your personality is the result of his thoughts. You are beloved, and you are beautiful. You have something to give your world that no other person has. Your family and your community of faith need the deposit that God has placed in your life. They will not be complete without you as you shine in your unique display of his image in you.

Be blessed in the name of God your Creator who made you and formed you (Deut. 32:6b).

10 Your Days Are Written In God's Book — Psalm 139:16-17

Spirit, hear God's Word for you in Psalm 139:16-17. "All the days ordained for me were written in your book before one of them came to be. How precious to me are your thoughts, O God, how vast is the sum of them."

Spirit, God nurtured you in the womb, and since your conception he has watched over you. Your days were not written haphazardly. Your life is not a random thing. His thoughts of you are precious and too vast to count. He thinks of you continuously and of new ways that he can bless you, just because you are his special child. He has written the script of your life. He chose every part of it. He is looking forward to reveal the chapters to the story he has already written.

God thought through all the details — your siblings, your birth order, large family or small family, city family or rural. He foresaw your pain, too. He knew that out of that brokenness comes a larger story, just like when Jesus took the loaves, and he blessed them, then he broke them, then he multiplied them to feed many. Because of his love, his power, and his blessing on you, he causes all the pain and negative things to be transformed into good things in his story for your life. So take courage. God has given you everything you need to be an overcomer, to have victory over the negative parts of your heritage, and to live in the beauty of all that he placed within you.

Spirit, in God's master plan and design he chose and designed every part of your spiritual heritage. He reached back into generations past and chose different parts of your heritage. Your generational blessings go back a thousand generations (Deut. 7:9). He chose the spiritual treasure chest of generational blessings that is set aside with your name on it. You are blessed to be an heir to this spiritual treasure. Seek God for it and ask him to release it at his appointed appropriate time.

Spirit, love is who God is and what he does. When he looks down from heaven, he says of you, "You are my beloved child, in whom I am well pleased." That's what he said of Jesus, and you are in Jesus and Jesus is in you. You are beloved. That is your incarnate identity. He pours out his lovingkindness on you every day in big ways and little ways. Be blessed to receive your belonging and worth in his love. Be blessed as God's love validates and affirms that you are special, his covenant child, a chip off the ole block. God thinks you are the best. Be blessed to celebrate your identity and legitimacy. Today be aware of your belonging, inclusion, significance, and worth in him.

Be blessed in the name of your Father who has carried you until you reached this place (Deut. 1:31).

11 His Competence In A Clay Pot — 2 Corinthians 4:7

Spirit, hear God's Word for you in 2 Corinthians 4:7. "But we have this treasure in jars of clay to show that this all-surpassing power is from God and not from us."

Spirit, your Father wants you to be completely whole in belonging and worth, in identity and legitimacy. Be blessed to know without question what a treasure you are to him. Be blessed to live as the special treasure you are. As you know who you are, you will understand the "why" of what you do. Be blessed with knowing your purpose and the specific blessings that God has stored up for you.

Spirit, be blessed in the name of the One who is all-surpassing power. Be blessed with knowing experientially that Jesus is the "how" of everything you are and do. Paul asked the rhetorical question, "What do you have that you did not receive?" (1 Cor. 4:7). And the answer is nothing. God is your competence (2 Cor. 3:5). Be blessed with knowing that it is "not by might nor by power, but by my Spirit," says the LORD Almighty (Zech. 4:6). You can be confident, knowing that apart from him you can do nothing (John 15:5), but in him you can do everything (Phil. 4:13).

Spirit, like Jesus you can be confident in the core of your being in following God's will, not your own; in speaking his words, not your own; in doing his work, as he does his work of intimately revealing himself. Thank God for your God-given competence, but don't allow your competence to become your identity. Be blessed with healing in your deepest doubts and your deepest wounds of identity, so that you do not have to strive to prove that you are worthy, legitimate, significant, and deserving of honor.

God designed you for some unique good works in Christ (Eph. 2:10). There are some things he placed you in the world to do that you can do better than anybody else, because of who he designed you to be. Be blessed in everything he designed you to be to fulfill his "your Kingdom come, your will be done" purpose on the earth. As you align yourself with who God designed you to be, you will be fulfilled, and the world will be blessed.

Be blessed in the name of the One who is your all-surpassing power (2 Cor. 4:7).

12 Jesus Loves You, This I Know — John 15:9; Galatians 2:20; Ephesians 5:25

Spirit, listen to the words of Jesus for you in John 15:9. “As the Father has loved me, so have I loved you. Now remain in my love.” Listen to the testimony of Paul in Galatians 2:20. “The Son of God… loved me and gave himself for me.” Listen to his message to us today in Ephesians 5:25. “Christ loved the church and gave himself up for her…”

Spirit, God your Father loves you. He has loved you from the moment he knit you together in your mother’s womb. He has watched you grow and mature into the fine person that you are. He is proud of you. He has heard your pleas in every trial of your life, days you thought would never end. He has plans for you, so keep open to his life — his love, peace, and joy. You need have no fear, for his love casts out all fear. He wants to show you love that you have never known.

Spirit, be blessed as you look into the face of Jesus the Son of God who loves you, this I know. He gave himself for you. Trust his love for you in all things, from the smallest to the greatest. He is with you. He is pouring out his love on you so that you grow into his beautiful likeness. Be ready for his great wisdom and great grace to be poured out on you. His wisdom and grace have no limits. Listen for his voice calling you, for he wants to talk with you and be intimate with you. Do not trust your own understanding, for his ways are higher than your ways. Trust him in a deeper way with all your being: spirit, soul, body. The more you trust him, the deeper he will take you. He will show you and guide you step by step.

The great theologian Karl Barth, one of the great minds of the twentieth century, was asked in his last years, “What is the greatest theological truth of all time?” I am sure the one who asked the question was poised with pen in hand to record the product of his great intellect. Instead, they got the overflow of his great heart. Without hesitation, Barth replied, “Jesus loves me, this I know.” That’s the greatest theological truth.

Spirit, God the Spirit loves you. God has poured out his love into your heart by the Holy Spirit, whom he has given you (Rom. 5:5). So you are thrice-loved — by the Father, the Son, and the Holy Spirit. He will open the eyes of your spirit so that you may see the wonders of his love that he has for you. Hear the refrain, “And wonders of His love, and wonders of His love, And wonders, wonders of His love.” -*Joy To The World*, Isaac Watts (1674-1748)

But be prepared that it will not be without warfare. The enemy will want to silence, steal, and destroy the love of God for you. He stands at your door daily with his lies. Do not allow him to gain a key to your heart.

Spirit, your covenant relationship with Jesus has changed your name. You are no longer called forsaken, unloved, or afraid. Your new name is confidence, joyfulness, and overcomer. Be blessed in the name of the One whose name is above all names (Phil. 2:11). Be blessed as his friend as you seek his face. Keep your eyes focused on him, and he will synchronize the desires of your heart with his. His love will be your strength in all your days to come. Feel his loving arms around you, precious one, and be strong in him. Be blessed in the One who is loving and faithful in all his ways to you (Ps. 25:10).

Be blessed in the name of the Son of God who loved you and gave himself for you (Gal. 2:20).

13 Choose Life — Deuteronomy 30:19

Spirit, listen to your Father's heart from his Word in Deuteronomy 30:19. "I have set before you life and death, blessing and cursing; therefore choose life, that both you and your descendants may live."

Spirit, come to the front and be blessed in the name of the One who is life. Your Father is pleased that Jesus his Son lives in you and his Spirit makes his home in you. Choose the abundant life of Jesus in you. He will never cease living in you. God chose your spirit to be his dwelling place before he created the physical body to place you in. Be blessed to choose life, his life in you. Your life is secure in him.

God pledges the full faith of his great name to you. His Word says in 1 Samuel 12:22, "For the sake of his great name the LORD will not reject his people, because the LORD was pleased to make you his own." You have the pleasure of the Lord. He is pleased that you are his. You belong to him. You are precious in his sight. You are a divine choice. Celebrate your chosenness. You are an expression of the embrace of the everlasting love of God. By his grace, seize your opportunities every day to choose life, to be life, to give life. Choose against what distracts you, confuses you, and puts in jeopardy the life of the Beloved in you. Choose to live from the loving heart of your Father.

Spirit, be blessed in the encouragement that comes from being united with Christ. Receive comfort from his love. Be blessed to choose fellowship with the Spirit. Bask in his tenderness and compassion. Make his joy complete by receiving his unshakable purpose for you in your Father (Phil. 2:1). You have not read the final chapter of his plans for you. He has written a future and a hope for you. In Jeremiah 29:11 God says, "I know the plans I have for you, plans to prosper you and not to harm you, plans to give you hope and a future." This verse was written to people who were exiled and captive in a foreign country for seventy years. God kept his promise, and they returned to the land he gave them.

The pain you feel is real, your circumstances are what they are, but be blessed with hope for your future in him who chose your life. Choose to believe in hope that he who called you is faithful. It is your choice. Spirit, be blessed with trusting his thoughts and plans for welfare and peace, for your good and not for evil.

Be blessed in the name of the One who has life in himself,
and his light is your life (John 1:4).

14 Sense Of Being — 1 John 3:1

Spirit, listen to the heart of your Father speaking to your heart in his Word in 1 John 3:1. "How great is the love the Father has lavished on us, that we should be called children of God! And that is what we are!"

Spirit, you bear the imprint of your Creator's fingerprints on your entire being. You are a special evidence of his continuing handiwork and creativity in the earth today. He chose generational treasures for you and your soul and body. He made you his child on whom he lavishes his love. Be blessed to feel with almost aching sharpness and clarity the truth that you are greatly loved. He calls you beloved. He likes you. In fact, he adores you. You are the apple of His eye. You are his special treasure. You are legitimate and worthy because he loves you, not because of anything you have done. Be blessed with a deep and abiding joy as a favored child of Most High God.

Spirit, God gave you your competence, your talents, and your personality. Beyond that is your identity of belonging and worth and your legitimacy in him as a covenant son/daughter. Be blessed with a healthy sense of being from a solid core of identity and legitimacy in him. Be blessed with physical, emotional, relational, mental, and spiritual sense of being in Christ Jesus. Be blessed to realize that you stand in his favor based on relationship, not performance. Be blessed with his approval and pleasure. Be blessed with awareness of all your spiritual blessings he has deposited in you. Be blessed with knowing you are set in a large place in the spirit realm, a place of authority in him.

Spirit, be blessed to know that you are loved, wanted, and needed in the world. Your Father placed you right where you are. Be blessed with relaxing in his perfect care in every detail, knowing he is lovingly watching over you. Be blessed with freedom from fear. You are immovable and unstoppable as you remain in that place of abiding in him and Jesus in you. Be blessed as God encourages and empowers you in his truth and purposes for your life.

Be blessed in the name of your Father who loves you as he loves his own Son (John 17:23).

15 You Are Beloved Of The Beloved Son — Song of Solomon 2:8-14

Spirit, listen to this about your Beloved in Song of Solomon 2:8-14. "My Beloved spoke and said to me, 'Rise up, my love, my fair one, and come away, for the winter is past, the rain is over and gone. The flowers appear on the earth… Rise up, my love, rise up, my fair one, and come away. O my dove, in the clefts of the rock, in the secret places of the cliff, let me see your face, let me hear your voice. For your voice is sweet, and your face is lovely.' "

Spirit, can you hear him inviting you to rise up and come with him? Receive him calling you his beloved, his fair one. Receive his loving shelter in the cleft of the Rock. Run to him in the secret place and see his face. He wants to hear your voice calling to him, because it is sweet in his ears and you are beautiful to him.

It may have been hard for you to hear his voice offering you his loving fellowship, protection, and intimacy because you have wounds that have cried loudly. You may feel your cries of pain have been unheard, because there were no earthly ears to listen.

But God has heard and he has seen…

… the pains of rejection, separation, and disappointment
… your isolation, fears, loneliness, and sense of insecurity
… feelings of being rejected, ignored, devalued, despised, left alone, and isolated
… feelings of competition, rivalry, comparison, and put-down
… feeling useless, worthless, unappreciated, and unloved
… feelings of shame and embarrassment
… feeling needy, vulnerable, unable to be of special value to one who matters
… emptiness of spending your effort and energy trying to earn esteem and worth
… overwhelming and relentless demands on time and energy
… inadequacy, discontent, frustration, and confusion about the course of your life
… doubt about your true calling in life, doubt about the meaning of your life
… exhaustion and despair never far beneath the surface of your existence
… no strength to get back in the arena with the lions seeking to devour you

Spirit, these feelings are not telling you the truth about you. Self-doubt and self-rejection are two great enemies. When they find fertile ground in your soul, they cause you to do something to try to prove your worth and earn the affirmation that you have desired. You don't have to contribute something so that the world will value you. You do not deserve to be pushed aside, forgotten, and abandoned. You don't have to be right to make a place or be on guard to keep your place. This assault could have overwhelmed you at points.

It is not easy to hear that you are God's beloved in a world that shouts, "You are ugly, you are no good, you are worthless, you are a nobody." The curses of lying voices do not tell the truth about you. These voices separate you from God's truth of who you are and who he made you to become. Don't waste time blaming and complaining. It is time to loose the soul from self-rejection that may go back generations.

Spirit, hear and receive deeply that you are the Beloved of the God of the universe. You are not a victim! Embrace your unique brokenness, for through it God is making you to become a beautiful testimony of his restoration and grace. In the darkest hour, he never left you alone, or rejected you, or counted you as worthless or a nobody. His Beloved Son died to make you beloved in himself. Embrace your brokenness, befriend it, make peace with it, and put it under his blessing. Be blessed to take your pain to his cross, and God will purify and deepen the blessing that rests upon you in your pain.

Spirit, receive this description from Isaiah 53:2-5,10 of the One who carried your pain. He had no beauty or majesty to attract us to him. There was nothing in his appearance that would cause us to desire him. He was despised and rejected by men, a man who suffered and was familiar with bitterest grief. We turned our backs on him and hid our faces from him. He was despised, and we didn't care. Yet he took up our weaknesses and infirmities, and our sorrows weighed him down. He was wounded and pierced for our sins. He was crushed for our iniquities, and his punishment brought us peace. He healed us by his wounds. It was the LORD's will to crush him and cause him to suffer and fill him with grief. God made his life a guilt offering for us. The will of the LORD will prosper in his hand.

Be blessed in the name of Jesus who bore your pain and sin in himself for you (Isa. 53:6b).

Based in part on *Life Of The Beloved*, ©1992 by Henri J. M. Nouwen. The Crossroad Publishing Company, New York, NY.

16 You Are Blessed To Be A Blessing — Genesis 12:2

Spirit, listen to God's Word in Genesis 12:2. "I will bless you…and you will be a blessing."

Spirit, come to the front to experience the total satisfaction of God's heart toward you. You are a blessing to him. Be blessed with listening to God's tender heart, the voice of El Shaddai to woo and nurture, to love and find pleasure in you. Feel his satisfaction in you, as you delight and fulfill his heart by simply being you. Be blessed with freedom to be the unique you that you are, the beautiful you that he designed. He is pleased when you dedicate everything about you to him — your gifts, anointings, birthright, your time and seasons, the land on which you walk and work and play and live, your likes and dislikes, your interests, your passions — every expression of who you are. Be blessed with joy and strength and grace as you resonate in sync with the Father of your spirit (Heb. 12:9).

Spirit, you are one of God's good gifts. Be blessed with spiritual eyes to see that he is leaving his fingerprints all over your life. Be blessed as you celebrate God's blessing in you, and let that blessing flow out of you. Be blessed in the way you discern, and sense, and feel, and express Jesus in you. It is uniquely you without apology, and it is God's gift to you and to others. Be blessed as you minister his good gifts, starting in your closest relationships. Be blessed with strong connection with him, so that it overflows into fresh connection spirit-to-spirit, heart-to-heart with others. Be blessed with restoring and deepening significant horizontal relationships and creating new ones, as God makes your love increase and overflow for others. You are a blessing to others, as you display his blessing inside and out.

Spirit, your Father will bless your risk-taking for whatever he says. Just do it. If you have never done it before, if you don't have a mentor or model, it's o.k. Look into God's face, and let the light of his eyes download into you what he is saying to you. He will go ahead of you. He is your way-maker and your confidence. Be blessed to see signs of God's goodness in specific ways that speak to you that he is present and involved, he is active and in charge. He is blessing you to be a blessing.

Be blessed in the generational name of the God of Abraham, Isaac, and Jacob (Exo. 3:15).

17 Liberty In The Lord — 2 Corinthians 3:17-18

Spirit, listen to the Word of God for you in 2 Corinthians 3:17-18. "The Lord is the Spirit, and where the Spirit of the Lord is, there is freedom. And we, who with unveiled faces all reflect the Lord's glory, are being transformed into his likeness with ever-increasing glory, which comes from the Lord, who is the Spirit."

Spirit, complete freedom is your birthright. Be blessed with fully knowing your birthright in the liberty of the Lord. From the Holy Spirit through you comes your legal right to identity, belonging, acceptance, worth, affirmation, competence, inheritance, and blessing. Be blessed with realignment of your body, your biology, your chemistry, all your physical being under God's direction, not the soul's direction. Be blessed with realignment of the mind, will, and emotion of the soul under your authority and direction, in God's light as he intended. Be blessed with knowing his joy and peace in your innermost being.

Spirit, take your rightful authority in Jesus, and take the scepter of his authority as he directs you to use it for his glory. You have a biblical commission. It is written in 1 John 3:8, "The Son of God appeared to destroy the devil's work." And it is written in Hebrews 2:14-15, "Since the children have flesh and blood, Jesus too shared in their humanity so that by his death he might destroy the devil who holds the power of death and free those who all their lives were held in bondage by their fear of death."

Spirit, in the victory of Jesus in you, stand in freedom. Jesus has already conquered all the works of the enemy, including the power of death and the bondage to the fear of death. Based on your life experience, this may feel like an impossible dream, but this is God's will for you. He is God of the impossible. Spirit, be blessed with the assurance of the Word of God that these things can be so and are so in you and that you are called to stand in them as a minister of life. Be blessed in all the liberty that is in the Spirit of the Lord in you.

Be blessed in the name of the Spirit of the Lord (2 Cor. 3:17-18).

18 What Do You Want? — James 1:17

Spirit, listen to the Word of God for you in James 1:17. "Every good and perfect gift is from above, coming down from the Father of the heavenly lights, who does not change like shifting shadows."

Be blessed to know that your heavenly Father gives good gifts to his children. Spirit, your Father is asking you, "What do you want?" Be blessed to give him your true answer with no fear of rejection or ridicule. Be blessed with being thoroughly and totally alive and real in your answer.

"I want a place to see the sunrise and the sunset."
"I want to feel the wind in a magnificent thunderstorm."
"I want to see the stars at night so close that I could reach up and touch them."
"I want to breathe free up high on a mountain and imagine I am soaring like an eagle."
"I want to be caught up in the rush of a waterfall and be moved by the power and beauty."

What do you want, spirit? Listen. Maybe you will be blessed to hear,

"I want to paint the colors I see inside." They're inspired by God's throneroom.
"I want to dance, because motion is in my essence." That's God's cosmic synchronization.
"I want to play the music that moves my innermost depths." That's the harmony of the sound of heaven.
"I want to sing opera." When that's what you were born to do, nothing else will satisfy the heart of God.
"I want to figure skate in perfect choreography with a partner so that we two move as one." That's a picture of Christ and his bride.

Be blessed as you reflect the One who is infinitely creative and share in the glory of his creation — the brilliant colors, the complexities of his designs, the varieties of his creatures, his thoughts that can't be counted. Every moment is an opportunity for seeing his fingerprints.

You, spirit, are finding your voice, and you are expressing who you are, so that you can come to a higher level of embracing, understanding, and accepting how God made you in his image. Listen to what you hear when you ask, "What do you really want?" and do it. Honor all the gifts that God put in you so they are released from deep within you with the power of divine grace operating in your whole being. Pursue the pure expression of who you are. Be blessed to line up and synchronize with the fullness of God's expression in you, so that there is less struggle inside of you between spirit, soul, and body. Be blessed inside with life-giving clarity, alignment, congruence, and harmony. Be blessed as God is calling you up higher into all that pleases himself when he thinks of you.

Be blessed in the name of the Creative One who saw all that he had made and called it very good (Gen. 1:31).

Your Father's Heart

19 Your Father's name: Father Of Our Spirits — Hebrews 12:9

Spirit, listen to God's Word for you in Hebrews 12:9b. "How much more should we submit to the Father of our spirits and live!" And in Numbers 16:22. "Moses and Aaron fell facedown and cried out, 'O God, God of the spirits of all mankind…' " And in Numbers 6:27. "So they will put my name on the Israelites, and I will bless them."

Spirit, you are the innermost part where God's Spirit resides. You pray and sing and bless him (1 Cor. 14:15-16). You connect with him at a deep level, as you gaze into the light of your Father's eyes. You take the soul beyond wounds, shackles, and iniquities into blessing and abundance. Invite your Father to bring more wholeness. Ask him to transform your life and remove everything that does not glorify Jesus. Tell the soul to release its grasp on what it has been holding on to. Receive a new grace to run the race of life free of weights and entanglements.

Spirit, your heavenly Father is writing his name on you. Listen to Revelation 3:12. "I will write on him the name of my God … and I will also write on him my new name." You have been carrying around a set of old labels and names. God is removing all labels and names which he did not author. Let his Spirit work with you, spirit, to transform your soul and change your body. Cut soul ties that have bound you to people and places where you do not belong. Release them from your spirit, soul, and body. Receive the new names that God is writing on you.

Romans 8:2 says in The Living Bible, "For the power of the life-giving Spirit — and this power is mine through Christ Jesus — has freed me from the vicious circle of sin and death." Spirit, you can release the soul from striving, frustration, conflict, and futility into the power of God's name in you. Be blessed to integrate the soul with you in all you do, as you live from the life of Jesus in you. He did what he saw his Father doing and said what he heard his Father saying. Be blessed to do the same, as you are freed in him more and more. Invite him to put in you his thoughts from heaven that will affect earth — creative thoughts, blessing thoughts, liberating thoughts that align with "Your kingdom come, Your will be done, on earth as it is in heaven."

The Father of your spirit wants you to understand your full rights as a free and legal son, a joint heir with Jesus to all the inheritance laid up in heaven for you. You have his blessing (Num. 6:27). You already have everything you need for life and godliness on the earth. Align with the Spirit of God and align your soul and body in their proper order. Be blessed as the God of all grace himself, who called you to his eternal glory in Christ, beautifies and restores all things and makes you strong, firm, and steadfast (1 Pet. 5:10).

Be blessed in the name of the Father of your spirit (Heb. 12:9).

20 The Seal Of Your Father's Pleasure — Mark 1:11

Spirit, hear God's Word in Mark 1:11. "And a voice came from heaven: 'You are my Son, whom I love; with you I am well pleased.' "

Spirit, God told his Son how he felt about him. He fed him with his words that nourished him with the vital emotional nutrients of sonship. If the Son of God needed these words from his Father, how much more do you! Jesus stood in victory when he was confronted three times by satan in the wilderness because he was strengthened in his inner being by these affirming words. Be blessed to be so formed and nurtured by your heavenly Father's words, "I am pleased with you," that you can face any battle and be victorious. Be blessed to hear your heavenly Father's voice first-person, saying to you "You are my son, or my daughter, whom I love; I am well pleased with you."

You longed to hear words like that from your earthly father. Let your heavenly Father father you. Be blessed to know by his Spirit speaking to you that you are a delight to him. Be blessed to know without doubt that you are his favorite son or daughter. Be blessed with fully realizing the work of the Spirit of sonship in you, working continuously to bring you to live in your birthright as your Father's beloved child. From that place of strength you can work on the soul to bring healing, recovery, and restoration from all wounding. You can go forward into all the potential that God planted in your DNA, both spiritually and naturally.

Spirit, your Father was pleased to make you his own (1 Sam. 12:22), and he is blessing you every day. Be blessed with a safe place to be who your Father intends you to be. Be blessed to receive a love letter from your Abba today and every day, so that you will know that you have worth, you are valued, and you are cherished. Be blessed to know that you are a treasure to him. Be blessed with knowing that he never stops being your dear tender Abba. He affirms, welcomes, loves, heals, comforts, coaches, guides, delivers, and corrects you for your good and his glory. He never loses his pleasure in you as the son or daughter he uniquely designed.

Spirit, your Father recorded in writing the intention of his pleasure in you. Hear and receive his heart for you in Ephesians 1:5-14 NLT (personalized for you). God's unchanging plan has always been to adopt you into his own family by bringing you to himself through Jesus Christ. And this gave him great pleasure. So we praise God for the wonderful kindness he has poured out on you, because you belong to his dearly loved Son. He is so rich in kindness that he purchased your freedom through the blood of his Son, and your sins are forgiven. He has showered his kindness on you, along with all wisdom and understanding. God's secret plan has now been revealed to you; it is a plan centered on Christ, designed long ago according to his good pleasure. And this is his plan: At the right time he will bring everything together under the authority of Christ — everything in heaven and on earth. Furthermore, because of Christ, you have received an inheritance from God, for he chose you from the beginning, and all things happen just as he decided long ago. God's purpose was that you who trust in Christ should praise our glorious God. When you believed in Christ, he identified you as his own by giving you the Holy Spirit, whom he promised long ago. The Spirit is God's guarantee that he will give you everything he promised and that he has purchased you to be his own. This is just one more reason for you to praise your glorious God.

This, beloved one, is the pleasure that your heavenly Father takes in you. Spirit, be blessed to receive these words your Father speaks to you. Be blessed with being settled in your being in the eternal realities of the goodness and kindness of your Father and in the sovereignty, authority, and dominion of who he is. He has sealed you in his pleasure.

Be blessed with the seal of his pleasure in his promised Holy Spirit (Eph. 1:13).

21 Sonship/Father Heart Of God — Romans 8:14

Spirit, listen to the Word of God for you in Romans 8:14. "Those who are led by the Spirit of God are sons of God."

Spirit, your heavenly Father blesses you with true biblical sonship. He wants you to receive it. Be blessed as he calls you to life, nurture, and enlargement. He is the source of your biblical manhood or womanhood and of the abundant life of generational blessing that is laid up for you. Be blessed with the most profound blessing that you need to receive. Receive the Father-heart of God. Rejoice in his special creation of you, his kind intention toward you, his matchless love for you, and his glory revealed in you. Be blessed with God re-parenting you in ways your earthly mother and father were not capable of doing. Be blessed to receive his healing in your soul's gaping holes and wounded fathering. Be blessed as he completely fills your daddy holes. Be blessed with your heavenly Father giving you all the father's blessing that you craved from your earthly father.

Be blessed with life-changing encounters with the Father-heart of God. Be blessed with your Father-God's best healing work in restoring your heart and soul according to his design that he had for you before the foundations of the world were laid. Be blessed with knowing your Father's heart nurturing belonging, inclusion, and worth. God can heal you to wholeness, and from that place of wholeness he will send you forth to do all that he designed you to do. He can bring forth your true birthright, to be all he wants you to be. Be blessed to be strengthened to implement the will of the Father in your life.

Spirit, be blessed with measurable growth in your being as a son — growth that is mental, spiritual, emotional, and relational. Jesus, the Father's beloved Son, grew in wisdom and stature and in favor with God and men (Luke 2:52). He lives presently in you with all the power of his Sonship relating to his Father. Be blessed with the Spirit of truth who bears witness to you concerning the lies you have believed, your fears, your wounds, the nurture you never received, the judgments and vows you made about relationships, the places in you that were not called to maturity, the agreements you made with the enemy, and other things in a fallen world.

Be blessed with a rich gold mine of identity and legitimacy from which to live out your birthright and destiny confidently and purposefully. Be blessed with God's exquisite fathering, and receive it as a special true son or daughter. Be blessed with fully realizing the life-changing truth of the Spirit of sonship in you, living in you to possess your birthright as your Father's beloved son. Be blessed to know his Spirit speaking to you, spirit, that you are a delight to him.

Be blessed to know without doubt that your Father is extending his favor toward you, assuring you of release into the full rights of your true identity and legitimacy. Spirit, be blessed with knowing this new grace place with your Father. This is the time of your Father's favor, a time of release of the life of sonship, as foretold in Malachi 4:5-6, "See, I will send you the prophet Elijah before that great and dreadful day of the LORD comes. He will turn the hearts of the fathers to their children, and the hearts of the children to their fathers." Be blessed with the alignment with a father's love that you have been seeking.

Be blessed in the name of your Father to the fatherless (Ps. 68:5).

22 You Are The Beloved — John 17:23

Spirit, hear and receive God's Word in John 17:23 NLT. "I in them and you in me, all being perfected into one. Then the world will know... and will understand that you love them as much as you love me."

At his baptism and transfiguration, your Father said to Jesus, "You are the Son I love. I am well pleased with you" (Mat. 3:17; 17:5). It was a great affirmation of his love and pleasure in his Son. Because you are in Him, the Father loves you with the same love (John 17:23,26). You are God's beloved; that is the most intimate truth about you. It has to be true, because Jesus said it to his Father.

Spirit, let these words reverberate in every cell. Be blessed to live from the blessing of belovedness, not trying to earn it. Hear your Father speak to you about his deep bonds with you, his deep attachment to you with cords of unfailing love (Jer. 31:3; Hos. 11:4). Hear him speak to you about trust, faith, and love that is much deeper than your mindset of survival. Hear him speak to you about your deepest yearnings, your wishes, your hopes, and your dreams.

Spirit, hear the soft voice of your Father speaking in the core of your essence: you are the beloved. On you his favor rests. He sees you as a precious being. You are welcome to exist. God celebrates your existence. Be blessed to know how you were infinitely loved before you were wounded. That's the truth of your life. There is no burden on you to prove you are worthy of being loved, of being heard, of being respected and honored and given dignity. Your life is an unceasing "yes" to the truth that you are beloved because of God's great love. In him you deserve to be valued.

Receive the different tones in which others say that to you, but always remember that it is your spirit connection with your Father that matters. People do not give you your legitimacy. True legitimacy comes from the One who chose you with everlasting love.

Your Father says, "I called you by name from the very beginning. You belong to me, and I know you as my own, and I am yours. You know me as your own true Father. I molded you in your mother's womb. I carved you in the palms of my Son. I hide you in the shadow of my embrace. You have my infinite tenderness, and I care for you intimately. I have counted every hair on your head, and wherever you go, I go with you. Wherever you rest, I keep watch. I give you food that will satisfy all your hunger and drink that will quench all your thirst. I will never hide my face from you. Nothing will ever separate us. Wherever you are, I am. Live your life as my redeemed child. You can reach out to true inner freedom and find it ever more fully."

That's the message of your life... you are chosen, and you are beloved. It's your sacred romance. Say "Yes" to your belovedness, your significance, your worth, and your belonging. His "Yes" is engraved on your heart. Spirit, rise up to your full stature and discover how to fulfill your deepest essence of who you are, beloved in God your Father and kept in his Son. You are accepted in the Beloved (Eph. 1:6 NKJV).

Be blessed in the name of the Beloved Son (Mat. 3:17 NKJV).

Based in part on *Life Of The Beloved*, ©1992 by Henri J. M. Nouwen.
The Crossroad Publishing Company, New York, NY.

23 You Are Secure As The Beloved — Deuteronomy 33:12

Spirit, hear God's Word for you in Deuteronomy 33:12. "Let the beloved of the LORD rest secure in him, for he shields him all day long, and the one the LORD loves rests between his shoulders."

Spirit, you can rest in the full truth that you are your Father's beloved. The voice of your loving Father resonates in you in a deep place. He called you his beloved from eternity. Taste deeply of love, of God, and of truth. Know the treasure you are to God. You are a chosen one, a special person, noticed in your uniqueness, eternally valued. You are priceless and irreplaceable, safe in his everlasting embrace, at rest in his non-comparing love.

Spirit, being the beloved, minister to your soul the truth that you are chosen of God. Increasingly be aware of your belovedness. You are precious in his eyes. Hear this so that you live with a stable, settled sense of true belonging. The good things you DO reveal what a beautiful person you ARE. Your real gift is not so much what you can DO as who you ARE.

Be blessed with your heavenly Father providing a safe, secure environment, without having to test him continually, fearfully asking the questions, such as "Are you still with me? Will you still be with me if…? Prove it by…" Be blessed to choose against the accuser's lies about your adequacy, identity, legitimacy, your past, present, and future. Be blessed to know that you can never be rejected or abandoned by your Father. Your loving God never leaves you alone. His love is your companion every step of the way. Be blessed with knowing his heart nurturing belonging, inclusion, and worth. Be blessed with healing of your soul's rejection wounds and the spirit abandonment wound that is deeper.

Your Father calls you to become who you are in totality — spirit, soul, and body. All your life is an opportunity to become who you are, to affirm your own true spiritual nature, to claim your unique truth, and to say "Yes" to the one who calls you the beloved. God's love gives you your being. Discover more fully who God is and whose child you are. Your legitimacy is settled in him. Trust what he wants you to see and hear.

God has given you great gifts of inner peace, joy of living, sense of well-being, solidness and strength inside, and healing. Share your life in encouragement, hope, and trust. When you are secure, your presence is a joy to those who know you.

Spirit, receive and drive a stake in this blessing as the truth that shapes your daily life. Get quiet, listen to the blessing, and listen to the voice of love saying good things to you. Trust the voice of affirmation; it is persistent, strong, and deep. It will never let you go.

Synchronize with the voice calling you the beloved, and continually align yourself with your belovedness. Don't be pulled out of your center in your belovedness. Be blessed to be attentively present to him to see his fingerprints and feel his closeness.

Be blessed in the life and in the name of the Chosen One (Luke 23:35).

Based in part on *Life Of The Beloved*, ©1992 by Henri J. M. Nouwen.
The Crossroad Publishing Company, New York, NY.

24 You're A Son In Your Father's Heart — 1 John 3:1; Galatians 4:6-7

Spirit, listen to the Word of God for you in 1 John 3:1. "How great is the love the Father has lavished on us, that we should be called children of God! And that is what we are!" And Galatians 4:6-7. "Because you are sons, God sent the Spirit of his Son into our hearts, the Spirit who calls out, 'Abba, Father.' So you are no longer a slave, but a son; and since you are a son, God has made you also an heir."

Beloved one, be blessed to be firmly established in your true identity as a son of your Father with his lavish blessings as his heir. Be blessed as he unveils and reveals to you who you are and affirms to you how he sees you in Christ, your hope of glory.

Be blessed with deep speaking to deep in you, the place where your heavenly Father calls forth your real essence as his beloved son. Your Father's heart is passionate for your full identity as his son, based purely on relationship, not competence. Be blessed as he calls you to life to fully possess the sonship you are due. You do not have to work for it. You can't earn it, and you can never lose it. Be blessed with perfect love that casts out the fear that you aren't enough, or you don't have what it takes.

Spirit, there is a blessing from your generations that you never got. This is the empty piece inside. The Bible was written in and to a culture that was steeped in blessing — blessing the child in giving him his name, passing the patriarchal blessing on to the children's children, giving and receiving the priestly blessing. Be blessed to receive in your heavenly Father the father's blessing that you craved from your earthly father and never got. As you receive, be blessed to think and envision generationally. Be blessed with being intentional about leaving a generational legacy, a trust fund of blessings for your spiritual and physical generations. You can't give to the next generation what you don't have. Your Father is passionate about the deep well of your belonging and worth. Be blessed with settled legitimacy as a true covenant son/daughter of God your Father who can never leave you or forsake you.

Be blessed with the deep and abiding nature of a son, who is marked by freedom, nobility of birth and character, confident identity, honor, dignity, legal authority, purpose, true personhood, access to your Father, deep intimacy with him and within his house, and family likeness. In your Father you have his assurance that you are an heir to this rich trust fund laid up for you in his heart.

Spirit, receive personally this prayer of Paul for his spiritual children in Ephesians 1:17-19. "I keep asking that the God of our Lord Jesus Christ, the glorious Father, may give you the Spirit of wisdom and revelation, so that you may know him better. I pray also that the eyes of your heart may be enlightened in order that you may know the hope to which he has called you, the riches of his glorious inheritance in the saints, and his incomparably great power for us who believe." Be blessed to receive the Spirit of wisdom and revelation and live in him. Be blessed to know him better and his power for you.

Be blessed in the name of your glorious Father who opens the eyes of your heart to know his glorious inheritance in you (Eph. 1:17-18).

25 Favor — Psalm 5:12; Job 10:12

Spirit, hear God's Word for you in Psalm 5:12. "For surely, O LORD, you bless the righteous; you surround them with your favor as with a shield." And in Job 10:12. "You gave me life and showed me kindness, and in your providence watched over my spirit."

Spirit, be blessed with the assurance of your Father's blessing, his presence, his favor, and his surrounding grace. Who you are and everything you have is the result of his favor. He is your sun and shield, and his honor validates you (Ps. 84:11). Your Abba wants to take you as his precious child right up next to his heart today. He will keep you close and make his face shine on you and be gracious to you (Num. 6:24-25). Your Father smiles on you today with his compassion and his full blessing as you seek him (Isa. 30:18). He has written this day of your life in his book. He knew you before you were born (Ps. 139:16). You are constantly on his mind (Ps. 139:17-18).

Spirit, be blessed to know that your Father's providence goes before you to provide for your every need. He is with you to strengthen you and keep you from harm (1 Chron. 4:10). Be blessed as his favor rests on his appointed work through your hands (Ps. 90:17), because his purposes and power for you are great.

Spirit, you need favor with your authorities whom God has placed over you and with those in decision-making positions (Ezra 7:27; Neh. 1:11). His Word says, "The king's heart is in the hand of the LORD; he directs it like a watercourse wherever he pleases" (Pro. 21:1). Be blessed as God breaks through all hindrances and uses all concerned with you to fulfill his will on your behalf.

Spirit, let your Abba protect your emotions, as he surrounds you with the shield of his presence (Ps. 5:12). He promises that weeping may endure for a night, his anger is but for a moment, but joy comes in the morning, and his favor lasts for your lifetime (Ps. 30:5). He keeps you today in the favor of his love and faithfulness (Pro. 3:3-4). He withholds no good thing from you as you live before him blamelessly (Ps. 84:11).

Be blessed in the name of the One who rejoices today in doing you good (Jer. 32:41).

Emotional Healing

26 God's Good News For You — Jeremiah 29:11

Spirit, hear God's Word for you in Jeremiah 29:11. "For I know the plans I have for you," declares the LORD, "plans to prosper you and not to harm you, plans to give you hope and a future."

Spirit, be blessed with the love of Christ for emotional healing. The psalmist said that his body was troubled, and his soul was greatly troubled (Ps. 6:2-3). Be blessed with peace and hope being restored to you. The mind may have witnessed an event it can't cope with. The body may react physically under duress, the soul weeps. It is a total body reaction. Be blessed, spirit, soul, and body, to be healed in the root cause of all disturbance of your peace. Be blessed to reject all lies at the root. Through the power of the Holy Spirit, address the lies and be set free.

Jeremiah wrote to people who were in captivity for seventy years. Hear the good news: It's not too late. In the defining message of his life in Luke 4:18, Jesus said that he would set the captives free. If you feel captive in any way because of emotional wounding, be blessed with his love, redemption, and power to flood you and release you. Be blessed in your brain, your mind, and your memory, particularly the part that is holding on to any issues. Receive the compassion of Jesus to address this emotional concern. He is mighty to deal with any depression or other aftermath or backlash. Receive the light of his healing grace into everything that is out of God's order.

Jesus opened the minds of the men on the way to Emmaus so that they could understand him in the Scriptures. Understand his words to you. Jesus said to Paul, "My grace is sufficient for you, for my power is made perfect in weakness." And Paul replied, "I will boast all the more gladly about my weaknesses, so that Christ's power may rest on me" (2 Cor. 12:9-12). Spirit, boast in your wounds by declaring that the power of Jesus is in you to heal them. You have the treasure of your life in a human "jar of clay" to show that he is your all-surpassing power to accomplish his plans for your welfare (2 Cor. 4:7).

Spirit, hear Jeremiah 29:11-14 NLT. " 'For I know the plans I have for you,' says the LORD. 'They are plans for good and not for disaster, to give you a future and a hope. In those days when you pray, I will listen. If you look for me in earnest, you will find me when you seek me. I will be found by you,' says the LORD. 'I will end your captivity and restore your fortunes. I will gather you out of the nations where I sent you and bring you home again to your own land.' "

God's thoughts toward you are for peace. His plans in you are for healing, not for hurt or negativity or sadness. He promised the all-surpassing power of his love. He will accomplish his hope, his future, and his well-being in you. When you seek him, he hears you. He lets you find him to bring you back from your captivity, whatever it is. His best for you is peace, wholeness, and security.

Be blessed today in the name of the Prince of peace (Isa. 9:6).

27 Journey Of God's Deep Healing — Psalm 42:11; 103:1-5

Spirit, hear God's Word for you in Psalm 42:5,11; 43:5. "Why are you downcast, O my soul? Why so disturbed within me? Put your hope in God, for I will yet praise him, my Savior and my God."

Spirit, be blessed in the light of God. You are a blessed covenant son/daughter of God Most High. You display his family likeness. You are awesome in him, and you are not lacking in anything that you need. Your Father is nurturing and growing you in all the spiritual DNA that he designed in you. His gifts and callings are irrevocable. Nothing that you have done or that has happened to you changes that.

Soul, all you have known is shame, fear, and control. Your life's work has been to control because of fear. You have controlled what the mind remembers and takes in and processes. You have distorted based on your agenda of not wanting to feel pain or risk. You have been captive in a prison of your own making of fear and control. You have sabotaged any reality you didn't want to feel or face. You have sabotaged areas of the spirit that relate to God because they are outside the realm of your understanding and identity. The spirit is growing and becoming healthier and asserting itself, and you fear losing control.

Soul, be free from critiquing or rejecting the blessings of God the Father. He is inviting you to put your hand in his and go into this unknown spiritual journey, because he is near and he is safe. Come into agreement with God, and let go of stress and anxiety. Do not be afraid of the "new you," because God made the spirit for such a time as this. Breathe in the love of God, breathe out anything not of him. Center yourself in the love of Christ and receive his love into all your concerns, and give them to him.

Listen as the psalmist speaks to his own soul in Psalm 103:1-5. "Praise the LORD, O my soul; all my inmost being, praise his holy name. Praise the LORD, O my soul, and forget not all his benefits — who forgives all your sins and heals all your diseases, who redeems your life from the pit and crowns you with love and compassion, who satisfies your desires with good things so that your youth is renewed like the eagle's."

Spirit, you understand this, as the psalmist did. Put the soul in touch with Christ the Healer, and receive and soak up his healing presence in these words. Minister to the soul, because it is incapable of understanding and speaking the Spirit's language. Be blessed to trust the Spirit of God revealing himself in you.

Spirit, you have felt the favor of these blessings. You can trust God's favor to forgive you, to heal you, and to redeem your life from the pit. You can trust him to crown you with his love and compassion and to satisfy your desires with good things. Praise his name for these blessings that you have received as a gift from your Father.

Be blessed in his holy name as the covenant child of always-faithful God (2 Tim. 2:13).

28 God's Healing Touch — Isaiah 42:3

Spirit, listen to God's Word for you in Isaiah 42:3. "A bruised reed he will not break, and a smoldering wick he will not snuff out. In faithfulness he will bring forth justice." And in Psalm 147:3. "He heals the brokenhearted and binds up their wounds."

Spirit, come to the promises of God for healing. In his humanity Jesus knew all your sorrows and griefs, your rejection and scorn, your shame and guilt, your infirmities and afflictions, your crushing and wounding, your oppression and suffering, your helplessness and your tendencies to go astray (Isa. 53:1-6). He identified with you in every respect, because he was made like you in every way, and therefore he is able to come to your help (Heb. 2:17-18). He understands feeling bruised, broken, wounded, and barren, and he turns them to shouts of joy (Isa. 54:1).

Healing prayer is about applying God's healing words to wounded, sinful, helpless, and hopeless places of life. Isaiah said that God takes our wounds as an opportunity to display his glory (Isa. 61:3). That's how God can be glorified in the broken places. And the greater the wound, the greater the glory. In the end he "will wipe every tear from their eyes. There will be no more death or mourning or crying or pain, for the old order of things has passed away" (Rev. 21:4). God can restore what the enemy plundered. He said, "I will repay you for the years the locusts have eaten" (Joel 2:25).

Spirit, let the Holy Spirit of truth bring those things to the surface that he wants to touch, and be blessed to partner with him to do his work. Bring all memories to him so he can shine his light into the darkness, into the nooks and crannies of the mind, in all storage areas of the brain and your emotional mind. Give him all blocks to healing, especially unforgiveness, inner vows, judgments, unworthiness, negativity, or hopelessness. Be blessed with the healing love and compassion of Jesus touching all wounds you have from the past. Be blessed with knowing that Jesus will stand as a filter between you and the memories of the past. Be blessed as he lifts from you the scar tissue of past wounds, be they physical, verbal, emotional, or mental.

Spirit, lead the way. Choose release, choose to open the doors of the prison of fear in the soul. Identify all burdens the soul is carrying of shame, guilt, and rejection. Identify the lies, confess them, and renounce them. Ask the Holy Spirit of truth to state the truth and expand on it, and let him bring you into his light. Be blessed as he heals emotional issues and painful memories. Be blessed with deep and profound healing at the root of the problem inside the core issue, not just a band-aid to cover over the injury.

Be blessed with the comfort of the Lord for disappointment, pain, loss, abandonment, grief, fears, and all emotions that landed in you. Look into the face of your tender Abba to heal them all. Allow him to address your pain and minister his healing to the soul and the physical memory that is prone to replay the past. Be blessed as he feeds you with gentleness and kindness, nourishing you with hope in him, gathering you under this wings, drawing you deeper into his grace.

Spirit, Jesus is your Healing Sacrifice. You can bear witness to him, "Surely you have borne our infirmities and carried our diseases. You were wounded for our transgressions, crushed for our iniquities. You were stricken by God and afflicted for our healing. By your stripes we are healed" (Isa. 53:3-5). Be blessed to receive this as completed present reality. He is I AM to be this for you now.

God told Hezekiah, "I have heard your prayer, I have seen your tears, I will heal you." That's quite a promise, and it is as true today as when it was spoken then. He responds to our tears with healing. Jeremiah said, "Heal me, and I shall be healed indeed." Spirit, be excited by those words. Rest in those words. Breathe in the love and healing of God. Breathe out any pain or hurt or anxiety. Breathe in the comforting essence of Christ, and breathe out "And I will be comforted indeed." God remains faithful to you. Your Comforter indwells you. He is now administering comfort and healing in every area of hurt. Be blessed in the peace of God that rests upon you with his joy and strength. Be blessed in the courage of the Holy Spirit. The risen Jesus living in you is bringing you resurrection power. The ascended Christ is showing you a foretaste of his majesty. Be blessed in the abundant life of Jesus, as his healing compassion fills the essence of your being, as you align yourself with the Spirit of Christ Jesus every moment of every day.

Be blessed as he rubs his oil into all the places that were barren, broken, and hurting. Be blessed as he washes those areas that were tender and raw. Be blessed as he brings back to life those parts of your being long denied or buried. Be blessed that he is everything to you that you need.

Spirit, be blessed in confidence that your heavenly Father honors your tears that seek him, your patience to wait for him, your eyes to behold him, your wisdom to perceive him, your heart to meditate on him, and your life to show him forth in the power of the Spirit of Jesus your Lord.

Be blessed to receive more peace, more love, more power,
more of him who is All and fills everything in every way (Col. 3:11; Eph. 1:23).

29 Generational Healing — Hebrews 4:15-16

Spirit, hear God's Word for you in Hebrews 4:15-16. "For we do not have a high priest who is unable to sympathize with our weaknesses... Let us then approach the throne of grace with confidence, so that we may receive mercy and find grace to help us in our time of need."

Spirit, come to the front to receive emotional generational healing. Be blessed with healing in every area of damage in your family line. Be blessed to see the light and truth of the Healer shining on the sins and the issues that have been passed down generation to generation. In his full cleansing, they have no more power. Be blessed with order and alignment in all generational warping that was passed down. When the Son sets you free, you are free indeed.

You are blessed that Jesus feels and understands what you have inherited from your generations, and he is present as your healer. He honors your yearning for his healing presence. Be blessed to receive his love into your wounds. Carry your concerns to the foot of the cross that you may be healed. As you approach him, receive his grace and mercy for his help now. Be blessed with the abundant strength of Christ who strengthens you with his holy presence. Receive his release from everything that is negative and is tying you to the past.

Receive his gift of forgiveness to flow in your family tree. Be blessed with strength to give him your concerns and leave them with him. Be blessed to take them from your shoulders and leave them in his hands.

Be blessed with his light shining into issues of weakness and concern. What is exposed by his light loses its power to bind you. Be blessed with feeling his loving eyes looking into yours. Be blessed with the light of Christ being very evident in your healing, as he brings everything to his light. In his light you have life. Be blessed to rise from death, darkness, and disease as the light of Christ infuses you. Jesus said, "Do not be afraid. I am the light of the world, and I am with you always." He said, "Fear not, little flock. It is my Father's good pleasure to give you the kingdom." Be blessed with being set free to enjoy your life to the fullest in God's love and greatness.

Spirit, be blessed to see and experience the generational deposits of blessings and legacies he has placed in your bloodline. God said that although iniquity is visited upon the third and fourth generation, he shows his love and blessings to a thousand generations of those who love him and keep his commandments. Be blessed with God's peace, grace, favor, justice, righteousness and much fruitfulness, as you reap 30-, 60-, and 100-fold to a thousand generations. Be blessed to believe your Father-God for spiritual generational breakthroughs. He is your faithful God, who keeps his covenant of love with you. You are fully alive in the generational blessings of his covenantal kingdom, through Jesus Christ your peace, your healing, your love, and your authority. Thanks be to God.

Be blessed in the name of your High Priest and Mediator (Heb. 6:20).

30 Healing Hurts From Parents — Psalm 22:9; 71:6

Spirit, hear God's Word for you in Psalm 22:9. "You brought me out of the womb; you made me trust in you even at my mother's breast." And in Psalm 71:6. "From birth I have relied on you… I will ever praise you."

Spirit, God has been present with you from the womb. Before your mother or father knew they were expecting, your Abba Father knew you were there, and he rejoiced as your Abba. God has blessed you with eternal life in the cross of his Son Jesus that transcends the life you had from your parents. You are a son/daughter of God, on the authority of his Word. He ordained you and brought you forth.

Spirit, you legitimately needed a mother's blessing and a father's blessing, but your earthly parents did not know your full need for it or how to give it. They didn't have it to give because they themselves were wounded. So come to the front to receive healing for wounds at the hands of your parents and other caregivers.

There are two types of history stored in everyone. There is the remembered history of events and experiences. There are also a subconscious history of emotions and feelings. Receive God's work as he cleanses deep wounds that you received from words and actions in your family of origin. Receive the ministry of Jehovah-Rapha, the healing covenant name of eternal God, as he works in the core of your being. As you go face to face with him, receive his healing and blessing and deep release, where no other prayer ministry has touched. The soul (mind and will) has repented of the judgments and vows over and over, but under the judgments and vows, there were emotions of fear, rejection, abandonment, anger, disappointment, shame, unforgiveness, self-hatred, etc., that sprang from specific wounds. Those remain imprinted in the organic brain and stored in you, the spirit.

Spirit, listen to God's Word in Psalm 46:4-5. "There is a river whose streams make glad the city of God, the holy place where the Most High dwells. God is within her, she will not fall; God will help her at break of day." You are that holy place, that temple where God dwells. The Spirit of Jesus lives in you to heal and make you whole. The Spirit of truth and the God of all mercy is ready to do a thorough work to bring new life.

Receive his river of cleansing from all feelings that God didn't author — that you were of no value, an imposition, or you were not wanted or were conceived and born at an inconvenient time. Receive God's river of cleansing from the feeling that you were a burden to be borne, or an object to be used, a fixture in someone's world instead of a precious little one to be loved, valued, protected, honored, and nurtured. Receive cleansing in that core sense of being that you were a disappointment, that you could never measure up or be good enough. Receive cleansing from comparison, competition, evaluation, and displacement. Be clean and be free of that deposit of blame, shame, guilt, confusion, and self-hatred.

Be free of the feeling that you had to be responsible to hold the family together, to make momma or daddy happy. Be free and be cleansed of false responsibility that you had to make peace in their irresponsibility, or absence, or emotional absence, or strife in the family. Be free and be washed clean of false responsibility for the conflict and pain, that everything that went wrong was your fault.

Spirit, hear this: It wasn't your fault. Your mother/father failed to be present because of their own problems. Be free and receive a river of healing for the denial of your legitimate needs because they were never met. Be healed of the hope deferred that makes the heart sick.

You have forgiven many times from your head, but your heart still hurts and brings old garbage to the table in current situations and relationships. Receive the healing to you, spirit, that needed parenting, so you can truly release your parent for failing to be the person you cried out for him/her to be.

Spirit, you have received a new filter of the blood of Jesus and your heavenly Father's love and the seal of the Holy Spirit. This is like dialysis when blood is put through a filter, and all the impurities are filtered out. Let your toxins and impurities go through the holy filter system of the blood of Jesus to filter out

- anxieties, fears, dreads, worry
- rejection, abandonment, emotional absenteeism, isolation
- worthlessness, inadequacy, inferiority, insecurity
- anger, hatred, revenge, murder in your heart
- bitterness, resentment, unforgiveness
- perfectionism, performance, self-protection
- control, manipulation
- role reversal, care-taking, being a substitute mate
- abuse of all kinds: physical, emotional, sexual, spiritual, verbal
- put down, shame, being ill-used
- infirmities of all kinds

Be blessed as God fills up the hole in your heart, those empty spaces, that bottomless pit that craves nearness, intimacy, affirmation, connection, and significance, and yet fears it, is unable to receive it, and runs away from it. Receive healing from the wound caused by lack of bonding with your parent. Receive cleansing from attachment wounds, as Father-God binds you to himself with cords that cannot be broken, as he promised. Be free and be whole, be healed of broken trust that resulted when you could not settle down and feel secure, safe, and trusting in your parents to be there for you. Receive a new basic "trust-er" nurtured by your heavenly Father who never lets you down, so that you can trust authority figures.

Spirit, chose to replace the lies that you have agreed with and thus made agreements with the father of lies. Some of the lies are that you were not important enough or worthy to be given time, priority, focused attention, communication; that you were a mistake, you're a victim, just a survivor, __________ etc. Choose to crucify your unreliable feelings on the cross of Jesus. Take captive the thoughts, emotions, and will of the soul for Jesus' sake. You can do it. You must do it for full victory, and nobody can do it for you. God is at work in you to will and to do his good pleasure. Receive his enabling grace. Be blessed with his strength to embrace his work as good and perfect and in perfect timing.

Spirit, give the Holy Spirit of truth permission to clean out all the poison of woundedness that the soul has known for years and receive his ministry to do it. Be courageous to seek the truth, to feel the pain, to lay the ax to all bitter roots for a thorough work at their deepest source, that they may be completely removed and not defile you and trouble many.

You have authority in Christ to bind up and cast out all the enemy's strongholds coming off your family relationships. Put the cross of Jesus and the empty tomb between you and the works and workers of darkness to get release from the familiar games they have played: anger, guilt, shame, blame, judgment, bitterness, non-feeling, control, uproar, victim-mentality, performance, secrets, compulsions, addictions, ____________ (etc.)

Spirit, be strong to embrace life as God intends for you and not run away, withdraw, build walls, or be self-protecting any longer. Drink deeply of the understanding that you are loved, cared for, significant, the apple of your Father's eye. He delights in you. He is happy you are alive. You give him joy. Receive this reality and let your broken love-receiver be healed, as your brokenness is displaced by a higher truth of your place in Abba's house.

From the light of the eyes of Abba Father, receive blessing in the seat of life, your inner being. Let it trickle down to soul, and heart, and emotions, and will, and identity, and legitimacy. God will rebuild what has been desolate and oppressed. He will restore the years the locusts have eaten. Be blessed to continue to receive the ministry of Abba supernaturally in those places where the little boy/girl within still cries out for mothering or fathering. He finishes what he begins.

Spirit, settle down in your El Shaddai in full security, acceptance, and blessing. He is always there for you. He invites you to connect deeply and intimately with him. Be blessed with new freedom of spirit from him, unhindered and holy. Awake to life as the joyful son/daughter of the King that he created you to be. Be blessed as he satisfies the birthright that he has placed within you.

Be blessed in the name of El Shaddai (Ps. 91:1)

31 Inner Healing Ministry Of Jesus — Luke 4:18-19

Spirit, listen to God's Word as Jesus began his ministry by defining his call and his eternal relationship with you in Luke 4:18-19. Jesus said, "The Spirit of the Lord is on Me, because he anointed me to preach good news to the poor. He has sent me to proclaim freedom for the prisoners and recovery of sight for the blind, to release the oppressed, to proclaim the year of the Lord's favor."

Spirit, be blessed to know the mission of Jesus in you, that his kingdom is now within you accomplishing his purposes. Jesus is now present-tense empowered, anointed, and appointed by God to bring good news to you, to release slavery of your soul, to give you the vision of being your Father's favored child, to lift those places that were bruised, crushed, and broken, to release you from bondages and oppression, to open your eyes to see the future he is holding for you, to call you forth to become the true son/daughter after his own heart that you are, and to embrace that it is time — now is the year of God's favor.

The resurrection power of Jesus is actively working in you and for you. He wants to do a deep and thorough work as you increase in confidence and in his likeness. Be blessed to cooperate with him and not to quench him. Be blessed with more spiritual discernment for fulfilling your birthright and potential and for relationships with others — every area of covenantal life vertically and horizontally.

Spirit, these are days and times God ordained and foreknew (Ps. 139:17). Turn to your heavenly Father for your life script and marching orders. Jesus said that this is the "day when salvation and the free favors of God profusely abound" (Luke 4:19, Amplified). This is the time of your Father's favor to release you into your full rights as his son, as foretold in Malachi 4:5-6, "See, I will send you the prophet Elijah before that great and dreadful day of the LORD comes. He will turn the hearts of the fathers to their children, and the hearts of the children to their fathers." Your Father has turned his heart toward you. The Spirit of the Father is extending his favor toward you, assuring you of the freedom and the full rights of your true identity and legitimacy in him. Your Father's favor is blessing you every day. Open wide and receive it. Be blessed with knowing this new place of grace in your Father's favor.

Be blessed in the name of the One who favors you for a lifetime (Ps. 30:5; Exo. 33:12).

32 Turning Curses Into Blessings In His Time — Acts 3:19-21

Spirit, hear God's Word for you in Acts 3:19-21. "Repent, then, and turn to God, so that your sins may be wiped out, that times of refreshing may come from the Lord, and that he may send the Christ, who has been appointed for you — even Jesus. But he must remain in heaven until the time comes for God to restore everything, as he promised long ago through his holy prophets."

Spirit, be blessed in your appointed season of refreshing, receiving, rebuilding, restoring, and reformation. Jesus was born in the fullness of time, lived a sinless life, died on the cross as the atoning sacrifice, and rose again. In his authority break all ties with the enemy that have caused you to reap the warping of time. Your place is in Jesus, your Kinsman-Redeemer, to redeem you from curses on time which you and your ancestors have brought on yourself and your family. His all-sufficient blood releases you from all covenants, pacts, and agreements with the kingdom of darkness. Revelation 12:11 says, "They overcame him (the accuser) by the blood of the Lamb and by the word of their testimony; they did not love their lives so much as to shrink from death."

Be blessed to live in your eternal covenant in the redeeming blood of the Lamb, the Lord Jesus Christ. He said, "It is finished." Revelation 12:10 bears witness to this. "Now have come the salvation and power and the kingdom of our God and the authority of his Christ. For the accuser of our brothers, who accuses them before our God day and night, has been hurled down."

Spirit, it is right to file your brief in the court of heaven to confess that you, beloved one, and your forebears have broken God's righteous decrees. Repent for and renounce all of God's commandments that were broken in your generational line. Repent for leading others to commit iniquity, causing blessings to be stolen.

Be blessed with the effective cleansing of blood of Jesus that removes anything that separates you from his presence and tears down all barriers to future blessings in your generations. Be blessed with a time of refreshing in response to your generational repentance. Be blessed as God turns the curses into blessings. Be blessed to be released into the full purposes of God, which he planned before time, for this time, this timing, and this season.

Spirit, make righteousness your plumbline and justice your measuring line, so that God can sweep away the enemy and his plans. Receive cleansing with holy fire where righteous time was stolen. Receive God's reinstatement of right alignment in his holiness in the family line. Be blessed to extend this cleansing and purging fire forward to physical and spiritual seed to a thousand generations. In every place where blessing has been stolen, bring into alignment everything that was perverted and sanctify it and make it holy.

Spirit, you are in strategic partnership with the Spirit of God to bring into alignment God's purposes for you. The soul has remembered too much of the badness and the toxicity of the past, but be blessed to bring to light memories of times when God was present and speaking to you and giving you a sign of his goodness. Be blessed to lead the soul to receive new disciplines and new ownership, as you take sanctified authority over everything that pertains to you and your family. Be blessed as disappointments are washed away, vision is renewed, aborted dreams and desires are resurrected, God-directed expectations are renewed based on his Word and his Spirit and his time. You have expectations that have been deferred. Be blessed as God works in them.

Be blessed to lay hold of renewed hope. Be blessed with special grace to do all the things God has whispered to you for yourself and your family. Be blessed with grace in this time as you make the most of appointed time and get in line with eternity in the time of his favor.

Spirit, maximize the positive childhood memories and the positive significant imprints and bring into focus those experiences that you haven't understood before. Be blessed with remembering a word, a touch, an event in your childhood in a picture and you will say, "Aha, God was there, he was speaking to me in that. He had his hand on me. I see how that mattered. I see what an imprint that was on me for good."

Be blessed everywhere that you are pregnant with something new, something that you have held in your heart. It is nine months for a human child, but often much longer in the womb of God before heaven invades earth with a fulfilled promise. Allow your Father's purposes to be worked into your family, increasing the pool of deposit from which you will bring generational transformation. Be blessed in this time of realignment and reconciliation of what is out of order, out of step, out of sync, out of harmony, out of line with God's appointed time and purposes. Be blessed to position yourself to receive the redemption of every curse. Be blessed to receive everything that God wants to give you and your family in his redeemed time, restoring all the years the locusts have eaten.

Be blessed in the name of the Ancient of Days (Dan. 7:22).

33 Healing Ministry — 1 Thessalonians 5:23-24; Isaiah 63:9

Come, Holy Spirit, into the greatest need of this precious one's spirit and minister to him or her the Spirit of the Father. Minister all the finished work of the cross for every need. Go into the deep, hidden, inarticulate broken places that are hungering for restoration, and reconcile and align everything that is twisted, warped, and needy.

Precious one, hear God's Word for you in 1 Thessalonians 5:23-24. "God himself, the God of peace, will sanctify you through and through. He will keep your whole spirit, soul and body blameless at his coming. He is faithful who calls you, and he will do it." And in Isaiah 63:9. "In all their distress he too was distressed, and the angel of his presence saved them. In his love and mercy he redeemed them; he lifted them up and carried them all the days of old."

Spirit, come to the front to be blessed. Allow the presence of your Father to minister his redeeming love and mercy. Be blessed to receive his healing love and grace. See how he has lifted you up and carried you to this time. Put yourself into the present hands of God your I AM. Allow his sword to cut between you and the past (Heb. 4:12). Your soul remembers well the last wound to your identity, your legitimacy, your worth, and your sense of inclusion, but that was not the first wound that you suffered. The recent wounds drill back to deep and inarticulate wounds known to your spirit.

Ask God for direction on generational repentance and cleanup.

In Jesus' name, spirit, stand in your authority over soul, mind, will, emotions, and all functions of the body. Look into the face of your Father and ask him how to clean up the garbage from the toxic waste of negative generational buildup. Ask him to show you repentance, forgiveness, and release from judgments, vows, and curses. Use the cross of Jesus the Redeemer to cut the ties between you and the old familiar games and unrighteous soul ties with family, past, present, and future. Renounce the strongholds of anger, guilt, shame and blame, self-condemnation, judgment, unforgiveness, with bitterness, revenge, anger, hatred, and murder in your heart, control, manipulation, uproar, predator/victim entanglement, numbness, non-feeling, dishonor, jealousy, performance, self-effort, perfectionism, addictions, infirmity, death and destruction, ____________ (etc. Ask God to lead you.)

Spirit, let the Holy Spirit be very specific about the captivities that he wants to release, because Jesus said, "The Spirit of the Lord is on me, because he has anointed me to preach good news to the poor, to bind up the brokenhearted, to proclaim freedom for the prisoners, to set the captives free, and to proclaim recovery of sight for the blind, to release the oppressed, to proclaim the year of the Lord's favor" (Isa. 61:1-2). This is the day appointed by God. In Jesus' name, bind up and send away the spirits coming off the family familiars and strongholds.

Receive the healing ministry of the Holy Spirit.

Spirit, receive from your Healer rivers of healing for the wounds that have left scars on the soul. Receive rivers of healing for the hurts and needs, burdens and troubles, and overwhelming pain of years and years, that inarticulate place of weeping. Let the Holy Spirit of truth pull out the poison of fiery word darts, contentious and hurtful actions and anger, and painful memories. Many of them are stored in the soul, but, spirit, as you are healed, as the poisons and toxic actions and memories are pulled out, you will minister the healing that the soul needs. Receive God's healing now, so you can heal the soul from your wholeness.

Receive the forgiving ministry of the blood of Jesus.

Spirit, let the blood of Jesus pull out all the hurt and pain of abuse, defilement, abandonment, rejection, self-rejection, self-hatred, inferiority, inadequacy, non-belonging, comparison, competition, jealousy, perfectionism, pride, and performance; guilt, false responsibility, blame, shame, and victim mindset. Allow Jesus to take all the anger, wall-building, distancing, and isolation; the stigma of people who have not listened to you, who devalued your person with dishonor, who made you feel that different was bad, __________ (wait as other wounded responses surface). Let the blood of Jesus wash away the poisons of all these and others which he will reveal.

Receive the healing that God planned from before the world was, to heal every origin point of wounds, disease, and brokenness. God is destroying the roots to bring deep healing, not just lopping off fruits this time (Mat. 15:13). Your Father God will pluck up by the roots everything he has not planted, as you give him permission and as you partner with him.

Ask God to reveal labels.

Spirit, listen as you ask God to reveal all spiritual labels that the accuser of the brethren has put on you, for example, no good, stupid, clumsy, not important, disappointment, ____________ (etc.) You know them all too well. Ask the Holy Spirit to reveal the holy labels, the new name, he has for you… my son, my daughter, my beloved, my princess, grace and beauty, goodness, honor, confidence, blessing, ____________ (etc.) Listen for the name the Holy Spirit puts on you.

Put in blessing.

Spirit, receive rivers of love, washing you with waves of liquid love, covenant mercy, compassion, comfort, and faithfulness. Jesus, who walked on the waters, walks on your storm saying "Peace, be still." Dial down and know that he is God. Receive him quieting the harassment of your spirit, soul, and body with his presence and healing Word. Spirit, rest in the love and mercy of your Father-God, knowing he pities his children. He has compassion on you. He is your consolation and comfort.

Receive rivers of the grace of God. He is Ancient of Days. He is the covenant-keeping God of Abraham, Isaac, and Jacob. He made a covenant of grace with you. You have been wounded by covenant-breakers, but God cannot break his covenant. Be blessed with an infusion of the faithfulness of the heart of covenant-keeping God.

Be blessed to receive rivers of his peace flowing in and washing away all the striving, the lack, the holes, the dryness with a fresh clear stream of pure restoration and reconciliation of you to yourself and to God. No more anguished cry of "God, where are you?" Be blessed with reconciliation of your spirit with your soul, with your body, and with others.

Spirit, receive Spirit rest, and tell your soul to rest, knowing that your loving Father will take care of you. You don't have to fix it, make it happen, or make it right. Be released of all self-effort and responsibility for how things turn out. Receive the peace of a child who does not have to be responsible. Be blessed with simplicity of faith and trust to turn everything over to your father God and know with assurance and confidence that he is working in your circumstances, your life, in your history, in your future, and he is utterly faithful in meeting all your needs. He will always be there for you.

In all the pieces that have been missing, be blessed with integration, with wholeness, with alignment, with healing of fragmentation and fracture. Be blessed with hope and tender restoration.

You are under God's covering.

Spirit, you are under God's spiritual covering. The Ancient of days watches over the man or woman after God's own heart that you are and the positive gifts of his Spirit operating deep within, that power of divine grace operating inside. You have holy prayer partners in Jesus who ever intercedes and the Holy Spirit who groans petitions and intercessions that you cannot articulate, according to what's already in the heart, mind, and will of your Father.

Take your responsibility and authority.

Spirit, you have authority in the ascended Jesus over the mind, will, emotions, other functions. Take back what belongs to you. God has given you authority; begin to possess it. Take authority over every place that the soles of your feet shall tread. Rise up, and seize this opportunity for blessing. Receive the opposite blessing of each of the curses and captivities you have suffered. Be released in all areas like unwrapping the grave clothes, until your entire being is revealed — whole, healthy, complete.

Take your authority and speak stability to the soul. Come into alignment, into sync with the fullness of God's purposes, so that there is less struggle between spirit, soul, and body. Speak cleansing of all places over which you have authority. Take charge of the unreliable soul feelings and take them to the cross. Take captive the soul thoughts, will, and emotions, and put them under orders to the Shepherd and Guardian of your soul. Assert your rightful place, your command presence, so that people will see and know that there is something different — more peace, more joy and confidence.

God will release your gifts and blessings.

Spirit, your Father-Creator will release the gifts that are deep within you. Honor all the gifts and bless their righteous expression in all that God intended. The Lord your Father will release his power of divine grace operating in you. Set apart everything you are to him: gifts, anointings, birthright, time, timing, and seasons, the place of your jurisdiction where you live life in all its fullness. Be blessed with peace, grace, favor, justice, and righteousness wherever God takes you. Be stretched in your borders, as Jabez prayed in 1 Chronicles 4:10. Be enlarged in your boundaries, receive the hand of the living God upon you in all that you are and all that you do, because he will be with you to either keep you free from pain and trouble or to keep you through the pain. It's his choice, his sovereignty, for his glory.

Be blessed in the name of the Shepherd and Guardian of your soul (1 Pet. 2:25 NASB).

Comfort

34 Comfort For All Who Mourn — Isaiah 61:1-3

Spirit, your Abba sent his Son who began his ministry on earth quoting Isaiah 61:1-3. He said, "The Spirit of the Sovereign LORD is on me, because the LORD has anointed me... He has sent me to bind up the brokenhearted ... to comfort all who mourn, and provide for those who grieve in Zion — to bestow on them a crown of beauty instead of ashes, the oil of gladness instead of mourning, and a garment of praise instead of a spirit of despair."

Spirit, come to the front to be blessed in the name of the Spirit of the Sovereign Lord. Jesus defined his call and his eternal relationship with you when he quoted this passage in his first public sermon. The kingdom of your Sovereign Lord is within you, and the indwelling Christ is anointed in your life to bring good news to you, to bind up your broken heart, and to comfort your mourning. He is faithful to comfort you in your grief. These days may not feel like his goodness or his faithfulness, but his Word promises that dark clouds are under his feet (Ps. 18:9). He never stops being your dear Father who invites you near him to love, guide, deliver, heal, and comfort you. All you love is in his hands. He hears your prayers and your tears when there are no words. He counts them as liquid intercession, which is precious to him (Ps. 56:8a). He is your Mighty Warrior and contends with those forces that are contending with you (Isa. 42:13; Ps. 35:1).

Be blessed with a still heart, while he fights for you (Exo. 14:14; Ps. 46:10). Be blessed in his covenant of love that can never be taken from you (Rom. 8:35,38-39; Ps. 18:19). Be blessed to know that everything is for his glory, so that the thanksgiving of many will overflow to you (2 Cor. 4:15). Believe that he is being glorified in you and in your soul and body.

Spirit, be blessed with his sure promise that he is able to guard what you have entrusted to him (2 Tim. 1:12). Receive his covering of his sweet presence and peace that passes all understanding in all your cares. He never loses sight of whom he designed you uniquely to be and whom he designed those you love to be. His plans for you are written on the palm of the nail-pierced hands of his Son, and those scars are eternally before his throne in heaven.

Be blessed to know him as your Father of compassion and God of all comfort, who comforts you in all your troubles (2 Cor. 1:3-4).

35 Comfort: His Holy Exchange — Isaiah 61:1-6; Luke 4:21

Spirit, in Luke 4:18-19 Jesus quoted Isaiah 61, in which God promises his Messiah would give a holy exchange: comfort for grief, a crown instead of ashes, gladness for mourning, and praise instead of despair. Listen to the words of Jesus in Luke 4:21. "Today this scripture is fulfilled in your hearing."

Spirit, be blessed to know the One who comforts you as a mother comforts her child (Isa. 66.13). Your comforter is speaking to you tenderly. He knows your grief, your ashes, your mourning, and your despair, but he is exchanging these with you for his mercy, compassion, and grace. He is ministering himself to you by the fellowship of his Spirit. His Spirit produces peace, the joy of the Lord, and hope in him that transcends your circumstances. By the blood of Jesus, he will deal with the hurts, wounds, unforgiveness, and grief that try to erect walls in parts of your heart. He puts the cross of Jesus between you and anything that lays scars on your soul. He brings his hope, as you trust him and give yourself into the nail-pierced hands of Jesus.

Be blessed with rivers of covenant mercy washing you, rivers of love, compassion, comfort, and faithfulness. Jesus, who walked on the waters, walks on your turbulence, and storm, and agitation of soul, saying "Peace, be still." Tell your soul to dial down and know that God quiets all harassment with his presence and healing Word.

Spirit, rest in the love and mercy of your Father, knowing he pities his children. He is tender in his compassion toward you. He is your consolation. He made a covenant of grace with you, and he cannot break his covenant. His promises are sure, his presence cannot leave you. Be blessed with his hope, comfort, and meaning. Be blessed with being settled in the eternal truth of his authority and sovereign control. He is still on the throne as the judicial Ancient of Days, the ruling Lord and King. Be blessed as you take refuge in the strong arms of the Prince of Peace. God remains faithful to you. He is God of all comfort and Father of mercy. Spirit, thank God that he is comforting you now. Thank Jesus that he is healing your broken heart. Thank the Comforter that he is administering healing in every hurting place. Spirit, be blessed to receive his holy exchange: comfort for grief, crowns instead of ashes, gladness for mourning, and praise instead of despair.

Be blessed in the name of the One who is the same,
yesterday, today, and forever (Heb. 13:8),
who says "Today this scripture is fulfilled in your hearing."

36 Brokenness And Glory — 1 Peter 1:3-9

Spirit, listen to the Word of the Lord for you in 1 Peter 1:3-4. "Praise be to the God and Father of our Lord Jesus Christ! In his great mercy he has given us new birth into a living hope through the resurrection of Jesus Christ from the dead, and into an inheritance that can never perish, spoil or fade — kept in heaven for you."

Don't miss the weight of these words from God, one phrase at a time. Tell your mind to let you, spirit, lead in connecting with the Spirit of truth in this passage.

Spirit, hear again verse 3. "Praise be to the God and Father of our Lord Jesus Christ! In his great mercy he has given us new birth into a living hope through the resurrection of Jesus Christ from the dead..."

Resonate with the words "living hope through Jesus!" He gave you birth to new abundant life in him. Be blessed as your life in him unfolds daily, one step of faithfulness at a time. Seasons end, new birth happens. It can be confusing, because God doesn't give you neat signposts. He wants you to keep your eyes on him, as Jesus is revealed in living hope. Be blessed with glimpses of God's purpose in it all.

Spirit, hear again verse 4. "...into an inheritance that can never perish, spoil or fade — kept in heaven for you..."

You are an heir to a rich inheritance — all the riches of Christ Jesus. His purposes for you are in his keeping power. They can never die, or spoil, or fade away without fulfilling his heart for you. You are right in the middle of God's process for you. You don't have to settle for God's second best, because of somebody else's choices or your own. As you are being who you are in him, you can do what you are supposed to do. You may have disappointments, but your life is his story with plot, depth, adventure, suspense, surprising plot turns, and darkness that Jesus defeated. Be blessed as you understand more of his story that he is writing in your life.

Spirit, listen to 1 Peter 1:5. "...who through faith are shielded by God's power until the coming of the salvation that is ready to be revealed in the last time."

God surrounds you with his favor as a shield. You are shielded by his power, so that in every dark thing you've experienced, you can live large and strong. God put you here on earth in your exact place for his specific purpose, and you are living in that purpose, even when you don't know it. Your soul may be grumbling and resisting, but you are living the story that God is ready to reveal to you. God is a lot bigger than you expect him to be. He's a lot bigger than your circumstances. He is the God of detail. When you seek his face, he is deeply involved in the small details of your life, but he has a "bigger yes" for you. Your true glory is the revelation of his splendor, revealed in you day by day.

Spirit, listen to 1 Peter 1:6. "In this you greatly rejoice, though now for a little while you may have had to suffer grief in all kinds of trials."

As Jesus is revealed in you, you can rejoice no matter what. The display of his glory often comes through your wounds. Your dark nights showcase by contrast his splendid dawns, your griefs contrast with his glorious joy. In brokenness, God works in you something beautiful, deep, and substantial to offer others. You are developing inner strength as you are being blessed, broken, and given as an offering in your trials. True strength comes from your desperate need of God. You are a joy to him as you offer your true self as a spectacle of his sufficiency. God can't trust a man or woman who hasn't suffered. Paul said he wanted to know Christ and be conformed to the fellowship of sharing his sufferings, knowing there's a resurrection coming (Phil. 3:10).

Your Father created you for this time, for these very circumstances. He knew exactly what would be happening in your life as you are living it now. He knows the impact for which he is preparing you that still awaits you. You are living into the purpose for which you were created — in spite of difficult people, through hard circumstances, and through tough challenges. Your purpose is in process. You won't get there overnight. You won't magically wake up with it one morning. But today you are closer than yesterday, and tomorrow you will be closer than you are today. Be blessed in him to know these things and rejoice in him.

Spirit, hear 1 Peter 1:7. "These have come so that your faith — of greater worth than gold, which perishes even though refined by fire — may be proved genuine and may result in praise, glory and honor when Jesus Christ is revealed."

Jesus is pleased because he already sees your life as the pure gold he is refining. He sees the real you, the true you, the man/woman he has in mind as he is making you shine like precious gold. You shine to reflect him, not to do for yourself the best that you can do and grit your teeth and merely survive. The walls you build against harsh realities keep your life from being opened up and transformed. God is doing for you something that is more wonderful. He is displaying his praise, glory, and honor in Jesus in you.

Spirit, you hold the key. God is making eternal precious gold. Look into his face to reflect him. Keep God-referenced, God-oriented. If you lose your connection with his face, you lose your orientation. He is your true north. In finding out where you are and where you are going, orientation is everything. God has written the treasure map of your life, the way to the gold, so let him be the marker that says "You are here." At times that may be all he will give you, just the witness that "I am here." He won't let you see the whole map, but he knows the place in time meant only for you and found by you only at that moment. He inhabits that place and that moment. Wait on him to interpret it and lead you there. Be blessed with real faith that has been tested and proved genuine. Be blessed with faith made strong by Jesus the author and finisher of your faith. Be blessed with the riches of faith that is worth more than pure gold.

Spirit, listen to 1 Peter 1:8-9. "Though you have not seen him, you love him; and even though you do not see him now, you believe in him and are filled with an inexpressible and glorious joy, for you are receiving the goal of your faith, the salvation of your souls."

Be blessed with trusting love that is certain that God is fulfilling his good purposes when you don't know what he's doing. Be blessed with love that is fully satisfied that he is keeping his faithful word to you, no matter how long it takes or how contrary your circumstances look. Be thrilled with inexpressible and unspeakable joy now, and be blessed with glorious joy that sees you to the other side of your difficult circumstances. Be blessed in the name of the faithful One who is totally worthy of your love and trust. Be blessed with the faith, love, and joy beyond words that believing him brings.

Be blessed in the love of the One who engraved you on the palms of his hands from beginning to end, whole and complete (Isa. 49:16).

Fruit Of The Spirit

37 Fruit Of Love — Galatians 5:22-23

Beloved child of God, listen while I speak your Father's heart and his ways for you in Galatians 5:22-23,25. "But the fruit of the Spirit is love, joy, peace, patience, kindness, goodness, faithfulness, gentleness and self-control. Against such things there is no law. Since we live by the Spirit, let us keep in step with the Spirit."

Spirit, you are beautiful in the beauty of God's Spirit living in you. He has given you the good gift of his love in you. He makes you more like himself as you give him freedom to transform you into his image. The Holy Spirit wants to reach into the deep places of your being and bless you to display his love in the world.

Listen to Romans 5:5 "Hope does not disappoint us, because God has poured out his love into our hearts by the Holy Spirit, whom he has given us." You can know how dearly God loves you, because he has given you his Spirit to fill your heart with his love. You were created of your Father's love. You are the evidence of God's love deposited in you in lavish measure in making you just the way you are. Know deep within that you belong to your Father who is love, and he speaks his love to you. You are not an "it." You are you, the real you, the essence, the inner being. He enjoys you and finds pleasure in who you are.

Spirit, be blessed with larger-than-the-universe love, before-the-foundation-of-the-world love, the faithful love of your infinite Father for you. Be blessed to know that you are shielded in his love that always seeks your highest good, no matter what you do. Be blessed with God's kind of self-giving love that gives freely without asking anything in return and does not consider the worth of its object. Be blessed with knowing deeply that you are accepted and affirmed in him. His love was forever settled on the cross, as the hymn writer said, "Did e'er such love and sorrow meet." [1] Be blessed with being completely persuaded that nothing can separate you from his love. He loves you with a mighty love that has no end. Marvel at the goodness of his holy love that you cannot get to the end of. His love extends its covering over a multitude of sins. He perfectly loves you, and you need have no fear before him.

Spirit, when God who is love is present in you, love is the fruit of his residence in you. You love others because he first loved you and lives in you to love through you. Be blessed with the love of Christ that compels you, that holds you in his unconditional grip.

Be blessed with 1 Corinthians 13 unfailing love in you, permeating you. His grace makes possible in you his love with no end and no limit and no measure. Paul said that love binds all the other virtues together in perfect unity (Col. 3:14). Be blessed as you let that love flow through you to your family and everyone around you.

Lean on the arm of your beloved for love's sake, as you love by choice, not by emotion. Love must give, whatever the cost. Be blessed with increasing and overflowing love for others (1 Thes. 3:12), because God who is love lives in you to will and to do it.

Be blessed to display the same fruit of the love of God that the Holy Spirit produces in you, your grace-empowered response from his love (Gal. 5:22).

[1] *When I Survey the Wondrous Cross*, Isaac Watts (1674-1748)

38 Fruit Of Joy — Nehemiah 8:10

Spirit, listen to God's Word for you in Galatians 5:22. "The fruit of the Spirit is … joy. And in Nehemiah 8:10. "The joy of the Lord is your strength."

Spirit, God's purpose in his creation was his own pleasure. He rejoices in all his works (Ps. 104:31). Job 38:7 says that God laid the foundations of the earth and marked off its dimensions and did all his work of creation while the morning stars sang together and all the angels shouted for joy. Imagine the same joy of God when he created you! Your Father is joy, and he plants his joy inside you in the person of his Son. Jesus, the laughing Messiah, lives in joy in you.

Spirit, be blessed to drink deeply of the joy that God your Father has in you as his beloved. He blesses you with a touch of his rejoicing in your inmost parts. Be blessed with his understanding of joy, not the world's fickle happiness. Be blessed to know the joy of the Lord that gives you the strength to go forward, press on, to endure hardship. God commands for you the blessing of life in the joy of the Lord, defeating depression, destruction, and death. Be blessed with his joy to prepare thoroughly, to face pain unflinchingly, to accomplish, and to fulfill. Be blessed with the oil of joy that flows from heaven upon your head, dripping down until you are totally soaked, down to your toes.

Joy is the quiet, inner sense of well-being in Jesus, but it also means to spin around with intense motion. Spirit, be blessed with jumping, leaping, and dancing with rejoicing in intensity that words cannot fully express. Be blessed with Christ's overflowing joy that bubbles up in you to flow out of you (Phil. 1:26). He promises joy that nobody and nothing can take away (John 16:22). Be blessed as you are filled with the joy that the Holy Spirit imparts in your place in the kingdom (Rom. 14:17).

Have you ever been blessed just to watch someone laugh? Very soon you were laughing too, for no other reason than that they were happy. Be contagious with joy that is centered in the sovereignty of your Father. Be blessed to stay connected to the source of your joy that is based on being strengthened with his glorious power and on gratitude that you share in the inheritance of his holy people who live in his light (Col. 1:11-12). Joy is also a daily decision and a battle. You can count it all joy in trials of any kind, when you know that your Father does all things well for you. Be blessed to be energized for each new day and each new challenge with joy that comes from inner contentment.

Spirit, be blessed with the joy of a kid in the presence of his favorite grandfather. Be blessed to be an ambassador of joy in a world filled with stress and sadness. Be blessed as you spread joy wherever you touch the lives of others. Be blessed as you point them to the unfailing springs of their source of joy. Be blessed to lighten the load of others and strengthen weary hearts with the joy of Jesus. Be blessed to brighten and refresh the weary spirits of others with joyful confidence in Jesus. Be blessed as you pursue the joy set before you, because Jesus is the incarnate joy-giver, the joy-maker. Be blessed to pursue him who is joy. Jesus came so that you can have this kind of joy. It is his gift to you (Rom. 15:13). Be blessed in the incomparable joy of Jesus (Heb. 12:2).

Be blessed with the joy that the Spirit of joy produces in you, your response to his joy (Gal. 5:22).

39 Fruit Of Peace — Galatians 5:22; Ephesians 2:14

Spirit, listen to God's Word for you in Galatians 5:22. "The fruit of the Spirit is … peace…" And in Ephesians 2:14. "For he himself is our peace…"

Spirit, peace is not an emotion. Peace is a Person. Be blessed with peace, not as the world knows peace, but the peace that is Jesus living in you. He can never be taken away from you, and you can be blessed with peace at all times that Jehovah-Shalom gives. It is a calm, quiet state of rest and a harmonious relationship with God, with yourself, and with others. Be blessed with the good news of peace: how pleasant it is, how sweet and delightful and wonderful it is, how ordained it is for brothers to dwell together in peace, in the unity of the Spirit of peace. Be blessed with the rule of the Prince of peace in your inmost being.

Peace stands in contrast to war, and you don't need peace unless conflict is a possibility. Be blessed with putting on the sandals of peace, being prepared at all times to bring the gospel of peace into all circumstances and to all people. Be blessed with living as a peacemaker, for you are the child of the Most High God of peace. Your Savior and Lord speaks his peace into you and into your world by the blessing of his presence in you, so that you say "Peace, be still" to turmoil of all kinds.

Spirit, be blessed as your God of peace keeps your whole spirit, soul, and body blameless and above reproach in challenging relationships (1 Thes. 5:23). Be blessed that you are adequate for the task of peace-making that your Father gives you. He has prepared you and equipped you. Be blessed with the peace that comes from knowing he is your partner in each task.

In his farewell words to his disciples, Jesus gave peace as a gift to them from himself (John 14:27). Be blessed with experiencing the God of peace obviously present with you (Rom. 15:33). He is the author of peace of mind, tranquility, harmony, reconciliation with him, and a sense of his favor. He is the source of the blessings of health, welfare, prosperity, and every kind of good. Be blessed with receiving the Lord of peace himself with you always in every way dispensing his peace to you (2 Thes. 3:16).

Be blessed with the fruit of peace that the Spirit of peace produces in you, your response to his peace (Gal. 5:22).

40 Fruit Of Patience — Galatians 5:22; 1 Timothy 1:16

Spirit, listen to God's Word for you in Galatians 5:22. "The fruit of the Spirit is ... patience..." And in 1 Timothy 1:16. "I was shown mercy so that in me, the worst of sinners, Christ Jesus might display his unlimited patience as an example for those who would believe on him and receive eternal life."

Spirit, be blessed to know that your Father's patience toward you is his mercy flowing to you. He shines in the weakness of your impatience, to show himself to be a God of second chances, for you and others. He welcomes you back to the Father's house after the most outrageous violations of his covenant (Luke 15:20-24,32). He remembers your frame, and he knows you are dust. Be blessed to know that you are a work in progress, and he is not finished with you yet. He doesn't give up on you, and he intends for you to mirror the likeness of Jesus.

Spirit, see examples of the patience of Jesus in the gospels with people in every circumstance of life...

...with the woman caught in the act of adultery and with her accusers (John 8:2-11) "Let him who is without sin cast the first stone. Woman, neither do I condemn you." What wisdom of restraint born out of patience!

...with his disciples, when they provoked him to cry out "O you of little faith!" or "Have I been so long with you and you don't know me?"

...with his three closest companions whom he took into the Garden in the hour of his greatest agony, only to find them sleeping. He gently and patiently said, "Can you not keep watch with me for one hour? The spirit is willing, but the body is weak."

Spirit, you come to One who was a human being like you in every way, so that he might become your merciful and faithful High Priest before God, representing your sin. Since he himself has gone through suffering and temptation, he understands your weaknesses. He can patiently help you when you are being tempted (Heb. 2:17-18). Be blessed to come boldly to the throne of your gracious God. There you will receive his mercy and find grace to help you when you need it (Heb. 4:15-16).

Spirit, be blessed with the unlimited patience that Jesus displayed, because he lives in you to show you his patience to you and through you. Receive him working his patience in you to bring about his purposes and plans. Be blessed with long-suffering, not just tolerance, and with grace and compassion with yourself and others. Be blessed with knowing that God is working long-suffering in you, especially when others are trying you. Be blessed with his patient endurance and encouragement in battles long fought. Be blessed with a holy infusion of your Father's long-suffering when yours has run out. Patience is a marathon, not a sprint. Be blessed to keep the marathon of patience, even when your legs feel like lead and your lungs are screaming for relief.

Be blessed with the fruit of patience that the Holy Spirit produces in you, your grateful response to his patience (Gal. 5:22).

41 Fruit Of Kindness — Galatians 5:22; Psalm 145:17

Spirit, listen to God's Word for you in Galatians 5:22. "The fruit of the Spirit is … kindness…" And in Psalm 145:17 NASB. "The LORD is righteous in all His ways, and kind in all His deeds."

Spirit, be blessed to know the depth of God's kindness that leads you to repentance (Rom. 2:4). His kindness to you is responsible for your belonging to his kingdom. He showed you the incomparable riches of his grace and the magnitude of his kindness to you in Christ Jesus (Eph. 2:7). He predestined to adopt you for himself as a son through Jesus Christ, according to the kindness of his will and to the glory of his grace, which he freely gave you in his beloved Son (Eph. 1:5-6).

The kindness and love of God your Savior saved you in his mercy. He renewed you in the Holy Spirit, whom he generously poured out on you (Tit. 3:4-5). You are a living heir of the hope of eternal life because of his kindness, which is God's goodness in action. His kindness is your strength and comfort, even when he sits as a friend with you and doesn't say a word. His kindness relieves your sense of aloneness. He is a kind companion who shares your life. You have tasted his kindness, so let it cause you to hunger for more of him, so that you grow up into him and look more like him (1 Pet. 2:2-3).

King David ministered the kindness of God daily to the grandson of his enemy (2 Sam. 9:3). King Jesus was kind to you when you were his enemy (Rom. 5:8). He is kind to the ungrateful and wicked, so be blessed to love your enemies, and do good to them, and expect nothing back from them. Be blessed to prove yourself to be a son/daughter of the Most High, because his kindness actively lives in you to be a peacemaker at all times (Luke 6:35; Mat. 5:9).

Spirit, kindness to others gives evidence that you have forgiven them (Eph. 4:32). When you don't feel kind, take your feelings to God to work forgiveness in you for them. His unfailing compassion toward you never runs out as the source of your kindness (Isa. 54:8). Jesus is sympathetic, affectionate, displaying the mercy of his Father toward you. His kindness saw sheep without a shepherd (Mat. 9:35). Because of his kindness, the hungry were fed, the blind saw, lepers were cleansed, and the ignorant and innocent were taught. He knows your pain, your grief, your difficulty in living in a world where others sin and have sickness that you can do nothing about. He cares, he reaches out to touch as he touched lepers and the rejects of the religious order of the day.

Be blessed to live in the sweet and compassionate disposition of God's Spirit living in you. Be blessed to pass on the kindness shown to you by doing what is best and profitable for others (Tit. 3:6-8). The kindness and compassion of your Kinsman-Redeemer sees and restores the alien and the desolate. Let him respect, appreciate, esteem, and honor others through you in all relationships, circumstances, and decisions. Spirit, be blessed with the nature of Jesus that does not cut others off or cut them short. Be blessed with his grace that pervades your whole being, softening all that could be harsh. Be blessed with being mellowed in the sweet character of Jesus, like wine that mellows with age (Luke 5:39). Be blessed to reflect the nature of the dove of the Holy Spirit in you in acts and words of kindness.

Be blessed with the fruit of kindness that the Holy Spirit produces in you, your grateful response to unmerited kindness (Gal. 5:22).

42 Fruit Of Goodness — Galatians 5:22; Exodus 33:19

Spirit, listen to God's Word for you in Galatians 5:22. "The fruit of the Spirit is … goodness…" And in Exodus 33:19. And the LORD said, "I will cause all my goodness to pass in front of you, and I will proclaim my name, the LORD, in your presence."

Spirit, God is perfectly good because he is God. He forever linked his goodness and his name and his presence. He invites you to taste and see that he is good (Ps. 35:8, 34:8) and that his name is good (Ps. 52:9). What he does is good and what he gives is good because it flows out of who he is (Ps. 65:4). Out of his goodness he created you, and because he is good he redeemed you. His enduring goodness showered upon you his covenant mercy and forgiveness and compassion. Be blessed as you enjoy the unmerited goodness of God in caring for you (Nah. 1:7).

Because he is good, he is merciful and forgiving. He is your good Father who welcomes a prodigal with a hug, a feast, and a party with music and dancing. Because he is good, he wants good things for you, and he is giving and generous and enjoys blessing you. He cannot change, his goodness is constant, never wavering or failing (Jam. 3:17). When you receive his goodness, you receive something of himself.

He is good when he allows tests to refine you into purest gold, and he is good to display his quick sympathy and his tender heart to you when you fall or fail. He is good as he picks you up and holds you in the palm of his hands and will not let you go. His faithful goodness continues through all generations.

Spirit, celebrate his goodness with thanksgiving (Jer. 33:11). Thank him for being good and for loving you with his abounding love that endures forever (Ps. 118:1,29). Be specific in thanking him for his goodness in everyday things: a sunset, a beautiful fountain, a child's hug, answered prayers, the kindness of a stranger, a tear of empathy. His goodness is always in evidence, if you are looking, for he is good.

See the acts of goodness in the parable of the Good Samaritan. His pity on the man who had fallen among thieves was the fruit of goodness and nobility of character. He was touched by the helplessness and the distress of another. He reached out to alleviate the consequences of sin that were causing the man to suffer. Be blessed as you, too, bind up the wounds of others, minister to their hurts, and bring them to the house of your Father for his care.

Spirit, the angels at the birth of Jesus connected the highest glory of God with his good will to men. They announced God's goodness at the entrance of Jesus to earth. Jesus went about doing good, and he imparts many expressions of his goodness into your being. Be blessed with the virtue of the goodness of Jesus worked into your life. Be blessed to feel the zeal of Jesus for goodness and be energized with his kindness and goodness for others. Be blessed with active goodness that does not think to repay evil with evil but considers how to leave a blessing, from the goodness of Jesus in you. Be blessed with goodness to act for the welfare of those who are taxing your patience out of the dominion of their souls.

Be blessed with the fruit of the goodness of God that the Holy Spirit produces in you, your empowered response from his goodness (Gal. 5:22).

43 Fruit Of Faithfulness — Galatians 5:22; Isaiah 49:7

Spirit, listen to God's Word for you in Galatians 5:22. "The fruit of the Spirit is … faithfulness…" And in Isaiah 49:7. "The LORD, who is faithful, the Holy One of Israel … has chosen you." He proclaimed of himself in Exodus 34:6, "The LORD, the LORD, the compassionate and gracious God, slow to anger, abounding in love and faithfulness."

Spirit, hear this: there is no surer testimony in Scripture than that your Father is the faithful God who keeps his covenant of love with you (Deut. 7:9). He binds himself to you in his faithful love, and he does no wrong (Deut. 32:4). Because of his great love you are not consumed, for his compassions and great faithfulness never fail (Lam. 3:22-23). Jesus is the faithful and true witness, whose name is Faithful and True (Rev. 3:4; 19:11). He is faithful to keep you in temptation and faithful to forgive, because he is a merciful and faithful High Priest. He is faithful because God called you into fellowship with him, faithful to his promises and faithful to strengthen you. He has to remain faithful, because he cannot deny himself.

Spirit, be blessed with his covenant-keeping spirit. He speaks his faithfulness into you, so that you are not blown about or given to fickleness. Your faithfulness clings to his faithfulness to keep his promises and accomplish his will, for God's eyes are on his faithful ones (Ps. 101:6). Be blessed to stand firm in your faith, trusting and believing in him. Be blessed with knowing whom you have believed and being persuaded that he will keep you faithful (2 Tim. 1:12) Be blessed with letting his steadfastness keep you according to the plumbline of his trustworthiness.

Spirit, cling to justice, mercy, and faithfulness which Jesus said were important for you to pursue (Mat. 23:23). Paul instructed his spiritual son to fight the good fight and hold on to faithfulness and a good conscience (1 Tim. 1:18). He told him to flee the evil desires of youth, and pursue righteousness, faithfulness, love, and peace, along with those who call on the Lord out of a pure heart (2 Tim. 2:22). He told him to guard the good deposit of faith that God placed in him, to guard it with the help of the Holy Spirit who lived in him (2 Tim. 1:14). He held his own life up as an example of teaching, purpose, faith, patience, love, endurance, and sufferings (2 Tim. 3:10). By God's grace, be blessed to make this your testimony, as you in faithfulness live out what God in Christ has for you, resulting in transformed character and a godly way of life.

Many tests that have come to you were not to prove the faithfulness of God, but to prove your faithfulness in spite of circumstances. Be blessed to prove true to your faithfulness to God and to others. Be blessed with constancy in your practical Christian faith, faith with legs, faith that is lived out to the glory of your faithful Creator and Savior (1 Pet. 4:19).

Spirit, be blessed in his faithfulness in you that bears all things, believes all things, hopes all things, and endures all things (1 Cor. 13:7). Be blessed to be faithful to the trust that he has given you (1 Cor. 4:2). Be blessed to be a wise servant over your Master's household, whom he calls good and faithful and whom he invites to share his happiness (Mat. 25:21).

Be blessed with the fruit of faithfulness that the Spirit produces in you, your appropriate response from his faithfulness to you (Gal. 5:22).

44 Fruit Of Gentleness — Galatians 5:23; Matthew 11:28-30

Spirit, hear God's Word for you in Galatians 5:23. "The fruit of the Spirit is ... gentleness..." And in Matthew 11:28-30. "Come to me, all you who are weary and burdened, and I will give you rest. Take my yoke upon you and learn from me, for I am gentle and humble in heart, and you will find rest for your souls. For my yoke is easy and my burden is light."

The gentleness of Jesus was seen in his days on earth with children, with women, with outcasts, and with his quarrelsome band of misfits. Isaiah 40:11 says that he tends his flock like a shepherd. He gathers the lambs in his arms and carries them close to his heart and gently leads those that have young. Spirit, Jesus invites you to come to his rest when you are weary and burdened. He invites you to take his easy well-fitting yoke made by the Carpenter of Nazareth. He invites you to let him off-load your burden onto the person and character of your gentle Shepherd.

Spirit, your Father knows your frame and remembers you are dust. He deals gently with you according to your weakness and ignorance (Heb. 5:2). The infinite God of the universe has all power and might, but he sees and cares when a sparrow falls, and he carefully clothes the lilies of the fields that are never seen by human eye. He cares about your tears and puts them in his bottle. His gentle personal attention is beyond comprehension, yet you can gladly receive it.

Spirit, gentleness is not weakness. It is the bridled strength of the infinite power of God under his direction. Jesus could have called more than twelve legions of angels to rescue him from the Roman and Jewish authorities, yet he submitted to arrest and crucifixion, because the power of his love chose suffering on the cross for you. He cared not for his own comfort or reputation that he might set you in glory with himself.

The ultimate picture of the restrained strength of Jesus is in Philippians 2:5-8. "Your attitude should be the same as that of Christ Jesus: who, being in very nature God, did not consider equality with God something to be grasped, but made himself nothing, taking the very nature of a servant, being made in human likeness. And being found in appearance as a man, he humbled himself and became obedient to death — even death on a cross!" Spirit, fall on your face before that magnificent portrait of Jesus, and rise to take your position in his humility and meekness.

Gentleness is biblical meekness, a positive quality, and Jesus commended it when he said that the meek will inherit the earth (Mat. 5:5). Spirit, be blessed to accept his dealings with you as good and with a humble heart that does not dispute or struggle or resist him. He does not merely deposit his gentleness in you. He lives the strength of his gentleness in you, so that at all times you can have his attitude of holy gentleness toward others.

Spirit, gentleness is the inner character quality of a woman commended by God — the unfading beauty of a gentle and quiet spirit, which is of great worth in God's sight (1 Pet. 3:4). Gentleness is closely linked with humility, as Paul says, "Be completely humble and gentle; be patient, bearing with one another in love" (Eph. 4:2). God tells you to clothe yourself with compassion, kindness, humility, gentleness and patience, as you bear with others and forgive their grievances against you as he did (Col. 3:12-13). He chose you as his holy and dearly loved one to wear gentleness in a way that reflects well on him.

Be blessed with his gentleness in dealing with all people, cutting them some slack, mellowing all that is sharp, or harsh, or short in your reactions. Tame your soul that at times may want to be harsh or demanding, because insults and injuries are Father-filtered for his purposes. Be blessed with the gentle answer of Jesus that turns away wrath. Be blessed with being wise as a serpent but gentle as a dove.

Spirit, be blessed with the wisdom of gentleness that is first of all pure, then peace-loving, considerate, submissive, full of mercy and good fruit, impartial and sincere (Jam. 3:17).

Be blessed with the fruit of gentleness that the Spirit produces in you,
your appropriate response from his strength (Gal. 5:23).

45 Fruit Of Spirit-Control — Galatians 5:22,25

Spirit, hear God's Word for you in Galatians 5:22. "The fruit of the Spirit is … self-control…" And in Ephesians 5:18. "Be filled with the Spirit." And in Romans 8:5. "Those who live in accordance with the Spirit have their minds set on what the Spirit desires." And Galatians 5:16,25. "Live by the Spirit, and you will not gratify the desires of the sinful nature. Since we live by the Spirit, let us keep in step with the Spirit."

Spirit, ponder the immense self-control of Jesus. Isaiah 53:7 says, "He was oppressed and afflicted, yet he did not open his mouth; he was led like a lamb to the slaughter, and as a sheep before her shearers is silent, so he did not open his mouth." When he was abused, whipped, and crucified, he uttered only forgiveness. He was taunted and insulted and did not retaliate, not one word of bitterness. When he suffered, he made no threats. Instead, he entrusted himself to him who judges justly (1 Pet. 2:23).

Spirit, hear the Word of God in Hebrews 12:1-3. "Therefore, since we are surrounded by such a great cloud of witnesses, let us throw off everything that hinders and the sin that so easily entangles, and let us run with perseverance the race marked out for us. Let us fix our eyes on Jesus, the author and perfecter of our faith, who for the joy set before him endured the cross, scorning its shame, and sat down at the right hand of the throne of God. Consider him who endured such opposition from sinful men, so that you will not grow weary and lose heart." Your suffering Jesus is the model of biblical self-control. The daily cross you take up is your opportunity to let your silent Lamb live through you the joy set before him in all circumstance of opposition, criticism, and shame.

Jesus was fully God and completely a man, and he learned obedience by what he suffered. He had to train his will to do his Father's will, so that he could be the source of your resistance to every temptation to surrender to sinful words and actions (Heb. 5:8-9).

Spirit, be blessed with your greatest weapon, the presence of the Spirit of God in you to do his will. Be blessed with victory that comes from having the nature of Christ in your heart and spirit. Be blessed with his correction and training in righteousness (2 Tim. 3:16) which yields peace for those who are conformed to it (Heb. 12:11). Be blessed to apply the same determination of an athlete for physical exercise to spiritual disciplines for training in godliness (1 Tim. 4:8; 2 Tim. 2:5). Be blessed with control in your spirit and dominion over your soul and body. Be blessed with being in control of your flesh and your mind and being free of the control of the appetites of the world, the flesh, and the devil. Be blessed with a disposition that is even-tempered, tranquil, and balanced in spirit, that does not react to self-indulgence, senselessness, and selfishness.

Be blessed with Proverbs 16:32. "Better a patient man than a warrior, a man who controls his temper than one who takes a city." Be blessed with transformation of your present and future by his Spirit in all circumstances. Be blessed to rise above circumstances and your history to be all God created you to be, neither trying to control nor enabling those around you but calling them as well as yourself to a higher standard in the Spirit of liberty.

Be blessed with the fruit of the Spirit's control that he produces in you, your response because he lives in you (Gal. 5:23).

46 Fruitfulness — John 15:16

Spirit, listen to God's determined fruitfulness for you in John 15:16. "You did not choose me, but I chose you and appointed you to go and bear fruit — fruit that will last. Then the Father will give you whatever you ask in my name."

Beloved one, your Father chose you and appointed you to bear the fruit of the nature of his Son within you. The more you abide in him, the more fruit you will bear. His Spirit is working in you his love, joy, peace, patience, kindness, goodness, faithfulness, gentleness, and self-control. Do not be discouraged when you feel that the fruit of your life is barrenness or ugliness. Jesus is the seed of God planted within you. He prunes, feeds, and nurtures you to your full potential of the beautiful fruit of the Spirit and all the full qualities of Jesus in you. You do not produce this fruit alone; he does. Rest in his nature and his power to live through you. He is the Fruit of the Spirit. Every good and perfect fruit is him living his life in you.

Precious spirit, hear and receive this familiar passage in 2 Peter 1:3-4. "His divine power has given us everything we need for life and godliness through our knowledge of him who called us by his own glory and goodness. Through these he has given us his very great and precious promises, so that through them you may participate in the divine nature and escape the corruption in the world caused by evil desires."

Spirit, receive the truth that you have already within you everything you need to bear the fruit that remains. In him you can choose to step into those inner qualities commanded in 2 Peter 1:5-7. "For this very reason, make every effort to add to your faith goodness; and to goodness, knowledge; and to knowledge, self-control; and to self-control, perseverance; and to perseverance, godliness; and to godliness, brotherly kindness; and to brotherly kindness, love." All these are spirit qualities that the Spirit of Christ Jesus works in you with your obedience and active participation. And you have God's own promise that you are blessed if you possess these qualities in increasing measure, because they will keep you from being ineffective and unfruitful in your knowledge of our Lord Jesus Christ (1 Pet. 1:8).

Be blessed as you let your Vinedresser take you through the process to be fruitful. God is tender to give the right amount of sun and rain for the branch that you are. He must fertilize, tend the soil, and prune you for maximum fruitfulness. Be blessed with fruitfulness in his determined and appointed place and time for you. Be blessed in your unique identity, legitimacy, authority, anointing, and birthright in the Spirit of liberty, for with him there is full freedom and fruitfulness. "The fruit of the light consists in all goodness, righteousness, and truth" (Eph. 5:9). That's the harvest of the nature of Jesus in you.

Paul poured out his heart for his friends in prayer in Philippians 1:11 that they would bear the fruit of their salvation. That's what the fruit of the Spirit is. Hear him praying this for you. "[I pray that you will be] filled with the fruits of righteousness which come through Jesus Christ, to the glory and praise of God." He prays again in Colossians 1:10, "[I pray that you will] lead a life worthy of the Lord, fully pleasing to him, bearing fruit in every good work ... "

Spirit, hear and receive this promise in Psalm 92:12-15. "The righteous will flourish like a palm tree, they will grow like a cedar of Lebanon; planted in the house of the LORD, they will flourish in the courts of our God. They will still bear fruit in old age, they will stay fresh and green, proclaiming, 'The LORD is upright; he is my Rock.' "

Be blessed in the Lord, in whom you flourish and bear fruit to old age (Ps. 92:14).

Be Enlarged In Spirit

47 Be Enlarged By Reading The Word — Psalm 119:18

Spirit, hear God's Word for you in Psalm 119:18. "Open my eyes that I may see wonderful things in your law." And in Luke 24:31-32. "Then their eyes were opened and they recognized him… They asked each other, 'Were not our hearts burning within us while he talked with us on the road and opened the Scriptures to us?' "

Precious one, you are formed from the essence of God. His words breathe life into you. Invite your spirit to take its rightful place of leadership over soul and body to receive all your Father has for you through his holy Word, as you read his words with your spirit.

Spirit, be blessed as you receive fresh manna and new revelation from God's Word. The Word is the food that the world doesn't know. Peter said, "Like newborn babies, crave pure spiritual milk, so that by it you may grow up in your salvation" (1 Pet. 2:2). Spirit, be blessed as you read God's Word for nourishment and nurture designed specifically for your growth. You can retain so much more than the mind can. Reading the Word by the Spirit of God in you is the "eat right, exercise, and drink plenty of water" that you do for your inner being. Job said, "I have treasured the words of his mouth more than my daily bread" (Job 23:12). Spirit, be blessed to eat right (read and meditate on God's Word), exercise (increase in faith), and drink plenty of water (draw deep from the Living Water).

Your Abba communicates with you in his Word, revealing who he is and who you are in him. Jeremiah said, "When your words came, I ate them; they were my joy and my heart's delight, for I bear your name, O LORD God Almighty" (Jer. 15:16). Paul said, "In my inner being I delight in God's law" (Rom. 7:22). Be blessed to receive his words as your joy and delight. Be blessed as you desire your Father's heart in his words to you. The psalmist said, "How sweet are your words to my taste, sweeter than honey to my mouth!" (Ps. 119:103). Be blessed as you fall in love with God's Word like that. It is more precious than silver (Ps. 119:72).

The God-breathed Word is the plumbline written in your inner being. Be blessed as you hide it in your heart and fix his words deep within (Ps. 119:11; Deut. 11:18). Spirit, be blessed as you read God's Word to be aligned with his perfect will and receive his counsel in troubled times and his direction in decision-making (2 Tim. 3:16). Be blessed to receive it to illuminate your path and give light to your eyes (Ps 19:8; 119:105).

God promises fruitfulness as you take in his Word deeply. Spirit, listen to this promise in Psalm 1:1-3. "Blessed is the man who does not walk in the counsel of the wicked or stand in the way of sinners or sit in the seat of mockers. But his delight is in the law of the Lord, and on his law he meditates day and night. He is like a tree planted by streams of water, which yields its fruit in season and whose leaf does not wither. Whatever he does prospers." His Word does not return to him void in your life or the life of others who will taste its fruit in your life. Be blessed as you let the word of Christ dwell in you richly (Col. 3:16) as a spring of living water that satisfies you and waters many.

Be blessed to be a letter of recommendation for Jesus when his Word is written in your life. "You yourselves are our letter, written on our hearts, known and read by everybody. You show that you are a letter from Christ… written not with ink but with the Spirit of the living God, not on tablets of stone but on tablets of human hearts" (2 Cor. 3:2). Be blessed as you allow God's Word to accomplish in you all that your Father has planned for you.

Be blessed in the name of the Living Word of life (1 John 1:1).

48 Be Enlarged By The Love Of God — Song of Solomon 7:6

Spirit, listen to the Word of God for you in Song of Solomon 7:6. "How beautiful you are and how pleasing, O love, with your delights!"

Spirit, be blessed with setting your spiritual compass heading to these words of God to you. You are his precious one, and he takes pleasure in you. Be blessed to be enlarged with the deep love of your Lover. Be blessed with knowing that you delight his heart.

Listen, spirit, as your Lover tells you again from the Song of Solomon 4:1,9-10 that you are his beautiful one. "How beautiful you are, my beloved! Oh, how beautiful! All beautiful you are, my beloved; there is no flaw in you. You have ravished my heart, my sister, my bride with one look of your eyes, with one link of your necklace. How fair is your love, my sister, my bride! How much better than wine is your love, and the scent of your perfumes is better than all spices!"

Spirit, now is the time for you to receive how deeply God really cares for you. Listen to his words to you in Song of Solomon 2:11-13. "See! The winter is past; the rains are over and gone. Flowers appear on the earth; the season of singing has come, the cooing of doves is heard in our land. The fig tree forms its early fruit; the blossoming vines spread their fragrance. Arise, come, my darling; my beautiful one, come with me, for your voice is sweet, and your face is lovely."

You have faithfully endured the hardship of winter. Even in winter months, the ground is not completely dormant. The process of life continues. And now, spirit, the spring has come. Let go of any fear or unbelief and fully embrace the spring. Rejoice! Sing! Breathe in the fragrance of spring. It is time to put the winter behind and arise in the new abundance that your Lover has for you.

Spirit, you are the object of heaven's fiery love. He calls you his darling, his beautiful one. His love for you can never diminish or fade, because he is the eternal I AM. He loves you freely with unchanging love (Hos. 14:4). How can you doubt God's love for you? He doesn't give you some of his love; he is love, and he gives you himself (1 John 4:16). You have all of him, so you have all of his love at all times. Receive his love, just because you are his. His great love for you is bathed in rich mercy (Mic. 7:18; Eph. 2:4). What more can he do to prove his love than by giving you his Son in exchange for your life (Gal. 2:20; Eph. 5:25)? Be blessed in the wonder of such an amazing love story.

Be blessed in the name of the God of love who is with you (2 Cor. 13:11).

49 Be Enlarged By The Wonder Of Seeing — Isaiah 64:3; 1 Corinthians 2:9-12

Spirit, listen to the Word of God for you in Isaiah 64:3. “You did awesome things that we did not expect.” And in 1 Corinthians 2:9-10. “ ‘No eye has seen, no ear has heard, no mind has conceived what God has prepared for those who love him’ — but God has revealed it to us by his Spirit. The Spirit searches all things, even the deep things of God.”

Spirit, be blessed to see the changing wonders of Majesty. Be blessed with seeing things that others don’t. Be blessed with paying attention to what is right before you, with being present to what God has done and is doing, as you see, and ponder, and adore. Be blessed to live assuming that God’s truth and presence is manifest at every moment, in every encounter, with every opportunity of every day. Be blessed with the gift of noticing, going through life with eyes open and spirit engaged. God-seekers have the gift of seeing God’s fingerprints and interpreting them for others and pointing others to God in them. The art of noticing is a cultivated skill. Your birthright, maybe even your obligation, is to be so alert to God-moments that you cannot help but see and celebrate God’s handiwork and his purposes all around you. Be blessed with being enlarged by seeing what God is preparing and freely giving you.

God-moments are sometimes fleeting and are only seen by those who are looking for them. Picture the dawn, as light breaks through the darkness and color bursts forth. It happens in a few moments, and then the color is gone. You’ll miss God’s masterpieces if you are not looking at the right time. Be blessed with recognition, attentiveness to something more, to Someone more.

Spirit, let God connect the dots of awe and wonder. Be aware of realities that result from revelation and reflection, the connection between things seen and unseen. These are the province of poets, psalmists, artists, writers, and of every awakened child of God. Be blessed with expression in creative, thought-provoking ways to speak of things hidden beneath life’s surface. Be blessed with expressing what God’s eyes see through you. Be blessed to turn the thing noticed into language, melody, movement, or image.

Enjoy the observations of others, but tune yourself to want to see deeper, longer, more clearly, more focused. In God’s Spirit, you live in another realm. Live each day as you will one day wish you had, making war on dullness with astonishment, not too jaded to see wonder in small things. Be blessed with a lifestyle and a lifetime of discovering the character and nature of your Father and Christ in you. Be blessed to discover who God is, and uncover and awaken to who you are in him. Be blessed with being all you can be.

Spirit, be blessed with living life energized with wonder. Be blessed to see the Wonderful One and all of his wonders. You are not meant to live dull, lifeless, and passionless. Every day is a series of wonders to be unwrapped as gifts from God. Be blessed to fall in love with life and set in motion the mysterious dynamics that cause life to love you back. Be blessed to stand on tiptoe and be wide-eyed and sensitive to the world at your fingertips and under your feet. Be blessed to be amazed and live to make visible the amazing majesty of God.

Be blessed in his great and awesome name (Ps. 99:3).

50 Be Enlarged By People Of Large Spirit — 1 Corinthians 16:18

Spirit, hear the Word of God for you in 1 Corinthians 16:18. "For they refreshed my spirit and yours also. Such men deserve recognition." And 2 Corinthians 7:13. "By all this we are encouraged. In addition to our own encouragement, we were especially delighted to see how happy Titus was, because his spirit has been refreshed by all of you."

Spirit, be blessed as you seek out people with large spirits. Be blessed and refreshed by large-spirited people who live life richly and draw you out to be better than you are. Be blessed with people of large spirit to strike sparks that will kindle a flame in you. Be blessed with experiencing the spark that jumps from another person's spirit to yours. When that happens, you are forever blessed and changed. As you share spirit-to-spirit with them, receive enlargement, vision, refreshment, and hope.

Be blessed with finding your fit in your family and community of faith where God placed you among large-spirited people. Everybody is designed by God with a piece to contribute to the whole. You are designed to fit your special piece together with other people. You complement them, and you are blessed to receive from them, and they are blessed to receive from you. That is synergy, and you cannot do alone what God alone has called you to do. You will be fulfilled when you fit with other people who are also fulfilling God's design and being who God has designed you all to be.

To be loved, to be openly admired, to be esteemed are basic human needs that change outlook, values, and goals in life. Be blessed with people like that who love you like that. Be blessed with finding someone to come alongside you who is wise, willing to share insights, unconsciously imparting positive attitudes. Solomon is known for his wisdom and great understanding, but no doubt it came out of the largeness of heart like the sand on the seashore that God gave him (1 Kgs. 4:29 NKJV). Be blessed in the mystery of what is transferred from God's Spirit to you and from one human spirit to another.

Spirit, be blessed with sudden flashes of holy transfer of spirit from the heart of an author of a book, a sermon, a song, or a line of poetry. Be blessed to receive life and joy from a friend, a stranger, or a child. It is God's spirit through them changing your spirit for the better. Be blessed with interest, warmth, humor, vitality, intensity, and alertness.

Be blessed in the name of the God of the spirits of all mankind (Num. 27:16).

51 Be Enlarged With Loving Community — Ephesians 3:16-19

Spirit, listen to Paul's prayer for his friends in Ephesians 3:16-19. "I pray that out of his glorious riches he may strengthen you with power through his Spirit in your inner being…that you, being rooted and established in love, may have power, together with all the saints, to grasp how wide and long and high and deep is the love of Christ, and to know this love that surpasses knowledge — that you may be filled to the measure of all the fullness of God."

Spirit, be blessed with being enlarged in a community of saints. Although God loves you singly and individually, there is a sense in which you grasp the love of God with others in a way that you cannot grasp it alone. Be blessed with strength through his Spirit so that Christ may dwell presently and richly in you to root and establish you in love in community with others. Be blessed with knowing that you are infinitely loved in every dimension. Receive it, spirit, and be blessed to feel God's love in the greatest dimension of its great depth, and length, and height, and width. How deep, and long, and high, and wide is God? Infinite! It is not about how much you know about his love but how much you receive his love. Be blessed with the love of God which surpasses all knowledge through the Spirit of God. You can never understand it with your mind. Your soul cannot comprehend or receive it, but be blessed with being filled to the measure of all the fullness of the love of God.

Be blessed with Spirit-ordained covenants of love in mutual commitment with other Christians of like spirit. Thank God for those who remind you of your deepest identity and legitimacy. Be blessed to reach out and meet the spirit of others with joy, because both of you will be changed for the better. As the community of spirit is synergistic, the whole is greater than the parts.

Be blessed with a loving network of mutual support, affection, and loyalty. Be blessed with those who care greatly and intimately, so that you face nothing alone. Be blessed with awareness of the life and reality in community and its power to unlock hidden capabilities and joys in yourself and others. Be blessed with coming out of isolation into a safe place where God's love prevails.

Acts of goodness and generosity to others align you with God and bring out the best in you and others. Acts of bitterness, pettiness, and anger put you at cross purposes with God and diminish you and others. As others express confidence in you, it builds you up and strengthens you. As others bless you, God calls forth passion, warmth, and life from you that are contagious. Spirit, be blessed to stay aligned with God in community to receive life and give life.

Be blessed in the name of the Father from whom his whole family in heaven and on earth derives its name (Eph. 3:15).

52 Be Enlarged To Give Yourself To Others — 1 Timothy 4:12

Spirit, listen to the Word of God for you in 1 Timothy 4:12. "Be an example to the believers in word, in conduct, in love, in spirit, in faith, in purity" (NKJV). And in Titus 2:7. "In everything set them an example by doing what is good."

Spirit, living for Christ is the overflow of living in Christ, loving as he loved, caring as he cared for people, being his hands and feet and heart in your world. Be blessed with being an example to others, as you extend yourself to them in service. Be blessed with finding what God needs you to do and doing it, led by your spirit, not your soul. Be blessed with open eyes to opportunities to be about your Father's business. Be blessed with knowing with your spirit which opportunities have your name on them. Be blessed to know when to be a part of God's divine appointments in other lives.

Spirit, listen to what Paul said to his Christian brothers in Philippians 2:17. "If I am being poured out as a drink offering on the sacrifice and service of your faith, I am glad and rejoice with you all." Be blessed with being poured out wine and broken bread to the tired and desperate, the thirsty and hungry, the hopeless and traumatized. Be blessed with empathy and passion, spending yourself to lift up the hurting and unfortunate. Be blessed with being strength to those who are in hard times. Be blessed with being infused with courage and boldness from God's Spirit in all difficulties. Be blessed to dwell in the brightness of God's presence so you can reflect his sunshine in dark places of loss and uncertainty.

Spirit, hear the Word of God for you in 2 Timothy 2:2. "The things you have heard me say in the presence of many witnesses entrust to reliable men who will also be qualified to teach others." Be blessed in the stewardship that God has given you as a faithful 2 Timothy 2:2 leader. Be blessed to entrust the truth to reliable men and women who will also be good stewards of God's truth. Be blessed as you pass on the baton in the relay of truth to faithful disciples who will multiply the message. Be blessed in your faithfulness to nurture and equip God's people for these times.

Be blessed with hearing from God who you are and what he has given you to do. Be blessed to fulfill it to the utmost. Jesus said to his Father, "I have brought you glory here on earth by completing the work you gave me to do" (John 17:4). Be blessed with that being your testimony, that you have fulfilled everything your Father told you to do and completed the work he gave you.

Be blessed in the name of the One who was always about his Father's business (Luke 2:49 NKJV).

53 Be Enlarged To Enjoy God's Purposes In Creation — Romans 1:19-20

Spirit, hear the God's Word for you in Romans 1:19-20 "For since the creation of the world God's invisible qualities — his eternal power and divine nature — have been clearly seen, being understood from what has been made..."

God has plainly made himself known in creation. Spirit, be blessed with gratitude for beauty around you, for the strength it offers, for the peace it brings. Appreciate creation as never before. Be blessed to hear creation sing your Father's love. Be sensitive to misalignment, warping, and defilement. Be blessed with empathy for land that is out of alignment or grieving. Be blessed to call forth, welcome, and sanctify the identity, the purpose, and the product of land.

Be blessed in that place in your essence that loves the sea, that can hear the heartbeat of creation as the tides ebb and flow, as the sun rises and sets, as the stars dance at night in the expanse of the darkened sky, as the birds swoop and dive, as the fish jump, as the sun shimmers on the water, and in the smell of the air. Be blessed to watch a wild thunderstorm with flashes of lightning lighting up the sky better than a fireworks show. Be blessed to feel the wind and lift your face to the rain to let it caress your face. Be blessed to say, "This is speaking deeply in my spirit. Something in this electrified air calls forth deep unto deep inside me."

Be blessed in that place in your essence that leaps at the sight of majestic mountains, that soars in response to their peaks, that hears them breathe and sigh as the wind blows across them, that tunes in to the music the water sings as it falls over rocks in keys of music that no man can re-create. Be blessed to seek out birds to bless them, to call forth their glory in their Creator. Celebrate their place in his creation as their birdsong brings your land or your neighborhood into alignment with his righteous intention.

Spirit, hear God's Word in Genesis 1:28. "God blessed them and said to them, 'Be fruitful and increase in number; fill the earth and subdue it. Rule over the fish of the sea and the birds of the air and over every living creature that moves on the ground.' " Hear the command that God has never cancelled: rule over creation. Be blessed in your stewardship of his command to have righteous authority over creation, including weather. James 5:17-18 tells us that "Elijah was a man just like us. He prayed earnestly that it would not rain, and it did not rain on the land for three and a half years. Again he prayed, and the heavens gave rain, and the earth produced its crops."

Spirit, be blessed with Elijah-like authority over weather in partnership with God at his instruction. Be blessed to direct a hurricane and say, "Weaken and go east," if God should so instruct you, and read in the newspaper that an unexpected burst of cool air came out of the Midwest and cooled off and steered a 175 mile-an-hour storm that was 150 miles across. Only the breath of God could do that. More of you, spirit, is waiting to rise to meet God's dominion, to rise to your full potential in the earth.

Be blessed in the name of the Most High over all the earth (Ps. 97:9).

54 Be Enlarged With Enjoying God's Purposes In Land — Acts 17:25-26

Spirit, listen to the Word of God in Acts 17:25-26. "God himself gives all men life and breath and everything else… He determined the times set for them and the exact places where they should live."

On the third day of creation, God separated the water from the dry land. He created land as a masterpiece of his purposes and design. He blessed land by depositing gifts in land on continental, national, regional, and local levels. He installed all righteous earthgates, lines, and portals from the foundation of creation.

Spirit, there is an inherent blessing in land for us, because God created all things for us to enjoy. He gave Adam and Eve the mandate to rule over the earth and subdue it (Gen. 1:28). God did not take that mandate back at the fall. He repeated it to Noah (Gen. 9:1-2). We are all sons of Adam, and if we know it or not, we all have sensitivity to land in some measure. Be blessed with resonating with God's purposes in creation of land. Be blessed to observe differences in land, even when you do not understand in your soul what your spirit feels. Be blessed with fully cultivating the land anointing that God put in you.

Some cultures have shown reverence to God by valuing the treasures in the land. Our generation and our culture as a whole does not honor God's creation. Our generation has abused and trashed some of the greatest gifts in land. Be blessed to love the land, whether it is the plot that you own, a park that you love, or a place that you enjoy going. It could be your city or state or a country you have visited. Ask God to increase your sensitivity to land. Notice the mysteries of land. Discover connections of land, sound, motion, and light. Discover synergies in land. Be blessed to experience and express the thing that grabs you about a piece of land, as you recognize God's presence there. Be blessed with God's revelation of his creation, because he loves it and calls it very good.

Be blessed to seek out places where great beauty prevails, where great history has been deposited, where great acts of courage still echo. Seek the long-ago footprints of heroes, martyrs, and ordinary faithful people. Search out their hallowed ground where they buried their dead with inscriptions on their tombstone like this: "Here lies my beloved who died of fever. Ever she sought the best, ever she found it." Be blessed in that place in your inner being that is sensitive to and invigorated by the spirit of an old homeplace or old church or some other righteous place where a generational deposit waits to be tapped.

Be blessed with "reading" land, with listening to land, with feeling land, whether it is sad or happy, living up to its righteous purpose or defiled and in confusion. Be blessed with depositing the blessing of holy presence wherever you set your feet.

Spirit, be blessed with eternal eyes, ears, taste, touch, and smell to get in touch with the earth, to bless the soil and seeds sown, to call down water from heaven and water it with your tears if necessary, and to steward the growth that only God can give to a harvest of fruit that remains.

Be blessed in the name of the Ruler of God's creation (Rev. 3:14).

55 Be Enlarged: There's A New You — 1 John 3:2

Spirit, listen to God's Word for you in 1 John 3:2. "Dear friends, now we are children of God, and what we will be has not yet been made known. But we know that when he appears, we shall be like him, for we shall see him as he is."

Spirit, be blessed to understand and receive these blessings in spirit and in truth. Receive them and minister the truth of them to your soul. Wherever you are with God right now, he says that you are not yet what you will be. Be blessed to be transformed, healed, and enlarged by his Spirit in you, because God promises that your inner man is being renewed day by day (2 Cor. 4:16). God is reviving you. Be blessed with believing and receiving this truth and seeing his results in your life. Be blessed with being enlarged in your inner being to know your Father more and more. Be blessed with his profound working in you for your sake and for others in your world.

There are many things that you were incorrectly taught, so many experiences that were wounding, so many absences of good nurturing. Be blessed as God goes back to your childhood and growing up days to heal, reprogram, and renew your inmost being. Be blessed with complete healing from and recovery from abuse and shame — physical, verbal, mental, emotional, and spiritual.

Spirit, be blessed to feel the Holy Spirit making real to you his truths and blessings in righteousness. Absorb from him and feel yourself being set free as he teaches, trains, and transforms you. Be blessed as he nurtures, challenges, stimulates, and directs you.
Be blessed with new revelation, insights, spiritual wisdom, and knowledge. Paul told his Colossian friends to put on the new self, which is being renewed in knowledge in the image of its Creator (Col. 3:10). The New Living Translation says it this way: In the place of the old man, "You have clothed yourselves with a brand-new nature that is continually being renewed as you learn more and more about Christ, who created this new nature within you." Be blessed with God's timing and process of making you more like Jesus in all your responses and actions and thoughts. Be blessed with seeing his fingerprints on your life.

God says that he is doing a new thing. Listen to Isaiah 42:9. "See, the former things have taken place, and new things I declare; before they spring into being I announce them to you." Receive Isaiah 43:19-21. "See, I am doing a new thing! Now it springs up… I am making a way in the desert and streams in the wasteland… I provide water in the desert and streams in the wasteland, to give drink to my people, my chosen, the people I formed for myself that they may proclaim my praise."

Spirit, in him receive his new thing. Don't let anything or anybody rob you of God's best. Be blessed each day with more peace, and joy, and encouragement, and boldness that you know have come from him through seeing him as he is and seeing yourself as you are in him. There's more! Reach out, be enlarged, and receive more of him.

Be blessed in the name of the One who is doing a new thing (Isa. 43:19).

Holy Boldness

56 Holy Boldness: No Fear In God's Promises — Psalm 91:1-8, 14-16

Spirit, hear the Word of God for you in Psalm 91.
1 He who dwells in the shelter of the Most High
will rest in the shadow of the Almighty.
2 I will say of the LORD, "He is my refuge and my fortress,
My God, in whom I trust."
3 Surely he will save you from the fowler's snare
and from the deadly pestilence.
4 He will cover you with his feathers,
and under his wings you will find refuge;
His faithfulness will be your shield and rampart.
5 You will not fear the terror of night,
nor the arrow that flies by day,
6 Nor the pestilence that stalks in the darkness,
nor the plague that destroys at midday.
7 A thousand may fall at your side,
ten thousand at your right hand,
but it will not come near you.
8 You will only observe with your eyes
and see the punishment of the wicked.

You know that life is not a picnic; you are in a war. Spirit, be at peace because you are sheltered in the safe place of the refuge of the Almighty. Under the wings of El Shaddai, his promises are sure. When your soul lacks faith and is afraid, you will be defended by his faithfulness as your shield and defense. Be blessed to make yourself at home in the hiding place of Most High and take your rest under the wings of the Almighty. He is the Lord your refuge, your fortress, your God who is trustworthy. Be blessed with security from all satan's snares and schemes. Be blessed with peace under the covering of his wings.

Spirit, be blessed to put into God's hands the terrors in the dark and the arrows that attempt to destroy you by day. God has heard your heart, and you can be assured in him that the schemes of your enemy will not come near you. Ask your Mighty Warrior to reveal the real battle that you are up against. Rest in your Commander of the Lord's hosts, stand steadfast, and see that the battle is the Lord's. No fiery arrows can pierce your safe place in your refuge under him. You can be confident that no weapon formed against you will prosper. In his sure promises, don't be disheartened or worry about the tomorrows that are yet to come. Don't waste a minute of the present with worrying about the future. Your times are in his hands.

Jesus is standing in you against all hindrances to possessing all your inheritance. You have his name and the authority of his blood, the cross, his resurrection, his ascension, and his glorification to the right hand of Most High God. The empty tomb of Jesus put up a stop sign on the past. Be blessed to take your stand in the armor of the One who has already triumphed. He has already defeated the adversary you are facing. For such a time as this you can stand in all the armor of light that Jesus has provided for you. In his name you have victory, because his rescue and protection is secured to those who acknowledge his name.

Spirit, listen again to Psalm 91.
14 "Because he loves me," says the LORD, "I will rescue him;
I will protect him, for he acknowledges my name.
15 He will call upon me, and I will answer him;
I will be with him in trouble, I will deliver him and honor him.
16 With long life will I satisfy him and show him my salvation."

Spirit, your intimate friendship with God grows sweeter in knowing and applying his names — Elyon, Shaddai, Yahweh, Elohim. Know that he sees your deep love for him. It draws out his compassion for you in your desperation. Be certain that he comes to protect and deliver you. In covenant with God you have a claim on his answers, and he answers with himself. Be blessed in the presence of Jesus with you and in you, and he is totally unafraid. Make him the focus of your expectancy and confidence. He has promised you eight "I will's:" "I will rescue him, I will protect him, I will answer him, I will be with him in trouble, I will deliver him, I will honor him. I will satisfy him, and I will show him my salvation." The Hebrew word for salvation is Yeshua. It means help, deliverance, victory, salvation, healing, welfare, well-being. Your God Most High assumes all responsibility for you. Totally. Your birthright is dwelling in all that Jesus your Savior is for you. Be blessed to be satisfied in his salvation.

Be blessed in his name Yeshua-Jesus (Ps. 91:16; Mat. 1:21).

57 Holy Boldness: No Fear In God's Dwelling Place — Psalm 91:9-16

Spirit, listen to the Word of God for you in Psalm 91:9-13.
9 If you make the Most High your dwelling —
even the LORD, who is my refuge —
10 then no harm will befall you,
no disaster will come near your tent.
11 For he will command his angels concerning you
to guard you in all your ways;
12 they will lift you up in their hands,
so that you will not strike your foot against a stone.
13 You will tread upon the lion and the cobra;
you will trample the great lion and the serpent.

Spirit, the Author and Finisher of faith in you enables you to trust the unfailing protection of God Most High. He is exalted, omnipotent, supreme, and overwhelming in his majesty. He is your tender Abba, and his sure promises are found in his names — Dwelling Place, Lord, and Refuge. He is your shelter, your place of hope and trust, your home. In his names no evil can conquer you. Feel his strength in these names. He is with you. The Commander of the armies of heaven will command his angels to guard you all the time, and when he commands, it is done. His angels will hold you up in their hands so you don't trip or stumble.

God has a destiny that he purposed in you before the foundation of the world. Yes, you will have to confront obstacles and be an overcomer, and some of the strongest obstacles are the lies that the enemy wants you to believe. Your adversary is the father of lies. You are blessed to take your stand in confidence that you will tread upon and trample down the roaring lion and the serpent, man's ancient foe, because Jesus already defeated him. You are a covenant son/daughter of God Most High. Be bold, be free, and take your rightful authority in your protector.

Spirit, remember the character of your Father: God of all grace, Righteous Judge, Holy One, Compassionate and Faithful One, God of the impossible. You have the privilege of coming into agreement with him. Your birthright is to live in honor, dignity, and authority in Jesus' name. You are on kingdom business every day everywhere you go under God's orders. You represent your King as you carry out the business of his kingdom.

Spirit, you can speak to God like this: "I am your child, Most High God. I draw close to you. I dress myself in the armor of light. I plead the blood of Jesus over myself, my family, and my friends. I stand in the promises of Psalm 91. With Jesus Christ, my elder brother and my covenant-keeper at my side, the adversary has no authority over me, my family, my friends, or anything that touches my righteous jurisdiction. I will take my stand in the authority and power that is my heritage in Jesus' name."

Spirit, this is how God answers you. Listen to the promises of Psalm 91:14-16.
14 “Because he loves me,” says the LORD, “I will rescue him;
I will protect him, for he acknowledges my name.
15 He will call upon me, and I will answer him;
I will be with him in trouble, I will deliver and honor him
16 With long life will I satisfy him and show him my salvation.”

God promises to rescue you because you delight in him. You have set your love on him and have bound yourself to him. He promises to protect you and make you inaccessible to your enemies, because you know him intimately and personally. You know his character, his honor, and his fame. He promises to pay attention to you, and respond to you and answer you when you pray to him. He promises to be with you in trouble, in all adversity, suffering, anguish, and distress. He promises to draw you out of a tight place and deliver you and give you the honor due you as the object of his affectionate care. His crowning promise is that he will fill you with the satisfaction of a full life and show you his help, deliverance from distress, victory, welfare, well-being, and total forgiveness. In that you can be truly satisfied. Be blessed to be strong and of good courage, for his banner over you is love.

Be blessed in the name of the One who is the Banner of love over you (Song of Sol. 2:4).

58 Holy Boldness: No Fear In God's Hiding Place — Psalm 32:7; 42:8

Spirit, listen to the promises of the unfailing Word of God in Psalm 32:7. "You are my hiding place; you will protect me from trouble and surround me with songs of deliverance." And in Psalm 42:8. "By day the LORD directs his [covenant] love, at night his song is with me — a prayer to the God of my life."

Spirit, be blessed to know that the God of your life sings over you as a mother soothes and comforts a fearful baby. In his arms, he surrounds you with songs of deliverance as you are led through the enemy's strongholds of fear and anxiety to a place of safety, assurance, and confidence. In any trouble, you can sing under the wings of the Most High in harmony with his songs of deliverance.

Your Father secured his covenant with you in his only Son, and he is a covenant-keeping God. He can never forget his covenant promises with you. Jesus in heaven bears on his body the marks of that eternal agreement. See his hands, his feet, and his side, as he showed his disciples after his resurrection.

Spirit, he has written your days in his book of the covenant, the Lamb's book. Listen to these words in Malachi 3:16-17. "Then those who feared the LORD talked with each other, and the LORD listened and heard. A scroll of remembrance was written in his presence concerning those who feared the LORD and honored his name. 'They will be mine,' says the LORD Almighty, 'in the day when I make up my treasured possession. I will spare them, just as in compassion a man spares his son who serves him.' "

Beloved one, receive the promise of this. You can tell others of your confidence in his name and his faithfulness. Your name is ever before him in heaven on a scroll of remembrance. He acts on your behalf, just because you are his. He cannot deny his own special treasure. He will rescue you as a compassionate father spares an obedient child.

Spirit, listen to how The Message expresses Malachi 3:16-17. "Then those whose lives honored GOD got together and talked it over. GOD saw what they were doing and listened in. A book was opened in GOD's presence, and minutes were taken of the meeting, with the names of the God-fearers written down, all the names of those who honored GOD's name. GOD-of-Angel-Armies said, 'They're mine, all mine. They'll get special treatment when I go into action. I treat them with the same consideration and kindness that parents give the child who honors them.' "

All spiritual warfare is about the majesty and supremacy of God being revealed. Live in the power and authority of his spiritual victory as GOD-of-Angel-Armies. He that is in you is greater than he that is in the world (1 John 4:4). The Commander of the armies of heaven is on your side, and you have abiding safety in him. His love covers you completely, his defense of you is invulnerable and never ceases. He is your defended place. When the heat is on, run to him, not just as your escape, but as your secret place of intimacy with him where he sings over you. His nearness is your good. You have undisturbed safety and fearlessness as you settle down and make your home in him. He prepares a table before you in the presence of your enemies.

Spirit, God will teach you to be biblically fearless, based on your covenant relationship with him. Believe and receive his unfailing perfect covenant love that casts out fear (1 John 4:18). Take this deep into your spirit and life-experience. You have his faithful promises that you are secure in his protecting presence. You can rest totally depending on the character of God. Be blessed to trust in the All-sufficient One who is enough, where no lies and no fear can penetrate. Be blessed to see what God is doing in your trouble that is a stepping stone to more of Jesus. Be blessed with new peace in Jesus as your shield of faith. In him nothing can destroy your joy, your hope, your relationships, your witness, or God's purposes. And the God of peace will soon crush satan under his feet.

Spirit, be blessed in the name of the one who will never forsake you, as he says to you:

> So do not fear, for I am with you;
> do not be dismayed, for I am your God.
> I will strengthen you and help you;
> I will uphold you with my righteous right hand.
> For I am the LORD, your God,
> who takes hold of your right hand
> and says to you, Do not fear; I will help you. Isaiah 41:10,13

Be strong and courageous. Do not be afraid or terrified because of them,
for the LORD your God goes with you; he will never leave you nor forsake you.
The LORD himself goes before you and will be with you;
he will never leave you nor forsake you. Do not be afraid; do not be discouraged.
Deuteronomy 31:6,8

Be blessed in the name of the God of your life (Ps. 42:8).

Hope In Disappointment

59 God's Perspective On Hope In Disappointment — Romans 15:13

Spirit, listen to the Word of God for you in Romans 15:13. "May the God of hope fill you with all joy and peace as you trust in him, so that you may overflow with hope by the power of the Holy Spirit." And in Hebrews 4:12. "The word of God is living and active. Sharper than any double-edged sword, it penetrates even to dividing soul and spirit, joints and marrow; it judges the thoughts and attitudes of the heart."

Spirit, be blessed with the word that God speaks to separate you from the soul's history and agenda. Let him free you from the soulish bonds that have held you captive in disappointment and hopelessness. Be blessed by your Father's will, his heart, and his words. Let him do his perfect work to enlarge you to receive more of his fullness and to move you into the authority that he gives you over soul and body. Look to Jesus for ministry. He will shine the light of his Spirit in you to show you who you are and who he is in you and for you. Welcome his light.

Spirit, the God of hope calls you to hope (Eph. 1:18). You were designed for hope. He wants you to know that you are his own special creation. He determined for you an appointed place and time. He has given you the good gift of himself to live in you as his temple. He has deposited in you his great love in making you just the way you are, the real you, your true essence. You are blessed as he celebrates, affirms, and validates your unique identity for your authority, calling, and birthright in him. Spirit, you can hardly receive these words if you have received wounds of disappointment. Your soul has done everything it knows to do to heal them, but still disappointment gnaws deep inside you beyond reach. Disappointments are spirit wounds that have never been addressed and healed. Jesus, your Kinsman-Redeemer, is ready to redeem the years that the locusts have eaten when you cancel the "appointments" that your soul made with its expectations.

Spirit, you were created in the mind of God for eternity forever with him. Satan can't take that away from you, so he has sent fiery arrows to rob you now, deeply penetrating missiles of disappointment with others, with yourself, and with God. People have disappointed you many times. Others whom you wanted to please have been disappointed with you, and their disappointment has landed deeply in you.

Jesus your Redeemer wants to pull the poisons out of the wounds in you, spirit, and in your soul. He wants you to know and respond to him as the Way, the Truth, and the Life, because he said, "You shall know the truth, and the truth shall make you free. And when the Son sets you free, you will be free indeed" (John 8:32,36). God is inviting you to see truth, to hear truth, to understand his truth coming to you. That's a powerful invitation. It is life-changing to see with your own eyes, to take ownership of what you are seeing and hearing, coming out of denial and truly allowing God's truth to come into you. Spirit, be blessed as you let God reach into the deep places of your being. Be blessed as you see your disappointments through his eyes, maybe for the first time. He wants you to exchange his hope for your disappointment, because he loves you dearly and has given you the Holy Spirit to fill you with his love (Rom. 5:5, NLT). Be blessed to receive his hope that does not disappoint.

Be blessed in the name of the God of hope who fills you with all joy and peace as you trust him (Rom. 15:13).

60 God's Bigger Picture Of Hope In Disappointment — Isaiah 49:23; Psalm 62:1-2; Romans 12:12

Spirit, hear God's Word for you in Isaiah 49:23. "Then you will know that I am the Lord; those who hope in me will not be disappointed." And Psalm 62:1-2. "My soul finds rest in God alone; my salvation comes from him. He alone is my rock and my salvation; he is my fortress, I will never be shaken." And Romans 12:12. "Be joyful in hope, patient in affliction, faithful in prayer."

Spirit, be blessed to see that hope is a promise of God, a position in him, and a command.

The Promise Of Hope — Isaiah 49:23

Listen again to Isaiah 49:23. "Then you will know that I am the Lord; those who hope in me will not be disappointed." Spirit, the supernatural presence of the Holy Spirit lives in you, filling you with assurance that he cannot disappoint you. Be blessed with confidence that the sovereign Lord of your life is in charge of your circumstances. When expectation delays, when your hope is waiting without fulfillment, when disappointment tries to overwhelm you, you can have confidence in your Father, because you know that he is in control. He is Lord; he can't get it wrong. He can do no other. When you are tempted with hopelessness, your Father says that those who wait for him, those who hope in him, will never be put to shame.

The psalmist said, "One thing God has spoken, two things have I heard: that you, O God, are strong, and that you, O Lord, are loving" (Ps. 62:11-12). Your confidence in him will never disappoint you, because he is strong and loving. Be blessed with security and safety because your hope is anchored in your Father's love and unchanging strength. Be blessed with the truth of Psalm 16:5-6. "He is my portion… He maintains my lot." Be blessed with knowing that your Father's eyes are on those who hope. Be blessed with ascendancy over your soul which will ask the wrong questions. Be blessed with asking your Father the right question as your gaze is fixed on him. The question is not "Why?" but "How?" Be blessed with knowing that he is your "how." Be blessed with this dialogue with your soul. "The Lord is my portion," says my soul, "Therefore I hope in Him!" (Lam. 3:24).

God comes to be with those who hope in him, and he is enough. Your Father speaks hope to you, hope in him that does not disappoint, because he dearly loves you. Be blessed in God's promise that the desire he gives leads where he wants you to go — learning to endure, developing strength of character, in confident expectation of seeing the glory of his purposes for you and in his joy in hope. Jesus is your promised hope.

Spirit, receive the prayer of Paul in Ephesians 1:18-21. "I pray also that the eyes of your heart may be enlightened in order that you may know the hope to which he has called you, the riches of his glorious inheritance in the saints, and his incomparably great power for us who believe. That power is like the working of his mighty strength, which he exerted in Christ when he raised him from the dead and seated him at his right hand in the heavenly realms, far above all rule and authority, power and dominion, and every title that can be given…" You are seated in heavenly realms in hope, in the name of your glorious Father.

Be blessed in the name of the Spirit of wisdom and revelation, so that you may know your Promise of hope (Eph. 1:17).

The Position Of Hope — Psalm 62:1-2

Spirit, listen to Psalm 62:1. "My soul finds rest in God alone; my salvation comes from him." Listen to the NKJV translation. "Truly my soul silently waits for God; From Him comes my salvation. He only is my rock and my salvation; He is my defense; I shall not be greatly moved" (Ps. 62:1-2).

Spirit, God of hope is the essence of your Father. It is who he is, and you are in him (Rom. 15:13). Be blessed with rest in the God of hope alone when your expectation is delayed. You are in the waiting room of the God of hope, anticipating and expecting as you are learning the meaning of hope. The Hebrew words for *hope* and *wait* come from the same root word. The Hebrew words translated *hope* mean confidence, twisting in labor pains, waiting, expectation, patience, trust, enduring, expectancy, something longed for.

Some of these meanings of hope are not for the faint of heart. Spirit, be blessed with faithfulness in the face of circumstances that look hopeless. Be blessed as you take refuge in him and take new courage. Be blessed as you connect with your Father in hope in a special and deep way. Be blessed with unshakable hope in him, when everything else is shaken. Be blessed with firmly standing on the solid rock of God's faithfulness and timing. Be blessed with rest and quietness deep in your being that come from Jesus in you. Receive secure hope in Christ Jesus in you, the life of God flowing to you, your hope of glory (Col. 1:27). He is all. Be steadfast in abundant hope by his presence in you filling up what is lacking that you can't humanly do.

Spirit, listen to the confident position of intimacy and hope the psalmist expressed in Psalm 84, and take your position in God there.

1 How lovely is your dwelling place, O LORD Almighty!
2 My soul yearns, even faints, for the courts of the LORD;
my heart and my flesh cry out for the living God.
3 Even the sparrow has found a home, and the swallow a nest for herself,
where she may have her young — a place near your altar,
O LORD Almighty, my King and my God.
4 Blessed are those who dwell in your house; they are ever praising you. Selah
5 Blessed are those whose strength is in you, who have set their hearts on pilgrimage.
6 As they pass through the Valley of Baca, they make it a place of springs;
the autumn rains also cover it with pools.
7 They go from strength to strength, till each appears before God in Zion.
8 Hear my prayer, O LORD God Almighty; listen to me, O God of Jacob. Selah
9 Look upon our shield, O God; look with favor on your anointed one.
11 For the LORD God is a sun and shield; the LORD bestows favor and honor;
no good thing does he withhold from those whose walk is blameless.
12 O LORD Almighty, blessed is the man who trusts in you.

Spirit, be blessed with knowing God intends you to pass through every valley of trouble with his wisdom and grace and hope. Be blessed as the God of hope makes a door of hope in your Valley of Trouble (Hos. 2:15).

Be blessed as the One who is your hope makes your trouble into springs of hope (Ps. 84:6).

The Command To Hope — Romans 12:12

Spirit, listen as your Father commands in Romans 12:12. “Be joyful in hope.”

The Greek word translated *hope* means desiring good and confidently expecting to obtain it. Hope that is seen is not hope at all, but your assurance is in your Father that he is Lord of everything, even your questions, doubts, challenges, opposition, and suffering. He knows the mysteries of your life, he knows what he’s doing, and he has a purpose for everything. Therefore, you can rest in him. Sometimes he stands as your only hope, but even so, be blessed with joyful hope and encouragement that he is unfolding your future.

Spirit, in Psalm 62:5-8 God gives words of command to your soul. “My soul, wait silently for God alone, for my expectation is from Him. He only is my rock and my salvation; He is my defense; I shall not be moved. In God is my salvation and my glory; The rock of my strength, and my refuge, is in God. Trust in Him at all times, you people; Pour out your heart before Him; God is a refuge for us. Selah.”

God commands hope in him, and what he commands, he provides for. Paul said, “Continue in your faith, established and firm, not moved from the hope held out in the gospel” (Col. 1:23). In your circumstances that you can see, hope will fail you. That is the reason God gave you his Word and his promise. “Everything that was written in the past was written to teach us, so that through endurance and the encouragement of the Scriptures we might have hope” (Rom. 15:4). He gave you the Scriptures so that you can have hope. Immerse yourself in his Word, like Hebrews 6:18-19. “By two unchangeable things in which it is impossible for God to lie, we who have fled to take hold of the hope offered to us may be greatly encouraged. We have this hope as an anchor for the soul, firm and secure.” Spirit, be blessed as you take hold of God’s character, his unchangableness, and his promises with confidence. Be blessed with being sure that your Father cannot and will not lie to you, and he will never change his mind about you. Be blessed as you run to his firm hope as the strong and trustworthy anchor of your soul. Be blessed with continued faith in his goodness and with his great encouragement. In him you have the resources of the ages to press through walls of disappointment, self-protection, separation, and pain.

Be blessed with hope as God washes away disappointments with new vision and renewed God-directed “appointments” and expectation. God has appointed this season of refreshing and receiving for you. Receive his touch to restore the places that have been bruised, and broken, and shut down. Be blessed as you allow your Father to replace your burdens with his faith, your disappointments with his hope, and your doubts with his love.

Spirit, be blessed with the full purposes of God in re-forming and rebuilding you, which he planned before time to be released to you now. Be blessed to be saturated with renewed and restored life, so that hope deferred can no longer make you sick and hold you captive. Be blessed with all joy and peace in believing that God is doing this work by his Holy Spirit in you filling you with hope (Rom. 15:13). Be blessed as you live in brighter light that streams from the face of the God of hope. Be blessed as the light of his countenance shines in you hope in him that does not disappoint. Be blessed with receiving the nurture, ministry, and full and abundant gifts of the God of hope.

Be blessed in the name of Christ Jesus, your hope (Col. 1:27; 1 Tim. 1:1; Ps. 71:15).

61 Seeing The Fingerprints Of the Unseen — Job 26:14

Spirit, listen to this majestic picture of God in Job 26:14. "These are but the outer fringe of his works; how faint the whisper we hear of him! Who then can understand the thunder of his power?" And 1 Peter 1:8. "Though you have not seen him, you love him; and even though you do not see him now, you believe in him and are filled with an inexpressible and glorious joy."

Spirit, I bless your sweet softness in the hands of your Father when you don't understand what he's doing. I bless your surrendered heart to look for him when he's not doing what you wanted or expected. Every season has its beauty and is invariably preparation for the next season. In this time of the hiding of his power, take faithful steps of faith and obedience, faith and obedience. Beyond obedience, even when you don't see him, be blessed to love him. Although you don't see him now, be blessed to believe in him and be filled with glorious inexpressible joy — his joy.

Be blessed with eyes to see the fingerprints of his ways in your ordinary days, knowing that he says, "My thoughts are not your thoughts, neither are your ways my ways. As the heavens are higher than the earth, so are my ways higher than your ways and my thoughts than your thoughts" (Isa. 55:8-9).

Spirit, when you know you don't understand and when you think you do, the earth keeps shouting to you that he is completely faithful. The words of his mouth go forth as faithfully as rain and snow water the earth and make it bud and flourish and yield seed for the sower and bread for the eater. That's the law of the harvest. He promises that his word to you is like that. "It will not return to me empty, but will accomplish what I desire and achieve the purpose for which I sent it" (Isa. 55:10-11).

Spirit, as you see seedtime and harvest in the natural yield its return every year, enter his gates with thanksgiving and come into his courts with praise that you will reap a spiritual harvest as you sow in faith and joy. Worship leads you to a place of rest and trust in his faithfulness, his sovereignty, and his love. Be blessed to see that God is there, increasing your knowledge and experience of himself. Know this: with each place he takes you in those sometimes not-your-first-choice circumstances, he draws you deeper into himself.

The length to which God takes his own is beyond comprehension. Spirit, even when you see only the edges of his ways, hear only his small whispers, and cannot understand him, he is the Best. Even when he seems to have withdrawn from you, he promises that "you will go out in joy and be led forth in peace; the mountains and hills will burst into song before you, and all the trees of the field will clap their hands" (Isa. 55:12). You can celebrate him in the growth points of your journey, even in his faintest whispers. Remember Elijah. God was not in the violent wind, or the fire, or the earthquake, but in the gentle blowing of the still small voice. Be blessed to line up with his still small voice practically and in prayer, praying what he wants. Be blessed with an "upgrade" of your image of God, because what you think about him, who he is to you, is the single most important element in pleasing him in every respect, bearing fruit in every good work (Col. 1:9-13).

Be blessed in the name of the King of the kingdom he promised to those who love him (Jam. 2:5).

Intimacy With God

62 Seeking God — Psalm 63:1

Spirit, listen to the Word of God and be blessed with the passionate cry of the psalmist in Psalm 63:1. "O God, you are my God, earnestly I seek you; my soul thirsts for you, my body longs for you." And in Psalm 42:1. "As the deer pants for streams of water, so my soul pants for you, O God."

Spirit, be blessed to live from that deep cry of seeking God in your innermost being, longing for more of him, digging in to know him more intimately. Your Father desires constant communion with you spirit to Spirit. Be blessed with directing the thirst of your soul to communion with him. Be blessed with getting out of your head and into your spirit, meeting God personally and profoundly.

Be blessed to know that God is who he said he is, and he can and will do what he says he can and will do. He is the I Am to do it in you today. He is personal and powerful, and he alone satisfies. Jesus is standing and knocking, waiting for you to open up to him for satisfying fellowship (Rev. 3:20). Jesus invites you to a table set for two. He wants your love, and he will be satisfied when you fulfill his heart by opening up to him.

Spirit, be blessed with knowing your covenant-keeping God of promise as you seek him and keep company with him in Spirit and in truth. Be blessed with more of his Spirit, not more how-to's to make you feel religious or guilty. Be blessed to discover him more as his Spirit lives in you to fulfill your deepest cries. Be blessed to encounter him in such dimensions that you feel as if you have never breathed spiritually before.

Be blessed in his name Rewarder of those who earnestly seek him (Heb. 11:6).

63 Intimacy With God — Psalm 25:14; Genesis 3:18

Spirit, hear God's Word to you in Psalm 25:14. "The LORD confides in those who fear him; he makes his covenant known to them." And in Genesis 3:8. "Then the man and his wife heard the sound of the LORD God as he was walking in the garden in the cool of the day."

Spirit, you are of the same essence of Adam and Eve. God wants to walk with you, and talk with you, and speak intimately with you. Welcome him to come into the garden of your heart, and fellowship with him as they did — no books, no Bible, no sermon, no ritual, no expectations, no agenda. Just be, spending time with him. Be free of chains of expectation or performance or "same-ole-same-ole" in worship. Your Father's heart will minister to you, and you will respond in abandoned adoration. Be blessed to be filled with new worship that is deeply satisfying to God and that exceeds all your previous definitions of "good worship."

Spirit, be blessed in your face-to-face time with the living God as you are spirit-to-Spirit with him. Communion is a function of the spirit. Be in touch with the Spirit at all times so that you enter into new communion. Hear the sounds of heaven as you fellowship with him in intimacy. Let him touch you more deeply than he has ever touched you before. Experience love, and trust, and deep emotional satisfaction in him. Intimate friendship with God is reserved for those who are crazy about him. Be free to know your First Love and to come into harmony with him. Nothing compares with intimacy with him in richness and beauty. You meet him in surrender and waiting on him in faith, hope, and love.

Spirit, God confided in Abraham and Moses. He called them his friends. Christ said to the disciples, "You are my friends," and he says to you, "You are my friend if you obey my Father's commandments." Friendship with God is cultivated by authenticity in loving obedience. You were designed to live in friendship with him and share your life with him. Claim your friendship with God by coming boldly to his throne of grace. Since friendship is mutual, you give to him, even as he meets the needs of the depths of your being.

Spirit, John 1:14 says that Jesus the Word "became flesh and made his dwelling among us." His presence is your true home. The tabernacle in the wildness pictured Jesus coming to earth because God wants to be close to you. Sit on his lap, feel his arms around you, listen to his voice, hear his heartbeat. Fall in love with him. Be bathed in his love and experience his presence. Your true identity is beloved of God, not worker for him. Know him intimately, and relentlessly pursue him with steadfast hunger for more. Live with humility of heart before him, and ascribe "worth-ship to him." Declare him with your voice, and reflect him in your life.

John 1:14 also says, "We have seen his glory, the glory of the One and Only, who came from the Father, full of grace and truth." See his glory that Jesus brought from his Father. Receive the fullness of his grace and truth.

Be blessed in the name of the One and Only (John 1:14).

64 The Light Of God's Face — Genesis 1:1,3-4

Spirit, hear the Word of God for you in Genesis 1:1,3-4. "In the beginning God created the heavens and the earth. And God said, 'Let there be light,' and there was light. God saw that the light was good, and he separated the light from the darkness."

Spirit, hear the sound of God's voice that continually speaks his creative power in you and to you. Listen to James 1:17. "Every good and perfect gift is from above, coming down from the Father of the heavenly lights, who does not change like shifting shadows." Spirit, be blessed in the light of your Father's face. Be blessed in his good gifts of mercy and peace. Be blessed in his unchanging intention toward you. Turn to his face and see him gazing at you in rapt attention. Receive his download from the light of his eyes. Receive long gazes from the light of his countenance. Let your Abba transcend your wounds — spiritual, emotional, and physical — and any scar tissue which has formed there. His grace and blessing are in the light of his face toward you (Ps. 67:1).

Join the psalmist's request in Psalm 31:16. "Let your face shine on your servant; save me in your unfailing love." Spirit, seek his gaze, and receive the unfailing love of your Father in the light of his eyes. Receive that you are your Father's precious one. You are his, you belong to his family of light. He turned you from darkness into his kingdom of light for a place in his inheritance in light (Col. 1:12-13; Acts 26:18). His light reveals that he is your Lord, and you are who you are because you are in him. You have value, worth, belonging, and abundant acceptance. He cherishes your company. You are blessed to see his name Jehovah-Nissi, Banner of the Lord, over you as a canopy of love. You are blessed to see that he makes beauty for ashes out of the darkest things, as he moves on the face of the turmoil of your life and speaks light in you.

Spirit, listen to Psalm 36:9. "In your light we see light." Receive the light of his heart toward you. The light of his face shines on you. Receive it because you are in Christ, in his cross, his resurrection, and his ascension to the right hand of the Father, and you are seated in him there. Rest there at his strong right hand and feel his strength as his light rises in you. Receive his light that consumes all darkness. Claim that light, and you will become light in him, because Christ in you, the hope of glory, will shine. Receive his light that lights your way. Receive the light of his flame of correction, burning away the chaff. Receive his purifying light with joy. Receive his light that warms all coldness.

Hold his gaze as he lifts you up and holds you, everything you love, everybody you love, and your future. He is holding you near in his arms of love. He has invested gifts of love in you all along. There is coming a harvest of redemption of every one of them and more in his purposes. God will stir up all the gifts and graces he has placed in you for the right season. He will redeem all devouring according to his alignment. He will redeem every blessing with your name on it. Spirit, receive his blessing in continuous moments of stewardship of life in the light of his face.

"The LORD bless you and keep you;
The LORD make his face shine upon you and be gracious to you;
The LORD turn his face toward you and give you peace" (Num. 6:24-26).

Be blessed in the name of One who said, "Let there be light" (Gen. 1:3).

65 Simple Devotion To Jesus — 2 Corinthians 11:2-3

Spirit, hear God's Word for you in 2 Corinthians 11:2-3. "I am jealous for you with a godly jealousy. I promised you to one husband, to Christ, so that I might present you as a pure virgin to him. But I am afraid that just as Eve was deceived by the serpent's cunning, your minds may somehow be led astray from your sincere and pure devotion to Christ."

Spirit, be blessed to know that God is jealous for your undivided affection. He pictures this in the imagery of two lovers. He counts you as a pure virgin engaged to his Son Jesus. When you are madly in love, it is easy to have eyes only for the one you love. You listen in rapt attention for the next word that comes from your lover's mouth, and any wish is your command. You let nothing disturb your communion.

Spirit, listen to the single commitment of a lover of Jesus. He said, "Only one thing is needed. Mary has chosen what is better, and it will not be taken away from her." Be blessed as you choose the one thing that cannot be taken away from you: fellowship in complete devotion to Jesus, filling your heart with him, hanging on his every word, and joyously abandoning yourself to the next thing he speaks. Be blessed as you quickly respond to his prompting. On this earth the spirit of Jesus was conscious of one thing — perfect oneness with his Father (John 10:30; 17:22). Be blessed with the simplicity that is in Christ, so that all you do is based on perfect unity with him.

Feel the love hunger of one of the greatest lovers of God. Among all the privileges of royalty, where no pleasure of the king was denied, David said in Psalm 27:4, "One thing I ask of the LORD, this is what I seek: that I may dwell in the house of the LORD all the days of my life, to gaze upon the beauty of the LORD and to seek him in his temple." This was the priority of a man after God's own heart — simple and pure devotion to seeking him, being in his presence, drinking in the beauty of his holiness, wanting nothing and nobody else.

In the months after Jesus ascended back to his Father, Peter and John amazed the most learned and powerful Jewish ruling body of the day. How did these common uneducated fishermen obtain the power to raise a crippled man and heal many others? Dr. Luke tells us. "When they saw the courage of Peter and John and realized that they were unschooled, ordinary men, they were astonished, and they took note that these men had been with Jesus" (Acts 4:13). Being with Jesus was their credential — being entirely dedicated and loyal to him, letting nobody turn them aside, being faithful to the power he imparted to them. Be blessed with the courage and boldness that mark the simplicity and devotion of being with Jesus. Be blessed with freshness and power that has others amazed and marveling at your purity in Jesus alone. Be blessed with no other agenda than being sold out to making the name of Jesus famous.

As he sat in jail near the end of his life, Paul boiled his life down to its essence. He said, "One thing I do: Forgetting what is behind and straining toward what is ahead, I press on toward the goal to win the prize for which God has called me heavenward in Christ Jesus" (Phil. 3:13-14). His single-minded devotion to Jesus baptized him with love that did not shrink from pouring his life out as a drink offering. He had eyes only for the prize — Jesus himself and his pleasure. Spirit, be blessed with the integrity of loving Jesus only and following him wholly.

Be blessed in the name of Jesus who is worthy to receive power and wealth and wisdom and strength and honor and glory and praise (Rev. 5:12).

66 Zephaniah 3:17

Spirit, hear God's Word for you in Zephaniah 3:17. "The LORD your God is with you, he is mighty to save. He will take great delight in you, he will quiet you with his love, he will rejoice over you with singing." Listen to it again from the Amplified Bible. "The Lord Your God is in the midst of you, a mighty One, a Savior — who saves! He will rejoice over you with joy. In his love he will rest in silent satisfaction. He will exult over you with singing."

Spirit, receive your Father's smile today. All the affectionate imagery you can muster is only a dim picture of how he feels about you. You have not yet heard or seen or known the majesty of all his great love. You have longed and ached for a father's embrace, and you have a Father whose heart longs for you. Be blessed as you receive his embrace. Look into his eyes to see him and yourself reflected there. He loves you in the way you were created to be loved. He loves you as the King of lovers, and his love is strong as death. He has come to overwhelm you, to ravish your heart. He will pour out over your life everything you need. He has saved the best till now.

Spirit, one thing is necessary: live at his feet and rest in his presence. Let his peace ease your mind. Let his love calm your heart. Don't settle for a puddle when he wants to give you an ocean. As your Abba delights in his Beloved Son in whom he is well pleased, he delights in you in the same way, because he is in you and you are in him. The prayer of Jesus was "Father, let them know deep inside that as you love me, so you love them, they in me and I in you" (John 17:21,26 paraphrased). He loves you way beyond what you deserve or can earn.

Spirit, let his love be the foundation of your life, and you will be filled again and again in all the promises he has spoken to you. He wants you to know that you are beloved in the Beloved Son and complete in the finished work of the cross. In the cross he dealt with all sin, wounds, words, and other hurtful things that separate you from his love. God delights in you. There's power in that little phrase. "I am the one God likes." We desperately need to live in this truth: "God LIKES me" — today, every day, every moment. That doesn't mean you do everything right, but when you do something wrong, you come to a throne of grace and find mercy to help you in your time of need. Be blessed as you receive mercy and grace there, that empowering presence of the Spirit to believe the truth and live in it. Allow God to remove all that is ugly and causes offense.

Spirit, coach the soul to let go of the past, the pain, the problems. Insist on it, and turn your back on them as you face your Father. You and he together will face the rest of your life. All that you have passed through and all that you currently are experiencing is all for the good. Be blessed with joy and a different peace and a greater rest than you have ever known. Be blessed with refreshing and renewal in his presence, as you pursue the days of fulfillment of what he has created you for.

Habakkuk 3:19 says "The Sovereign LORD is my strength; he makes my feet like the feet of a deer, he enables me to go on the heights." Spirit, run with him upon the hills, leap upon the mountains. Do not fear the high places. He made your feet sure-footed. Do not be afraid. He holds you in his heart, and he will hold your hand.

Spirit, receive and be blessed by one worshiper's personal translation of Zephaniah 3:17. "The eternal self-existent God, the God who is three in one, he who dwells in the center of your being — is a powerful valiant warrior. He has come to set you free, to keep you safe and to bring you victory. He is cheered, and he beams with exceeding joy and takes pleasure in your presence. He has engraved a place for himself in you, and there he quietly rests in his love and affection for you. He cannot contain himself at the thought of you, and with the greatest joy he spins around wildly in anticipation over you. He has placed you above all other creations and in the highest place in His priorities. He shouts and sings in triumph, joyfully proclaiming the gladness of His heart in a song of rejoicing, all because of you. *Dennis Jernigan's personal translation of Zephaniah 3:17*

Spirit, be blessed in your Father's house where there's a party just for you, in your honor, to celebrate you. He wants to dance with you in the ballroom of the Great King. He is a dancing warrior who captivates the heart of his beloved. He'll teach you to dance, because he's a dancing King, the dancing Lover of your soul. Dance on the places of fear with him. Dance through the night with him. He will lead you. He will give you victory. Most of all, he will give you his unspeakable joy and abundant hope.

Spirit, hear it again and be blessed in this truth. The Lord has arrived to live among you. He is a mighty Savior. Be blessed as he gives you victory. Be blessed as he rejoices over you with great gladness. Be blessed as he loves you and does not accuse you. Be blessed in the wonderful sound of the Lord himself exulting over you in happy song. Be blessed to hear a new song from your Father.

Be blessed in the name of your dancing Warrior (Zeph. 3:17).

67 Holy Exchange — Isaiah 61:1-3

Spirit, listen to the Word of God for you in Isaiah 61:1-3. "The Spirit of the Sovereign LORD is on me, because the LORD has anointed me… to bestow on them a crown of beauty instead of ashes, the oil of gladness instead of mourning, and a garment of praise instead of a spirit of despair."

Spirit, come to the front to be blessed with the holy exchange of Jesus. In Luke 4:21 after Jesus quoted Isaiah 61, he said, "Today this scripture is fulfilled in your hearing." Jesus offers you an exchange of his life for yours — his sinlessness for your sin, his life for your death, his power for your weakness, his freedom for your bondage, his comfort for your grief, his beauty for your ashes, his gladness for your mourning, and his praise for your despair. He said that it is fulfilled today in him, and your life is hidden in him today (Col. 3:3). Be blessed to receive the connection he gives you with your Father's tender heart, and exchange his peace for your clamor and chaos. Receive from him his comfort, love and joy, just because you are his. He offers you his vision and his hope in exchange for your disappointment, because he sees so much more than you do.

Spirit, he crowns you with glory and honor, instead of ashes, heaviness, and hopelessness. You sparkle as a jewel in the crown of beauty of the Lord Jesus Christ. He gives you a new dawn in his rising glory. Be blessed as a powerful growing testimony of his presence, freedom, and grace. Be blessed as you are enlarged in all of who Jesus is in you and what he does for you.

Spirit, listen to the Word of God for you in Isaiah 43:4. "Since you are precious and honored in my sight, and because I love you, I will give men in exchange for you, and people in exchange for your life." Be blessed to know that you are honored and loved by God. The smile of his eyes validates you. Be deeply grounded in that. That's your unshakable identity and legitimacy. Two of the Hebrew words in this verse have the idea of weight. You are a "heavyweight" in God's eyes. You are precious, and Jesus is the weight of glory in you. Be blessed as you are centered in the honor of your own preciousness, significance, and worth, as he does awesome things in you.

Because of this, God promises that he will give people in exchange for your life. You are laying down your life to live Jesus in front of some people. You are being a testimony of Jesus to them, ministering Jesus to them, representing Jesus to them. As you do that, God will exchange everything he has allowed in your life, every trial and hurt you have endured, every victory you have won — he will exchange all that for healing and freedom in the lives of others. He will reproduce your victories in others. Be blessed with his restoration come full circle, as you pass on what you have received. He who promised is faithful, and he will do it.

Be blessed in the name of your Faithful God (Heb. 10:23).

68 The Presence — Exodus 33:14

Spirit, listen to the Word of God in Exodus 33:14. "The LORD replied, 'My Presence will go with you, and I will give you rest.' "

Spirit, be blessed with the ministry of the presence of God. Be blessed with visitations in the night seasons of rest in your spirit, a holy hedge around your bedroom, where you can rest and receive downloads of everything that you need from the presence of the Spirit of your Father. Be blessed with being enriched in communing with him in the night seasons, as the evening is the beginning of the day in God's order. Be blessed to nestle into the Spirit of God to let him work in the deepest core of your identity, belonging, and worth while you sleep. Be blessed to rest in your full legitimacy in Jesus his Son as your Father ministers to you.

From the ministry of his presence, be blessed with waking up in the morning refreshed and greatly anticipating another new day in joy, and peace, and hope, and in communion with your Father, your Redeemer, your Friend. God ministers himself to you. You are not limited to ministry from someone else. You do not need an expert. You don't have to have somebody pray for you. Receive the grace of the presence of the Lord with you and the release of his blessing of presence around you and on you and in you and through you.

Spirit, in him be proactive. Take authority in his name and his presence in you over every place and situation you go into. Actively bless every place where you go with the presence of the holiness and the alignment of holy God in all places of your God-given jurisdiction. By his presence in you, be blessed as you carry the holy blessing of the Lord, the blessing of cleansing and restoration in Jesus' name.

Be blessed in the name of the Presence who lives in you (Exo. 33:14).

Living In Your Spirit

69 Living In Resurrection Power — John 11:25

Spirit, hear God's Word for you in John 11:25. "I am the resurrection and the life." And in 1 Peter 1:3 "Praise be to the God and Father of our Lord Jesus Christ! In his great mercy he has given us new birth into a living hope through the resurrection of Jesus Christ from the dead." And in Ephesians 1:18-20. "I pray also that the eyes of your heart may be enlightened in order that you may know … his incomparably great power for us who believe. That power is like the working of his mighty strength, which he exerted in Christ when he raised him from the dead and seated him at his right hand in the heavenly realms."

Spirit, be blessed to know that you are identified with the death, burial, and resurrection of Jesus. You are united with him in his resurrection (Rom. 6:4-5). You live in the fullness of the risen and ascended Christ every day because God raised you up with him. It is no longer you who live but the Spirit of him who raised Jesus from the dead is living in you (Rom. 8:11). He is your life in the fullness of his resurrection (Phil. 3:10).

Because of what Christ did, you are hidden in God, sealed by the power of the Holy Spirit. Be blessed to live seated with him in the heavenly realms in Christ Jesus (Eph. 2:6). Be blessed in the reality of your new life, your sanctification, and all the finished work of Christ's resurrection and ascension.

Spirit, you are created to hear and commune with God and represent him to the soul and body. You are the team leader, leading the soul and the body. You have been given all spiritual blessings in the heavenlies in Christ Jesus. As the Holy Spirit makes these blessings active in your life, he applies to you all of the power and gifts in Pentecost. Be blessed to live unto him in all things, giving him total claim to your life.

All authority in heaven and on earth has been given to Jesus, and you are raised with him to the right hand of the Father and established with him in his authority. Receive all the authority of his ascension by which you have his power and dominion over spiritual forces of darkness. Be blessed to stand in Christ, having all authority to overcome the power of the evil one. You reign in life through Christ.

Spirit, the glories and the benefits of the resurrection and ascension of Christ on your behalf are huge. You can compare the trials in your life now with the darkness of the hours after the crucifixion. You are waiting to emerge triumphant in the dawning of resurrection with the rebirth of life and hope and joy.

Spirit, there is a huge bank account of spiritual riches that is in your name. But it's not yours until you make a claim against it, until you write a check on it and cash it. You can be rich and go hungry if you never write a check or access the ATM. You are making a claim on the resurrection power of Jesus when you say, "I am no longer a slave to sin. Because of what Jesus did, I am not under the spirit of the law of sin and death." You cash a check on the resurrection power of Jesus every time you bow your knees and ask forgiveness or access his grace to go to someone and ask their forgiveness.

You put in a claim on the resurrection power of Jesus when you are faced with something you can't handle, and you look to him and throw yourself on his sufficiency. You make a claim on the resurrection power of Jesus when you feel rejected and remember that in your Father you are not rejectable, and he can never reject you.

You make a claim on the resurrection power of Jesus when you feel unloved and abandoned, and you counter that with the truth that "Nothing can separate me from my Father's love; he cannot leave me or forsake me." You put in a claim on the resurrection power of Jesus when you live in the fullness of him who fills everything in every way, and you put everything in your life under his feet and make him your head over everything in your life at all times.

Spirit, Jesus came to show you his Father and your Father. Be blessed that your Father's purpose and power is to restore you to be who he designed, and in Jesus you can access it. The more you exercise your freedom of choosing Jesus, the easier it is to stay in your spirit. Be blessed to understand your true position in Christ. Spirit, receive it and chose to live in it, not allowing the soul or the body to take over. The Spirit of Christ Jesus is present every day in you so that you can live always from your spirit.

Be blessed in the name of the Spirit of life in Christ Jesus (Rom. 8:2 NKJV).

70 Forgiveness — 1 John 1:9

Precious one, I invite your spirit to step up and lead your soul and body into the complete work of forgiveness and cleansing that is the great and wonderful gift of God. Spirit, listen to God's Word in 1 John 1:9. "If we confess our sins, he is faithful and just and will forgive us our sins and purify us from all unrighteousness."

Spirit, I bless you to look into the face of your Abba and ask him to reveal any area of your life that needs his work of forgiveness. God's Word says, "For all have sinned" (Rom. 3:23). We are separated from God, a people needing the removal of sins. Jesus said in Matthew 26:28, "This is my blood of the covenant, which is poured out for many for the forgiveness of sins." Forgiveness means to release sin from the sinner. This required Christ's sacrifice as the just and full punishment of sin, putting away sin, and the deliverance of the sinner from the power of sin.

Jesus made forgiveness very important to our fellowship with God. In Matthew 6:14-15 he said, "For if you forgive men when they sin against you, your heavenly Father will also forgive you. But if you do not forgive men their sins, your Father will not forgive your sins." We receive and give forgiveness. In Matthew 18, Jesus taught about a servant who was forgiven of a great debt by his master, but another man owned him far less, and the servant had him thrown into jail. When the master found out about it, he had the servant thrown into jail to be tortured. Then Jesus said, "This is how my heavenly Father will treat each of you unless you forgive your brother from your heart" (Mat. 18:35). Unforgiveness puts us in prison and torments us.

Spirit, listen to the Word of God. "But if we walk in the light, as he is in the light, we have fellowship with one another and the blood of Jesus, his Son, purifies us from all sin" (1 John 1:7). Walking in the light speaks of a right relationship with God. When we have a right relationship with God, we are to have fellowship with others, living in forgiveness. Then the blood of Jesus is continually cleansing us from sin. Forgiving others is crucial to seeing the life and power of Jesus flowing in and through us.

Precious child of God, unforgiveness is the result of a wound not dealt with, which leads to anger, resentment, and bitterness. The soul will react to the degree that it is not healed from woundedness. Spirit, be blessed as you look to Jesus and receive cleansing for the unforgiveness which the soul has held onto for so long. Respond to what your Father is saying, and be blessed to lead in forgiveness, or the healing for the soul will be lacking. Complete forgiveness brings freedom. The complete work is forgiving others, forgiving ourselves, and repenting for judging God.

Be blessed with all wisdom and discernment as you forgive everyone who has ever done anything against you. Your soul may justify your resentment for the terrible thing. You may even feel that you have a right to hold a grudge, or that the person does not deserve to be forgiven. But God is very clear. He commands you to forgive from the heart, and in forgiving from the heart, not just with your will, you will receive healing for your soul. I bless you to forgive others to the point that you actually feel yourself cleansed of resentment and bitterness, allowing the cleansing and healing to flow to your soul until you can pray for them and bless them.

Spirit, look into the face of Jesus and ask him to help you forgive yourself. Receive the cleansing of forgiving yourself, as he removes your transgressions from you "as far as the east is from the west" (Ps. 103:12). Be blessed to lead your soul to release all self-condemnation, self-judgment, or self-punishment and receive the cleansing of the sufficient blood of Jesus.

Spirit, ask your Father if there is anything you hold against him. Consciously or unconsciously, is there any resentment or bitterness or anger about what he has allowed in your life? This is hard self-examination but imperative for a clear relationship with your Abba.

Be blessed to receive cleansing and healing of soul and to allow the complete work of forgiveness to reach the body. The body can hold the effects of your sin of unforgiveness. The blood of Jesus is not like a spot remover which you use to clean the spot in the carpet on the surface, and later the stain comes back again from down in the fibers. The cleansing power of forgiveness goes deep into the fiber of your being, laying the ax to the root (Mat. 3:10; Luke 3:9). Spirit, you bring life to the body as you lead in complete forgiveness.

Be blessesd, spirit, to lead soul and body to receive the deep, complete work of forgiveness in intimate, personal relationship with Jesus Christ. Forgiveness enlarges your capacity to love and brings you close to the heart of Jesus, the sacrifice for sin. He prayed on the cross, "Father, forgive them; they don't know what they are doing." Let the grace of God do the deep work of removing the root of bitterness in you (Heb. 12:15). Forgiveness brings you into freedom and life. Unforgiveness shackles you in torment. Be blessed to choose freedom and life.

Be blessed in the name of Jesus who paid the complete price for sin on the cross (Col. 2:13-14).

By my good friend and wonderful ministry partner Debbie Sample

71 Direction — Isaiah 11:2-3

Spirit, listen to God's Word of God in Isaiah 11:2-3. "The Spirit of the LORD will rest on him — the Spirit of wisdom and of understanding, the Spirit of counsel and of power, the Spirit of knowledge and of the fear of the LORD — and he will delight in the fear of the LORD. He will not judge by what he sees with his eyes, or decide by what he hears with his ears."

Spirit, be blessed in the name of the seven-fold Spirit of the Lord. The prophecy in these verses was perfectly fulfilled in Jesus. God put you in relationship with his Son so that he lives in you to be all of himself for you. In him you have the Spirit of wisdom and understanding, the Spirit of counsel and power, the Spirit of knowledge and the fear of the Lord.

The living Word inhabits his written Word in hundreds of promises about his tender direction of you. Seek his face as you cry out to him, "Show me your ways, O LORD, teach me your paths; guide me in your truth and teach me" (Ps. 25:4-5). Be blessed as he responds to you as he said in Psalm 32:8. "I will instruct you and teach you in the way you should go." This pictures someone walking beside an ox, goading it along. It is the idea of coaxing, directing, instructing, and training until the ox is accustomed by practice to doing it the master's way. But God promises something more: "I will guide you with my eye." He can lead you with one look of his eyes, like that meaningful look you give your child eye-to-eye without a word being spoken. Be blessed to be always looking into his face to see his guidance.

Spirit, God promises precise direction that you will hear in Isaiah 30:21. "Whether you turn to the right or to the left, your ears will hear a voice behind you, saying, 'This is the way; walk in it.' " Be blessed as you hear him whisper direction, "This is the way. Walk this way." If his word is to fight, let it be for his glory. If he says to wait, let it be with hope and grace secure in his timing and sovereign hand. If his word is to flee, let it be with his permission and at his direction. If he tells you to offer a sacrifice of praise, let it be with thanksgiving that is a sweet savor to him. Be blessed to be confident that he is working out all things for good, whether you see it or feel it now.

Spirit, be blessed as you follow his faithful direction. He will teach you his ways and make you sensitive to his hand on your life. Be blessed with assurance that you don't go anywhere today without your personal Guide. Be blessed with his open door before you that no one can shut, according to his sovereign will, and with closed doors that are outside his purposes for you (Rev. 3:7-8). Let the blessing of his presence lead you. Don't go where he does not bless (Exo. 33:12-16).

Be blessed as you seek his face, for his eyes are open to all your ways (Jer. 32:19). Let your expectation be centered in him (Ps. 62:1,5). As he directs your paths, he gives you peace, because he promises that he will keep in perfect peace those whose eyes are fixed on him, because you trust in him (Isa. 26:3). Be steadfast and fix your hope completely in him and rely on him, as you know that all things are totally in his hands, for Jesus' sake.

Be blessed in the name of the One who guides you in paths of righteousness for his name's sake (Ps. 23:3).

72 Endurance And Encouragement — Romans 15:4

Spirit, listen to God's Word for you in Romans 15:4. "For everything that was written in the past was written to teach us, so that through endurance and the encouragement of the Scriptures we might have hope."

Spirit, you have experienced the debilitating invasion of discouragement. You have been assaulted and assailed from every side. One of the assignments of the evil one against the people of God is to oppress them by wearing them down (Dan. 7:25). In the name of the Ancient of Days, you can resist the oppressing assignments of the adversary by stepping behind your hedge of protection in the blood of Jesus. Spirit, hear God's words in 2 Chronicles 20:15 and 17. "This is what the LORD says to you: 'Do not be afraid or discouraged because of this vast army. For the battle is not yours, but God's. You will not have to fight this battle. Take up your positions; stand firm and see the deliverance the LORD will give you, O Judah and Jerusalem. Do not be afraid; do not be discouraged. Go out to face them tomorrow, and the LORD will be with you.' "

You have a choice: to be afraid and discouraged because of the vast army against you, or you can be unafraid and encouraged because God is with you. He is your hope and your victory in the battle in which you are so weary. In his great heart he has a plan for your welfare, to give you a future and a hope. You are anointed with grace to stand with more hope and encouragement today than yesterday and more positive assurance of seeing his goodness at work in everything in your life. Run to the joy of the Lord that is your strength. Be blessed with endurance and encouragement as you stand in the One who fights your battles for you.

Spirit, look up into the face of your Father in heaven in complete devotion and trust. His name is God who is there with all those who are discouraged and not at peace. He cannot deny his name. He cannot lie. His presence never leaves nor forsakes you. The name of the Lord is a strong tower to which the righteous run and are safe (Pro. 18:10). Hide there in him from the devourer and the accuser. Hide in him from the spirit of heaviness and discouragement. He wants to cover your weariness in every area with his blanket of strength.

Spirit, you have celebrated his intervention in your life many times and many ways in the past. Be blessed to remember how he has shown himself strong to you. Be blessed today in the name of the One who gives endurance and encouragement. Be blessed to anticipate that he will continue to reveal himself to you in the future.

Once Jesus rebuked winds and waves, saying "Peace be still." You are blessed in the name of the One who stills the storms (Mark 4:39). Another time, Jesus commanded Peter, "Come to me." Peter stepped out of the boat onto the wind-driven waters, and when he took his eyes off Jesus and looked at the waves, he sank. Whether Jesus stills the storm or invites you to come to him on the water, that's his choice. You will be steadfast, immovable in him, unless you look at the tempest. Keep your eyes fixed on Jesus. He will come alongside, lift you up, strengthen, encourage, and refine you to bring about his sure purposes. You can stand in the rule and dominion of the Prince of peace. Be blessed in his great faithfulness to you that is new every morning.

Be blessed in the name of the One who bids you come (Mat. 14:29).

73 Refreshment — Isaiah 40:31

Spirit, hear God's Word for you in Isaiah 40:31. "Those who hope in the LORD will renew their strength. They will soar on wings like eagles; they will run and not grow weary, they will walk and not be faint."

You are exhausted and at the edge of your endurance from running the race of life. You are weary and weighed down by demands and tensions. You need strengthening and refreshment with God's holy strength to receive his enabling grace for each day. Be blessed as you are lifted into your Abba's presence to receive his love. Spirit, lift your eyes to him, and receive his eye-to-eye, face-to-face connection of the fresh touch of his love in all its fullness. He has given his word that he sets the godly ones apart for himself. He committed himself to you as your Abba and he will meet all your needs today, because those who seek him will not lack any good thing. He has covenanted to heal and strengthen you spirit, soul, and body. He pledges to defeat Satan's plans of attack in physical and emotional areas that are vulnerable.

Spirit, receive his Spirit of revelation, wisdom and understanding, so that you take only his yoke and do the things that fulfill his divine purposes. You can be confident in his ability and presence at work in your life in everything that touches you. You have his favor and blessing as a shield.

Spirit, remember your God-given place in his scheme of things. See the cross and run there and hide from all stresses and pressures. His resurrection power and his ascended authority and glory outshine all the plans of the enemy to oppress you. He will lighten your steps as you mount up with wings as an eagle, as you run and do not grow weary, as you walk and do not faint. That's his sure word to those who wait on him. Be still inside, and look to him and receive a fresh touch of the power of the Holy Spirit. Let him re-fill and rejuvenate you so that you will have a full cup from which to water others. Hear God speaking to you as you draw close to him.

Spirit, God gives you grace for today, and then tomorrow he gives a whole new supply of himself. Receive his sweet presence each moment, and rest in feeling secure in him. When you don't know the outcome of your situation, it is safe not to know, because he is good. Be blessed to open up to new trust in your Father. It is his will and design that you take your full God-given authority, evicting all fear and doubt and discouragement, because God's perfect love casts out your fear.

Spirit, the blood of Jesus heals where there is pain and hurt. His hands hold the answer in the situations closest to your heart, the ones that have wearied you the most. Know that God holds the key for every person and circumstance that has claim upon your spiritual, emotional, and practical responsibility. God's reconciling grace is ready for all relationships to enjoy his unity and the sweet fellowship of his presence. Exchange your strength for his. Be blessed in the power and the glory of his great strength.

Be blessed in the name of the Lord who is your strength and your song (Isa. 12:2).

74 God's Abundant Blessings — Matthew 10:16

Spirit, listen to God's Word to you in Mark 10:16. "He took the children in his arms, put his hands on them and blessed them." As a beloved child of God, receive these eight blessings from the fullness of his abundant blessings for you.

Be blessed with spiritual blessings — Ephesians 1:3-6

Spirit, you have been "blessed in the heavenly places with every spiritual blessing in your Lord and Savior Jesus Christ. He chose you in him before the creation of the world to be holy and blameless in his sight. In love he predestined you to be adopted as his child through Christ Jesus, according to his pleasure and will — to the praise of the glory of his grace" (Eph. 1:3-6). He is watching over your love relationship with him. He is calling you up higher into sweeter fellowship with himself. He is calling you to himself to know him better and to love him more intimately and to worship him more whole-heartedly. The truth of his Word is alive to you as never before, as he opens his Word to you and feeds you fresh manna, new and personal every day. Be blessed as he leads you to set your will to follow him fully, to stand strong in him, and to be single-minded in seeking him. Be blessed as he establishes you to live in his Spirit in deeper ways. Be blessed as he calls you beyond obedience and duty into the delight of intimacy with him and desire to please him and honor him in all you are and all you do.

Be blessed with emotional blessing — 2 Corinthians 7:6

Spirit, your God of all comfort is giving you his tender consolation, as he comforts the downcast, as he promised (2 Cor. 7:6). Be blessed as he surrounds you with his covenant mercy, compassion, and grace. Be blessed as he ministers to you by the special fellowship of his Holy Spirit and causes you to feel his love for you. Be blessed as he establishes you in who you are in Christ. You are a jewel in his crown. Be blessed as the grace of his Spirit produces peace and joy and hope in him that goes beyond your circumstances. God will show you any hindrance that is holding you back. By the blood of Jesus, he will dissolve the hurts, wounds, and unforgiveness that erect walls in parts of your heart. He puts the cross of Jesus between you and anything that has laid scars across your soul. Be blessed in his healing touch, as you trust him and give yourself into the nail-pierced hands of Jesus.

Be blessed with mental blessing — Romans 12:2

Spirit, be blessed with the transformation of a renewed mind, so that you test and approve God's good, pleasing, and perfect will (Rom. 12:2). Receive God's refining fire to burn out the wood, hay, and stubble, so that only pure thoughts and words remain. Receive his cleansing and renewing in his truth to counter the lies you have believed. Be blessed as you hear his voice and receive his wisdom and revelation. Receive from him new meditations and praises in your heart and new words of life in your mouth. Listen for his practical guidance each day in his Word and in the fellowship of his Spirit. Be blessed in his promises to keep you one step at a time on the path he has marked out for you, especially when you can barely see his footprints. Be blessed to know with confidence that when you can't see his hand, you can trust his heart.

Be blessed with personal blessing — Ephesians 3:20

Spirit, give God glory that he is able to do immeasurably more than all you ask or imagine, according to his resurrection power that is at work within you (Eph. 3:20). His incomparably great power is at work for you. Lift up to your Father's heart the desire that you have watched over the longest and most fervently, the one you have all but given up hope on. Receive from him protection from discouragement in spite of hope deferred. You can safely put your expectations in him in all circumstances and relationships. Be blessed to know that he will fulfill in fullest measure all the things that he has ordained for your life. Be blessed as he gives you his best answer in his time by his risen life.

Be blessed with right relationships — Philippians 2:2

Spirit, be blessed to love others, being like-minded, being one in spirit, working together with one heart and purpose (Phil. 2:2). Let God lead you into righteous submission to your authorities as he ordains, so that his order of love is established. Seek him to show you where to break all ties that bind you unrighteously. Be blessed with the strength of spiritual friendships, right loyalties, and trustworthy relationships. Be blessed with a healthy community of like-spirited encouragement and fellowship. Be blessed with the synergy of others of like vision.

Be blessed with physical well-being — Proverbs 18:10

Spirit, run to the name of the Lord, the strong tower of the Most High for deliverance and safety from every evil power that seeks to harass, intimidate, or hurt you. The name of the Lord keeps you in his strength, according to the needs of each day. Be blessed in your Keeper of your health under his protecting power, for you are the apple of his eye. Be blessed in all the provision of Psalm 91 that is available to your life. He assigns his angels to go before you and protect you day and night. Be blessed as you run to the safety of his shelter in the secret place of the God Most High.

Be blessed with financial blessing — James 1:17

Spirit, God is your source of every good and perfect gift, and he gives you faithful and timely provision. Be blessed to know him as your source, your supply, and your security. Be blessed as he enlarges and establishes your faith in his goodness to supply. Know that he is good, he is generous, and he knows his own (John 10:14). Because he is your good shepherd, you will lack no good thing (Ps. 34:10) as you seek him. Because he is Lord of all your life, be blessed as you trust his heart toward you to never forsake you in time of need.

Be blessed with fruitfulness — John 15:16

Spirit, you did not choose God, but he chose you and appointed you to go and bear fruit — fruit that will last. Your Father blesses his eternal work through your hands. Receive his new thing in your journey with him. Be blessed as he calls forth the new thing he wants to do in you and through you. Be blessed as he gives you the fruit of your labors. Be blessed as he leads you in great wisdom and gifting in new paths of opportunity in his kingdom. Be blessed with faith, a mantle of praise, refreshing, assurance, and boldness, as you maximize every opportunity to glorify God with your life. In Jesus stand firm in faith, declaring his righteousness and victory and resisting all the works of the evil one. Be blessed in your life to be a blessing to many others and bring forth fruit that will last.

Be blessed in the name of the One from whom all blessing flows.

75 Possess Your Freedom — Galatians 5:1

Beloved one, listen with your spirit to God's Word for you in Galatians 5:1. "It is for freedom that Christ has set us free. Stand firm, then, and do not let yourselves be burdened again by a yoke of slavery."

Spirit, be released into your full freedom in Christ to be entirely whole – spirit, soul, and body. Receive ministry from your Father in the same areas until your inner being knows exactly who you are and is strong, as he takes all hindrances, encumbrances, and baggage and replaces them with the life of his authority in you. You are not meant just to survive. You are meant to thrive and be whole, and free, and complete.

Right where God has placed you, there are things that he has put in you that you don't know now, and fruits in your character that he is building in you in this season, and treasures in you that he has not yet revealed. Be released from all yokes of bondage to be the man/ woman after God's own heart that you are. Be blessed to possess your freedom to which he has called you.

Spirit, receive the tender correction of your Shepherd. Sometimes he uses his rod and staff to guide you, lest you stray from his care in paths of righteousness, but your soul resists. Welcome your Shepherd's discipline for your good. He guides you to persevere into full freedom in himself that is your right in him. Persist and stand firm in him. Be blessed with all the liberty of the Lord. It's yours, because Jesus set you free. Be blessed in his purpose for you to live free in full confidence.

Be blessed in the name of your Deliverer (Jer. 15:11).

76 Fountain Of Life — Psalm 36:9; 46:4-5

Spirit, hear the Word of God for you in Psalm 36:9. "For with you is the fountain of life." And in Psalm 46:4-5. "There is a river whose streams make glad the city of God, the holy place where the Most High dwells. God is within her, she will not fall; God will help her at break of day."

Spirit, you have received the water of eternal life that Jesus gave you. When you feel that you're in a wilderness, be blessed to drink from living waters that stream from the hard places because he is your Spiritual Rock (1 Cor. 10:4). Psalm 114:7-8 says that the presence of the God of Jacob turns the rock into a pool, the hard rock into springs of water. Be blessed in the water of his presence. Psalm 107:35 says, "He turned the desert into pools of water and the parched ground into flowing springs." Be blessed with the Fountain of living waters welling up in you. Isaiah 49:10 says that his compassion will guide you and lead you beside springs of water. Drink often of his thirst-quenching water. Be blessed with rejoicing in his unfailing springs of joy and mercy. God will make the Valley of Trouble into a place of springs, and you will go from strength to strength in him (Ps. 84:6). Be blessed from his righteous spring of blessing that is flowing to you. Let him fill you up and pour you out to others who are thirsty. Be blessed to touch those who haven't tasted the fountain of life and point them to the source of the water of life.

Spirit, listen to the promises of God to the poor, the needy, the parched, the barren:
Isaiah 41:17 "The poor and needy search for water,
but there is none; their tongues are parched with thirst.
But I the LORD will answer them; I, the God of Israel, will not forsake them.
18 I will make rivers flow on barren heights, and springs within the valleys.
I will turn the desert into pools of water, and the parched ground into springs.
19 I will put in the desert the cedar and the acacia, the myrtle and the olive.
I will set pines in the wasteland, the fir and the cypress together,
20 so that people may see and know, may consider and understand,
that the hand of the LORD has done this, that the Holy One of Israel has created it."

Be blessed in the healing stream from the holy place where the Most High dwells. You are blessed to stand in God's river flowing from his throne, carrying the sound, motion, power, and fragrance of heaven to you. Be blessed to live in his healing crystal river filled with justice and righteousness, flowing from his throne (Rev. 22:1-2). Be blessed in the name of Lamb who leads you to springs of living water, and he will wipe away every tear (Rev. 7:17).

Be blessed in the name of the One who is Living Water,
who invites you to come to the waters (John 4:10; Isa. 55:1).

77 Shalom — Covenant Fulfillment And Completion — Judges 6:11-22; 8:28

Spirit, listen to the Word of God in Judges 6. "Gideon built an altar to the LORD there and called it The LORD is Peace. To this day it stands..." God said to Gideon, "I am with you, mighty warrior... Go in the strength you have and save Israel out of Midian's hand... Am I not sending you? ... I will be with you... Peace, do not be afraid... With 300 men I will save you and give the Midianites into your hands... Place a trumpet and a lamp with a torch inside in each of the men's hands... Shout, 'A sword for the Lord and for Gideon!' Sound the trumpet, and the Lord routs your enemies." During Gideon's lifetime, the land enjoyed peace for forty years (selected from Judges 6:11-22; 8:28).

Spirit, come to the front and receive the covenant name Jehovah-Shalom in Judges 6:24. And receive Ezekiel 37:26. "I will make a covenant of peace with them; it will be an everlasting covenant." And Psalm 85:8 NKJV. "I will hear what God the Lord will speak, for He will speak peace to His people and to His saints." And Ephesians 2:14. "For he himself is our peace."

Jehovah-shalom is one of the covenant names by which God has bound himself to you. Spirit, be blessed with the full understanding of what God means when he tells you he is your peace and will speak peace to you. You have all the blessings of shalom in Jesus in the covenant that was cut in his body. He lives in you to keep his covenant of total peace, all the peace you need. Your covenant of peace is for security, welfare, and well-being, not just the absence of strife, struggle, or war. Be blessed as he ministers to you more than freedom from fear. Be blessed to know that it is wholeness, safety, and joy, and health and soundness of your spirit, soul, and body. Be blessed to stand in its provision of positive good condition, success, and comfort, not just neutral tranquility. Be blessed with the benefits of his covenant of peace in harmony with yourself and with God and with others. Be blessed with harmony of spirit, soul, and body, both externally and internally. Be blessed with full assurance that everything is all right because God has everything under his control, more than just being unharmed or unhurt.

Shalom means completeness, harmony, and fulfillment, not just superficial satisfaction or happiness. It is the state of blessing in Jesus that you enjoy that is not buffeted by the winds and waves of tumultuous circumstances or the strife of people in your life or self-doubt or struggle. Jesus in you, your Prince of peace, means that you, spirit, are settled and at rest in an unconcerned state of blessedness in him. Receive the blessing of shalom from your covenant-keeping God. Be blessed as he gives you his peace in your sense of well-being in him. Be blessed as he is the government of his peace in your life. Be blessed in him, your true source of shalom. He alone is your complete and total fulfillment. Be blessed to receive a new work of the God of peace in you. Be blessed that the Person of peace, your hope of glory, lives in you and cannot leave you.

When someone asks you, "How are you doing?" Answer honestly, "It is well," regardless of your circumstances, because it is so. Be blessed with God's unshakable peace from the inside out. Be blessed with his peace as your covering, so your heart knows his fullness.

Spirit, be blessed with all the words implied in shalom: calmness, confidence, contentment, courage, and completeness. Be blessed with restoration to God's original design and purpose for you in Christ, back to the place of his first intent for you, at total oneness with himself in every part and as a whole. Be blessed to know the healing power of his presence and his restoration of every broken place. Be blessed by his mighty power giving you victory over every enemy through his light that shines out of your broken earthen vessel.

Be blessed to be whole in spirit, soul, and body as a result of being in harmony with God's peace and his purpose for your life. Be blessed with unshakable faith that, through his sufficiency, he meets every need that you face by his limitless resources of everything.

Spirit, be blessed as he fulfills his covenant promises in your life and in your family, in your mission and ministry, and in your times. Be blessed as he brings you the greatest and deepest measure of satisfaction and fulfillment and completeness that you can possibly know.

Be blessed in the name of Jehovah-Shalom (Jdg. 6:24).

78 Stirred, Not Shaken — Psalm 15

In the world today and even in the church, you will encounter the subtle and not so subtle workings of the enemy of God's best for you — the "little white lies," the dwelling on thoughts that "no one will know," the compromise "for the greater good." Precious one, call your spirit to its place of authority, and tell your soul to align itself under your spirit and your body under your soul. Let the Word of God in Psalm 15 invite you to come into his presence and live there. Let God stir within you those things required so that you cannot be shaken.

Spirit, listen to God's Word for you in Psalm 15.
1 LORD, who may dwell in your sanctuary? Who may live on your holy hill?
2 He whose walk is blameless and who does what is righteous,
who speaks the truth from his heart
3 and has no slander on his tongue,
who does his neighbor no wrong and casts no slur on his fellowman,
4 who despises a vile man but honors those who fear the LORD,
who keeps oaths even when it hurts,
5 who lends his money without usury and does not accept a bribe against the innocent.
He who does these things will never be shaken.

Precious one, God is inviting you to his appointed place where you feel his presence. He is inviting you to live with him as a person of honesty, genuineness, and sincerity, both morally, ethically, and spiritually. Proverbs 11:3 NAS says, "The integrity of the upright will guide them, but the falseness of the treacherous will destroy them." Be blessed to put on the whole armor of God, especially the belt of truth, and let your Father sanctify you in his truth.

Spirit, be blessed with purity of heart that Jesus works in you, for out of the overflow of the heart, the mouth speaks. Be blessed as you receive the Word of God to cleanse you, spirit, soul, and body, "by the washing with water through the Word" (Eph. 5. 26). Hebrews 4:12 says, "For the word of God is living and active. Sharper than any double-edged sword, it penetrates even to dividing soul and spirit, joints and marrow; it judges the thoughts and attitudes of the heart." Be blessed to let the Word do in you what your Father intends.

Be blessed to let God control your words. I bless your tongue to sing of God's righteousness (Ps. 51:14) and tell of his righteous acts (Ps. 71:24). Be blessed to speak life-giving words and to let the praises of God be continually in your mouth. Spirit, be blessed to be a person who fears the Lord and who honors those who fear the Lord. Psalm 25:14 says, "The LORD confides in those who fear him; he makes his covenant known to them." I bless you to always be zealous for the fear of the Lord (Pro. 23:17b). I bless you to honor God in everything you do and all you say.

Spirit, be blessed with the blameless character of one who wants to be intimate with Jesus. Be blessed with the manner of life that can draw near his presence and live on his holy hill. Be blessed with integrity that admits you into fellowship with holy God. Be blessed with God's approval and security. Be blessed to know that you will never be shaken as you live in harmony with God's ways.

Be blessed in the name of the Father, Son, and Holy Spirit who invites you to draw near to him (Jam. 4:8).

By my good friend and wonderful ministry partner Debbie Sample

79 Widow's Oil — 2 Kings 4:1-7

Spirit, listen to God's Word in 2 Kings 4:1-7. "The wife of a man from the company of the prophets cried out to Elisha, 'Your servant my husband is dead, and you know that he revered the LORD. But now his creditor is coming to take my two boys as his slaves.' Elisha replied to her, 'How can I help you? Tell me, what do you have in your house?' 'Your servant has nothing there at all,' she said, 'except a little oil.' Elisha said, 'Go around and ask all your neighbors for empty jars. Don't ask for just a few. Then go inside and shut the door behind you and your sons. Pour oil into all the jars, and as each is filled, put it to one side.' She left him and afterward shut the door behind her and her sons. They brought the jars to her and she kept pouring. When all the jars were full, she said to her son, 'Bring me another one.' But he replied, 'There is not a jar left.' Then the oil stopped flowing. She went and told the man of God, and he said, 'Go, sell the oil and pay your debts. You and your sons can live on what is left.' "

Spirit, at the place where you have nothing at all, in the place of your desperation, be blessed to look and see the "little oil" that you have, not what you don't have. It may be financial need, or the grace to handle a difficult person, or the courage to try something new. Your identity may be at stake, because in the Old Testament world when a woman's husband died, she lost her identity and standing in the community. Do not major on your inadequacy or lack. Don't bind yourself with vows like "I can't..." "It's impossible..." "I'll never be able to..."

Look into the face of God and listen for his voice and follow his instruction. Whatever he says, do it quickly and thoroughly. Gather "empty jars" and not a few. Behind closed doors, in your prayer closet, present the vessels to him in the secret place. By faith pour oil into each one until it is full. The Bible says, "She kept pouring." Keep doing whatever God says. The oil flowed until all the vessels were filled, as many as the widow presented to God. Today be blessed to know that whatever empty "jars" you present that represent your emptiness, God will fill them full with provision for today and for the future.

Spirit, be blessed as you protect this process of obedience to him. The widow did not tell the neighbors what she was doing. Some people cannot understand your journey. Everyone does not see what you see or have the relationship with God that you have. You are uniquely in process with him. Others may try to talk you out of your faith, or discourage you, or make you feel inadequate and unworthy. Listen to God and protect his communication with you by knowing when to speak and when to be silent.

Spirit, be confident that your Father takes good care of what is his. Sparrows find nesting places, and panting deer find water. You are more valuable than all of these (Mat. 6:26). He numbers the hairs on your head, and he knows your needs (Mat. 6:32). He promises to feed you with the finest wheat and satisfy you with honey from the rock (Ps. 81:16). He himself is your provision. Be blessed in his daily blessings, answered prayers, and undeserved favors.

Be blessed in the name of the Eternal God,
whose everlasting arms uphold you (Deut. 33:27).

80 Generational Legacy — Oak Of Righteousness — Isaiah 61:3

Spirit, hear God's Word in Isaiah 61:3. "They will be called oaks of righteousness, a planting of the LORD for the display of his splendor."

Spirit, God is making you an oak of righteousness, his planting for the display of himself. He wants his beauty to be known through you. He wants you to be a showcase of his character and to give evidence of his glory. As St. Francis of Assisi said, "Preach Jesus, and if necessary, use words." Be blessed to live the life of the Righteous One in you. Be blessed as you bear the fruit of his righteousness as he lives in you.

Be blessed as you give life in the same way that an acorn becomes an oak and produces other acorns. Oak trees feed squirrels, provide a place for birds to nest, and give shade to people, are beautiful to the eye, and exchange carbon dioxide for oxygen in the atmosphere by photosynthesis. But that's not their primary essence. God made them to live to reproduce themselves. In every acorn is an oak. They live generationally by reproducing. Oak trees have a generational legacy. This is your finest fulfillment — a legacy of righteousness that outlasts your life.

Spirit, God has placed you in the refreshing stream of Living Water flowing from his throne for healing. Jeremiah 17:7-8 says that you are blessed when you trust him and have confidence in him. Then you are like a tree planted by the water that sinks its roots deep by the stream (Ps. 1:3). You do not fear when heat comes; your leaves do not wither. They are always green. You have no worries in a year of drought, and you never fail to bear fruit. Let your roots tap deeply into Jesus your Source so that you can keep on keeping on in the demands on you that God has allowed where you are. Be refreshed each moment in Jesus who is eternally with you and in you and you in him. You display his keeping power, as he watches over you and keeps you flourishing in hard times to pass on your legacy of life.

John 15 says that God has chosen you for fruitful seed-planting for fruit that remains. Be blessed as you are faithful to plant in fertile soil and let God multiply. The oak does not strive to produce acorns. It does its "oak thing," and God provides the increase from the essence of the oak. You will reproduce who you are, regardless of who you are. Live the "Jesus life," and he will provide the increase from his life in you. As you are about your Father's business, he blesses you with the sure reward of generational fruitfulness for his name's sake (Pro. 11:18). Isaiah 32:17 says, "The fruit of righteousness will be peace; the effect of righteousness will be quietness and confidence forever." Be blessed to display the fruit of God's peace, and quietness, and confidence. Be blessed with a harvest of righteousness as you sow in peace (Jam. 3:18).

Be blessed in the name of Jehovah-Tsidkenu,
the Lord your righteousness (Jer. 23:6).

Time

81 Time — Ecclesiastes 3:1

Beloved child of God, listen to God's Word for you in Ecclesiastes 3:1. "There is a time for everything, and a season for every activity under heaven." And in Ephesians 5:15-16 (NKJV). "See then that you walk circumspectly, not as fools but as wise, redeeming the time."

Spirit, your Father loves you so much that he has given great thought and care to the days and times of your life. He planned you in his mind before the foundation of the world. He has recorded all your days in his book, and then he spoke you into existence. In the instant of your conception, he said, "Let there be you!" His word does not return to him void. He dropped you into your place and into this time to display his heart and his purposes in your generation. Be blessed to know that he determined for you an appointed place, time, and purpose (Acts 17:26).

God is outside time as we know it on earth. He is the eternal I AM. The past, present, and future are all the same to him (Heb. 13:8). God's reality is a present-tense now. But we live in the chronology of time and history. There are some things that only make sense in the convergence of events and people in this particular time. If they had happened or been spoken or written at any other time, they would not have the same meaning as they have now. Be blessed as God causes these things to come into alignment in this precise window of time. Just as the sun and moon must align to create an eclipse, God is synchronizing and aligning your spirit, soul, and body with time, space, matter, energy, light, and revelation. God will redeem time. Receive the significance of his alignment of time.

Jesus said in Luke 4, "The Spirit of the Sovereign LORD is on me… to proclaim the year of the LORD's favor…" The favor of the Lord in this time is your rightful spiritual inheritance in Jesus. It is the fruit of his incarnation into earth time and existence. Be blessed in God's appointed time for you. He chose for his Son to live in you in this time. Be blessed to receive and agree with the seasons of God. Be blessed as God's favor permeates his time for you. Be blessed as God invites you to see with your eyes, to hear with your ears, and to understand the time of his favor.

Spirit, recognize the time, seize the moment of God's favor, and open the door for yourself and others. Expect and receive the acceptable time of his favor. This is a time of sowing and a time of reaping. Sow to the spirit to reap the things of the Spirit. Be blessed in the law of Spirit and life, not the law of sin and death. Be blessed with sowing some things that others will reap. Be blessed with a harvesting time for which you have not sown, as you reap what your righteous ancestors have sowed. Be blessed to reclaim the righteous deposit of your godly ancestors.

Be blessed with the full purposes of God, which he planned before time, to be released to you in this time, in this season. Spirit, be blessed with anticipation, active participation with him, and hope of fulfillment. Be blessed in the dawning of greater light within you that is a union of you, spirit, and the Spirit of God. Be blessed as his light radiates and shines forth from you in this time.

Be blessed in the name of the eternal I AM (Exo. 3:14).

82 Redeeming The Time With Restoration — Isaiah 58:12

Spirit, listen to God's Word for you in Isaiah 58:12. "Your people will rebuild the ancient ruins and will raise up the age-old foundations; you will be called Repairer of Broken Walls, Restorer of Streets with Dwellings."

Spirit, be blessed with the fulfillment that Isaiah foresaw in this verse. God wants to bless this time with his presence, power, and purposes for you to complete the tasks concerning ancient ruins, waste places, age-old foundations of many generations, and broken down walls and gates. The people under Nehemiah rebuilt the wall in 52 days with a sword in one hand and the tools of reconstruction in the other. God will instruct you when to fight and how to use the tools of rebuilding. There is a time to fight and a time to build. Be blessed to arise and rebuild instead of criticizing the ruins and the toxic waste places. Be blessed with resources of wisdom, revelation, and truth bathed in love to be released to you and in you for rebuilding ruined lives and ruined cities and nations.

Be blessed in God's time of restoration, taking the old and precious generational treasures and new strategies in his timing to rebuild the desolations of families and the devastations of many generations. Be blessed in his time to rebuild and restore all that he intends for your family. Be blessed as you partner with him to turn the ruins into fortresses of righteousness, as Isaiah foresaw in Isaiah 58:12. Be blessed to be fathered and to spiritually father generations as a righteous adult son in the flow of the generations of God's household. Be blessed to store up a generational blessing for a thousand generations to come.

Spirit, be blessed in the authority that comes from intimacy with God. Be blessed to connect with his heart, his purposes, and his plans in new ways. Be blessed as you partner with God to extend the kingdom of heaven on earth into every place of your righteous authority in him. You are his expression that glorifies him in the world. That's the power of your life now. When you are who God wants you to be, you can restore, rebuild, and renew.

God's people will rebuild the ancient ruins, raise up the former desolations, and restore places long ago devastated. They will repair, renew, and revive ruined cities, the barrenness and emptiness of many generations. Spirit, be blessed with getting your eyes off what's been devastated, or desolate, or ruined, or empty, even for many generations. Be blessed not to be paralyzed by the ancient ruins, the former days. Push aside the roadblock of regret, live for the present, and move forward for the future. See the issues of your ancestral past under the redemption of Jesus. Be blessed with calling to your generations the blessings of restoration, well-being, and hope that God is nurturing in you, because you will be an ancestor one day. Spirit, you are dynamic, fruitful, and life-giving. As you take your place as a rebuilder, be blessed with generational blessings flowing in your family line.

Be blessed in the name of the Living Cornerstone
on whom the whole building is fitly joined together
and rises to become a dwelling in which God lives by his Spirit
(1 Pet. 2:4 NLT; Eph. 2:20-22).

83 Redeeming The Time With God's Alignment — Genesis 2:2-3

Spirit, listen to God's Word in Genesis 2:2-3. "By the seventh day God had finished the work he had been doing; so on the seventh day he rested from all his work. And God blessed the seventh day and made it holy, because on it he rested from all the work of creating that he had done."

God was completely aligned with himself and all that he had created over the first six days of creation. He rested on the seventh day, not because he was tired, but because he was at peace and at rest in himself. God sanctified time when he blessed it on the seventh day of creation, and he rested. Spirit, let God's peace and rest define your days. You can be standing in the middle of a vortex, like the eye of the hurricane, and have peace in your spirit because of your fellowship and intimacy with him in this time. God is at work. He is right on time, and you are progressing in his time. Be blessed in this time of God's purposes in your life and in his kingdom in the earth.

Spirit, be blessed as the Father, Son, and Holy Spirit righteously align your time. Be blessed with timely connection with him. Be blessed as you partner with his time to extend all the fellowship and purposes of the Father and Son through the Spirit in you, from heaven to you, into your God-given assignments — personally, financially, emotionally, relationally, spiritually, vocationally, in ministry. Be blessed to be in step with God's alignment and movement in Spirit, in truth, and in grace. Be blessed to meet God's pregnant time of purpose with intentional availability. Be blessed to touch God and partner with him, so that you realize the fullness of the ordained time of his favor. Be blessed in the revelation, wisdom, and kingdom of heaven on earth which will flow when you align with God's time.

Spirit, be blessed in this appointed time as you participate with God's timeliness to release more liberty, more healing, more of his life. His presence and love are with you now. He will bring all areas into harmony and stability, with the soul and body submitting to the direction of the spirit. Be blessed to cooperatively function with the people of God, the land, and all creation for the full purposes of God in the earth.

Be blessed in the name of the One whose name is the First and Last, who blesses your time (Rev. 1:17; Isa. 44:6).

84 Redeeming The Time In New Purpose — Jeremiah 1:5

Spirit, hear the Word of God for you in Jeremiah 1:5. "Before I formed you in the womb I knew you, before you were born I set you apart."

Spirit, be blessed with great peace and joy because your Father set you apart for his purposes in this time. He knew who you would be before he formed you in your mother's womb. He had purposes for you before you were born. This season is not for hanging on by the whites of your knuckles. It is more than survival. It is about abundant life that is truly life. Be amazed at the timing of God, as you see his fingerprints and reflections all around you. Breathe more deeply, see more sharply, and hear more clearly. Be blessed with spiritual prosperity, as God will enlarge you to release the full covenant promises he has held in store for you.

Spirit, the fullest expression of who you are comes from going spirit-to-Spirit with God, looking into his face and receiving from him his eternal purposes for you. Out of this intimacy with him you know your identity and rejoice in being who you are, nothing false, no facades, and no dishonor. Be free to be you. You are the most perfect you that your Father ever created. Be blessed in this time to be the very best you that you are, because you have been touched by his presence. The Jewish leaders in Acts took note of Peter and John because they had been with Jesus (Acts 4:13). He wants to reveal himself to the world through you.

Spirit, God says in Psalm 138:8 NKJV, "The LORD will perfect that which concerns me." Be blessed as God reveals his perfections concerning you. Be blessed as your life unfolds daily, one step of faithfulness at a time. Be blessed to know and express the gifts which he has placed in you to come to fruition in his time. Be blessed to live in the new mantle and the new name that God is placing on you for such a time as this, and be alert to refuse and remove old labels that lie about your true identity.

Be blessed as you look into your Father's face and apprehend his heart, his purposes, and his plans in new ways. Be blessed in the authority that comes from intimacy with him. Be blessed with redeeming the time in the fullness of God's purposes for you, as he releases everything for which he set you apart.

Be blessed in the name of the Almighty who reigns in your times (Rev. 19:6; 1 Cor. 15:25).

85 Right Time To Be About The Father's Business — Psalm 139:16

Spirit, listen to God's Word for you in Psalm 139:16. "All the days ordained for me were written in your book before one of them came to be." And in Luke 2:49 NKJV. (Jesus speaking) He said to them, "Why did you seek Me? Did you not know that I must be about My Father's business?"

Spirit, there are things which God knows are yet to unfold in your life. Be blessed with being in God's time, aligned with his timing and his purposes, not running ahead and not lagging behind. Be blessed with knowing his will and doing his will in the right time, the right place, and the right way, with the right people alongside you. Be blessed with being in the right timing of the call of God on your life.

Be blessed with waiting at seemingly closed doors, for Jesus holds the key. What he opens no man can shut, and what he shuts no man can open. Be blessed with open doors to go forward in God's time and timing, so you may experience the fulfillment of being everything he has called you to be at the right time and in the right place. Be blessed with some closed doors that keep you from doing things that God did not intend for you to do — good things, maybe, but not his best for you because they are out of sync with the sound, rhythm, color, and light of heaven for you. Be blessed with waiting and looking in the face of God to see where he wants you. It is disobedience to do what he did not purpose you to do or to be where he has not called you to be.

Spirit, God makes his way known to his friends. Look into his face and find out from him what is your piece of kingdom business for today. There you will be fulfilled. Be blessed with his fulfillment as you live in the timing of what he has already written in his book for you.

Be blessed in the name of the one who is Author and Finisher and who is always right on time (Heb. 12:2 NKJV).

86 Alignment Of Time — Psalm 31:15; Daniel 7:25; Revelation 1:8

Spirit, hear God's Word for you in Psalm 31:15. "My times are in your hands." And in Daniel 7:25. "He will speak against the Most High and oppress his saints and try to change the set times and the laws." And in Revelation 1:8. "I am the Alpha and the Omega," says the Lord God, "who is, and who was, and who is to come, the Almighty."

Spirit, let God bring every portion of your spirit, soul, and body into alignment with his divine time. Choose to stay in the present tense of God's time. Be blessed as you understand the wiles of the enemy to change God's times. He is trying to manipulate some things that God has appointed in the divinely orchestrated timeline of your history and your family line. Ask God to deal with all warping of your time. Be blessed in every part of your spirit to be in harmony with God's time. Ask him about time, timeliness, and bringing time into alignment, so that you stand in his victories and the breakthroughs already won.

Spirit, be blessed with intentionally lining up the soul and body with each other and with your birthright and with God's divine time, so that no portion of your being or spiritual identity or inheritance is out of kilter. God who is out of time can keep your spirit, soul, and body in right relationship to the flow of his days for you. Be blessed as you anticipate his timing on your coming and going. Be blessed to see his fingerprints upon everything that concerns you. If it concerns you, it concerns him. Look for and receive his nurture, and grow and increase and be strong in all that your Father has for you to receive. You have worked hard over time to overcome brokenness. Trust God to push you forward, because he is nurturing your whole spirit. Fragmentation is a thing of the past as God brings all of you to full stature, as Jesus grew in wisdom and stature and in favor with God and man. Be blessed with being whole in every part — spirit, soul, and body.

Spirit, be blessed to know the fullest dimensions of what God has placed inside you. Be blessed in the perfect harmony of all seven gifts: prophet, serving, teacher, exhorting, giving, ruling, and mercy, all singing the same tune in the same key of music. One may sing the lead at times, and then another, but none will overpower the beauty of all seven gifts together in divine symphony. Be blessed with knowing your identity in Christ for such a time as this. Be blessed to understand what your Father designed you to do and how he wants to implement your gifts to accomplish that work with authenticity. He is mentoring and coaching you in the completeness of Christ's likeness. Be blessed with receiving that spiritual deposit now. You have a powerful destiny and purpose. He is guiding and equipping you to demonstrate his magnificence.

Recognize that God's hand is on every circumstance of your life, as he gives you opportunity to learn and to express all the gifts he has placed in you. Be blessed as you accept the giftedness he has placed in you, and know that you are a gift from him to all the people in your circle of influence. Be blessed today in God's redeemed time. He made everything beautiful in his time.

Be blessed in the name of the Alpha and Omega, with whom time has no beginning or end (Rev. 1:8).

Physical Healing

87 Physical Healing In The Name — Luke 5:17; Hebrews 13:8

Spirit, listen to the Word of God for you in Luke 5:17. "The power of the Lord was present for him to heal the sick." And in Hebrews 13:8. "Jesus Christ is the same yesterday and today and forever."

Spirit, you are light, made of the same light as God. He wants you to be complete spirit, soul, and body (1 Thess. 5:23). You are named first, indicating that you are made to have dominion over the soul and the body. God designed you to rise up and take charge as you get your instructions from him. You are not passive. Be alert and large and strong and in charge.

Spirit, stand in the healing presence of God. Look into his face and connect with Jehovah-Rapha the Healer in you. Get your instructions from him and do exactly what he tells you to do for healing. Take your authority over every cell of the body, including physical ailment, and over the soul, including fear, and over body memories of infirmity or pain. Expedite the healing: take charge of the antibodies, the immune system, the blood flow, the body chemistry, the rebuilding of tissue, all the systems in the body, ____________ etc.

Speak to your own body as Peter spoke to the lame man in Acts 3:6-7. "Then Peter said, 'Silver or gold I do not have, but what I have I give you. In the name of Jesus Christ of Nazareth, walk.' Taking him by the right hand, he helped him up, and instantly the man's feet and ankles became strong." Peter boldly testified of the power of the name of Jesus in healing in Acts 3:16. "By faith in the name of Jesus, this man whom you see and know was made strong. It is Jesus' name and the faith that comes through him that has given this complete healing to him, as you can all see."

Spirit, seek the name of Jesus for getting the body to working in perfect harmony in every cell and tissue. Be blessed in God's alignment in the body for his highest purposes and glory according to his design for your total health. To Him be all the glory.

Be blessed in the name of Jesus the Healer (Luke 5:17).

88 Physical Healing In The Compassionate Healer — Luke 6:19

Spirit, listen to the Word of God for you in Luke 6:19. "The people all tried to touch [Jesus], because power was coming from him and healing them all." And in Mark 3:10. "He had healed many, so that those with diseases were pushing forward to touch him." And in Matthew 14:14. "When Jesus landed and saw a large crowd, he had compassion on them and healed their sick."

Spirit, be blessed in the compassion of Jesus. His compassion never fails. His touch is as powerful as when he walked the earth. God means for you to be whole spirit, soul, and body, and for the soul and the body to submit to his order. Take up your ministry to the emotional mind and organic brain and physical body. Erase with the blood of Jesus the bad body memories of sickness and pain and infirmity, even generational memories, and nail all residual effects and lingering familiar pathways to the cross of Jesus. Separate the "now" from the past with the cross.

The body has re-arranged God's intended alignment of spirit, soul, and body. Jesus the healer relieves the body of any dominion that it took over spirit and soul. Seek God's face for healing of pathways of the body that are harboring anything not of him. No more following the trail of the body's pain that distorts God's alignment of spirit, soul, and body.

Spirit, receive the touch of God in the roots of your being. Look into the face of God for wisdom and direction. Download alignment which is the opposite of a body at war against itself. Tell the body to return to the perfect creation that God envisioned in eternity past. In the place of misalignment, speak alignment and reconciliation to health and wholeness. Claim your rightful godly inheritance in the physical and emotional being that God chose. Take your place in God's design and purposes to call forth healing in soul and body. Receive the healing touch of Jesus down deep into your soul and your body. Let it infiltrate and fill every cell.

Spirit, God doesn't waste pain. He will use this present circumstance somehow to avenge himself on the enemy of your body. God's compensations will be larger than the worst that disease and disorder has inflicted upon you. He will tap deeper into the treasure that you are. Focus on the treasure to be revealed in your renewed earthen vessel.

Spirit, you never slumber nor sleep, because God doesn't. Nestle into the Holy Spirit for a download from him as you are resting in him at night. Listen as God instructs you how to bring his designed functioning to all the body. While the brain sleeps, while the soul is out of the way, access the health and wholeness that God designed for you before the foundation of the world. Do whatever God says from the light of his Spirit. Awake each new day with re-creation and refreshment, new health, energy, vision, and dominion in a healthy earthen vessel, because the surpassing greatness is of Most High God.

Be blessed in the name of the compassionate One who is good to all and has compassion on all he has made (Ps. 145:9).

89 Physical Healing In The Power of Jesus — Matthew 4:23-24

Spirit, listen to the Word of God for you in Matthew 4:23-24. "Jesus went throughout Galilee, teaching in their synagogues, preaching the good news of the kingdom, and healing every disease and sickness among the people. People brought to him all who were ill with various diseases, those suffering severe pain, the demon-possessed, those having seizures, and the paralyzed, and he healed them."

Spirit, be blessed with Jesus the Healer filling you and going to all areas that need to be healed. Be blessed with the good news that he has power to heal, washing over you and flowing to every cell in your body. He is your healing, your well-being, your wholeness. Spirit, look to God and receive the healing light of Jesus and direct your body to receive it in every cell that needs to be restored. Receive him for your bones, discs, tendons, muscles, sinews, joints, your blood, your marrow, your heart, your lungs, your immune system, the brain, nerves and nerve endings, the organs, all systems of the body, and in every place you need healing. In the authority, love, and compassion of Jesus Christ, be blessed with his light penetrating like a laser to bring accurate healing right into the physical distress that is controlling your life.

Spirit, speak to all cells that are misbehaving within you for whatever reason, and bring them under the control of Jesus. Minister his healing that sets them free from physical disease and pain. One desperate man of faith said to Jesus, "Say the word and my servant will be healed." Be blessed with faith to believe that through your asking and his authority that Jesus will heal you. Be blessed with a measure of faith to believe for your healing, as the woman who touched the hem of Jesus' garment and felt his healing strength flowing out to her. Be blessed with believing that he is present, and his power is present for you to be healed, well, and whole.

Be blessed with the healing of the Lord Jesus Christ living in you as you trust him in all things. Be blessed with open spirit eyes and spirit ears to receive the full word of God and his peace and healing grace in all your body.

Be blessed in the name of Jesus of Nazareth, whom God anointed with the Holy Spirit and power, so that he went around doing good and healing, because God was with him (Acts 10:38).

90 Physical Healing In The Unchanging Jesus — Matthew 10:7-8; Hebrews 13:8

Spirit, listen to the truth of God's Word in Matthew 10:7-8. Jesus commanded his disciples to heal the sick. "As you go, preach this message: 'The kingdom of heaven is near.' Heal the sick, raise the dead, cleanse those who have leprosy, drive out demons. Freely you have received, freely give." Hebrews 13:8 says, "Jesus Christ is the same yesterday, today, and forever."

Spirit, be blessed with the love and power of Christ the Healer filling you and going to all areas that need complete health for his sake. Be blessed in all your physical body where there is infirmity. Be blessed with the healing essence of Jesus, flowing in every cell, to bring into line that part of the body that needs to be aligned with God.

Look into the face of God to receive his fullness and his grace at the root of your physical lack of health. You can receive and give a powerful and accurate blessing to your physical distress in the authority, love, and compassion of Jesus. Refer all the cells that are misbehaving within you to Jesus. Allow him to speak to the core issues, whether it is hereditary issues or the environment or another root cause. Be blessed with the healing touch of Jesus that heals you and sets you free from physical disease and disorder.

Spirit, in the present moment focus on your connection with the healing power of God more than the soul's or body's concentration on the pain or sickness or weakness. If pain increases, grace will much more increase. Do not look back, and do not think ahead to what might happen. That is the domain of the soul. Both bring unrest. One leads to being stuck in the past and being paralyzed by it, the other to fear and worrying about the future. Both waste the present.

Spirit, your place in the present moment is in your abiding place in Jesus and him in you. He is the I AM in you. Immerse yourself and saturate yourself in God's wonderful presence now, infused with the ever-present Jesus. Soak up his love and healing presence. It is the time to receive all that the Lord wants you to have, so that you minister to the soul and body.

Jesus the Healer is the same yesterday, today, and forever, so allow his compassion to flood you and flow to every cell in your body, to heal every link and neuronal pathway. He is your healing, your well-being, your wholeness. He wants you to be whole for all his purposes for your gifts and birthright. Be blessed with boldness to receive what is yours in his name Jeshua, which means more than salvation. It means deliverance, healing, health, wholeness, and well-being.

Spirit, receive from God and be blessed with alignment of spirit, soul, and body with his power for physical healing. But more than pursuing your physical healing, be blessed with a holy time of inner quiet and worship with the Healer. Be blessed with being with him in adoration and devotion, in powerful intimacy and connection. Be blessed as you reach out to him for life, for a fresh touch of the Holy Spirit.

Be blessed in the unchanging name of the King of his kingdom (John 18:36-37).

91 Physical Healing — Matthew 21:13-14

Spirit, listen to the Word of God for you in Matthew 21:13-14. " 'My house will be called a house of prayer'... The blind and the lame came to him at the temple, and he healed them."

Spirit, you have an area of responsibility to see that the body complies with the perfect design God intends. God calls you and your physical body the temple of his Holy Spirit, and he still heals in his temple. The Word of God is living and active, quick and powerful (Heb. 4:12). That is a healing term in Greek, meaning the Word is effective medicine. On the basis of his covenant name and character, Jehovah-Rophe is your attending physician. Be blessed as you come confidently to Jesus the Healer for complete healing in his covenant mercy. God delights to show covenant mercy to you — spirit, soul, and body (Tit. 3:5).

You have God's promises. He sent his word and healed them and delivered them from their destructions (Ps. 107:20). His word is forever settled in heaven (Ps. 119:89). Come boldly to the throne of your gracious God, so that your body may receive his mercy and find grace to help you in your need (Heb. 4:16). Take your position of active participation and authority in your healing. Under God's direction line up all the cells in the body in exact order, sequence, and alignment, proper ratios, levels and times, in every dimension, and from every perspective.

You can plead God's ownership. He made you and bought you with the death of his Son on the cross. You belong to your Abba, the King of creation, and he takes care of what is his. Your Father cares personally, individually, and specifically. He is touched by the feeling of your infirmities. Jesus stopped to compassionately minister his healing virtue from his spirit to one woman who touched the hem of his garment. Healing is consistent with his holy, sovereign character. He is strong and sovereignly able, and he shows himself strong on your behalf. His faithfulness is steadfast, and his resurrection power is unlimited.

Spirit, look into the face of your Father to receive his healing strength on your behalf. You have a right to make a claim on your covenant relationship with him and ask, "Oh, God, do it again, and do it for me." God has healed before, and he will do so again. Appeal to God's unchangeable purposes for your life. In God's Spirit identify them, claim them, and don't be denied. He will watch over every day that he has written in his book for you to fulfill his purposes in your generation (Ps. 56:8b; 139:16). He has given you everything you need for life.

Spirit, God is a God of order. Disease, infection, and degeneration are disorder in the cell structures of the body. On the authority of the Lord of the universe, petition him to command every cell in the body to bow to his command and come to order and align with his will. God is a Mighty Warrior. He contends with those forces of darkness and destruction that are contending with your health (Isa. 42:13; Ps. 35:1).

Spirit, take charge of the soul and tell it "Peace, be still" while God fights for you (Exo. 14:14; Ps. 46:10). The Prince of peace is present to still your fears and comfort you with knowing that you are in his hands. God loves you. He will never take his covenant of love from you (Rom. 8:35,38-39; Ps. 18:19). He delights in you (Zeph. 3:17).

God is good and gives good gifts to his children (James 1:17). Your Father has heard your prayers, your tears of pain. He has heard tears of exhaustion and not feeling well and having to trudge on. He has received them as liquid intercession which he stores up in his presence (Ps. 56:8a).

Spirit, thank God for the years of life and good health that he has given you. Don't take that for granted. Thank him for reflections of himself that he has allowed you to show to others. Be blessed to look for God's glory. God delights to reveal his glory, so that many will give him thanks (2 Cor. 4:15). Jesus prayed, "Father, glorify your name!" The Father's voice came from heaven, saying, "I have glorified it and will glorify it again" (John 12:28). So keep believing him to do what glorifies him the most in the health of your soul and body. By the power that raised Jesus from the dead, your Father will do far abundantly beyond what you ask or imagine, according to his power at work in you (Eph. 3:20-21). Receive his sweet presence and be at peace, because you know whom you have believed and are convinced that he will guard what you have entrusted to him (2 Tim. 1:12). Be blessed as you let the One who is your peace fill your temple with peace that is beyond all understanding (Eph. 2:14; Phil. 4:7).

Be blessed in the name of the One who heals in his house of prayer (Mat. 21:14).

Seven Covenant Names of God

Blessing In The Seven Covenant Names Of God

Everything that pertains to life and godliness is already in us. A lot of Christian experience is trying to get something from God for the inside of us. Because we've not experienced the deposit of God in us, we don't know that it's in us. It's like a child who has the ability to walk and talk, but he needs to be cultivated and nurtured as he grows into walking and communicating.

God revealed himself in Scripture in his names. His covenant names reveal his nature. His covenant names are for fathering us and bringing us into mature sonship with him and living in our authority as sons of God on the earth. Jesus died on the cross, not just to save us from our sins, but to reveal the Father to us and to connect us to him as sons in God.

That's an important key as we begin to nurture ourselves and grow our spirits up in the Lord. The seven gifts found in Romans 12:6-7 are on the inside of every person—prophet, servant, teacher, exhorter, giver, ruler, and mercy. One of the covenant names of God expresses itself very powerfully to each part of our nature made in the image of God, each one corresponding with one of the gifts:
Jehovah-Jireh, the first covenant name, God our provider
Jehovah-Rophe, the second covenant name, God our healer
Jehovah-Nissi, the Lord our banner
Jehovah-Shalom, the Lord our peace
Jehovah-Rohi, the Lord our Shepherd
Jehovah-Tsidkenu, the Lord our righteousness
Jehovah-Shammah, the Lord ever present with us.

My friend Deborah Brunt said, "Knowing God by name involves more than reading a name or mentally understanding it. Knowing him by name involves speaking his name, experiencing his name, receiving and reflecting and responding to the One the name reveals. Thus, we come to know our Father as we praise Jehovah-Shammah, as we cry to Jehovah-Jireh, as we follow Jehovah-Rohi, as we rest in Jehovah-Shalom, as we cling to Jehovah-Tsidkenu, and as we exult in Jehovah-Rophe. Knowing him by name, we come to honor, love and trust God the Father." [1]

Jesus Christ paid the price so that these seven attributes of fathering from God could be ours. Jesus went to his Father, so his Father could become our Father. Once we get the revelation of our Father's nature, we will begin to grow exponentially in spirit, and we will begin to live in legitimacy. We begin to live and act more like God as his nature is revealed more in us.

Let each covenant name of God speak deeply to all of your spirit in the following blessings.

[1] Deborah P. Brunt, "Spirit of the Living God," What's a Woman to Do? e-column, May 2008, www.keytruths.com.

92 Jehovah-Jireh — Prophet Portion — Genesis 22:13-14

Spirit, I invite you to hear how God revealed his name and nature in Genesis 22:13-14. Abraham was instructed by God to go to Mt. Moriah and to sacrifice his son Isaac. When he got there, he was willing to obey God and sacrifice his son. When he got the knife poised ready to kill his own son in obedience to God, an angel came and grabbed his hand, and a ram was found in the thicket. God introduced himself to Abraham and to us as Jehovah-Jireh, the provider who sees the need and makes the provision for what is needed.

Prophet portion, be blessed with the name Jehovah-Jireh, your provider. I bless you with knowing that God has seen your desperation without him and has provided everything you need. Be blessed in the Father nature that revealed the sacrifice of his Son Jesus to prove to you that you do not have to earn favor or acceptability with him. That price has already been paid in the Son, the perfect and acceptable sacrifice for sin, so that you can have relationship with God. You can do nothing to make him love you more, and you can do nothing to make him love you less. Jesus has already proved that on the cross. Be blessed with knowing that Jesus is your provided Redeemer. Be blessed with deep gratitude for every provision he made for you to be his.

Be blessed in the freedom that Jesus, your Jehovah-Jireh, has already provided for you to live a righteous life with God. In his finished work on the cross he provided full satisfaction for every need of spirit, soul, and body. He is the provision; he himself is everything you need spirit, soul, and body.

Prophet, be blessed with being willing to give everything you are and all that you have as an act of love and submission to your loving Savior. Be blessed with willingness to run into the arms of him who has declared you unconditionally loved and accepted. Be blessed with forgiving yourself because of him, not in spite of what you have done. Be blessed with wonder, awe, and worship rising up in you for his love.

Be blessed with brokenness over the sinfulness of others in your world but not with condemnation or judgment. Be blessed with directing your heart and your spirit to others who have done wrong, to hold out the redeeming hope of God's forgiveness, cleansing, and healing through your healed heart and his grace.

Be blessed in the name of Jehovah-Jireh,
the one who provided for your greatest need (Gen. 22:14).

93 Jehovah-Rophe — Servant Portion — Exodus 15:26

The second covenant name of God revealed in scripture is found in Exodus 15:26. God brought his people into the wilderness where he revealed himself to them as Jehovah-Rophe, God who heals. He said, "I will put none of the diseases upon you that I placed upon Egypt, if you will listen to me and obey my commands and keep my ordinances." God told his people that if they would serve him, he would take all sickness from them.

Servant portion of the spirit, be blessed as a child of God to know the ordinances of God, and obey them, and live in divine health and prosperity. Be blessed to know God as healer to bring cleansing for you. God wants to reveal himself to cleanse you from all your past pain, wounds, bondages, and the toxicity of life that you've received from your parents and past generational curses.

You are a product of generational blessings and curses you inherited from your parents. You were born with both a gold mine and toxic waste dump. Your parents did not know to clean up their physical toxicity, emotional woundedness, and spiritual bondage before having children. They passed on some negatives to you.

Servant spirit, the good news is that your Father is not limited by the imperfections of your parents. Your heavenly Father wants you whole in spirit, soul, and body. Be blessed with the covenant name of Jehovah Rophe, your healer. Be blessed with cleansing from the defilement of past generations and from your own wrong choices. Be blessed with God sanctifying your spirit to such a degree that you hunger and thirst for the will and the Word of God and the communion of his Holy Spirit. Be blessed in the name of your Father who is the healer of broken hearts. Be blessed with healing of broken heartedness. Be blessed with a spirit that's healthy, alive, alert through his healing presence. Be blessed with cleansing in your soul from every generational wound and stronghold of lies. Be blessed with the cleansing blood of Jesus for negative words spoken to you, about you, or against you. Be blessed with washing away all defilements of mind, will, and emotion. I bless you to love and be loved, to enjoy life and to enjoy your Father and to be enjoyed by him, to have peace with yourself, with others, and with God.

Be blessed with freedom to hear from God, to respond to him and to be used by him as a restorer, healer, and a counselor. Be blessed with cleansing your physical body from susceptibility to diseases in this world. Be blessed with your Father's cleansing of your blood, since life is in the blood. Be blessed with health and wholeness in your autoimmune system, which is anchored by the bloodstream. Be blessed with health in every organ, system, and cell of your body.

Be blessed in the name of Jehovah-Rophe, your healer (Exo. 15:26).

94 Jehovah-Nissi — Teacher Portion — Exodus 17:15

God revealed himself as Jehovah-Nissi, the Lord who fights our battles. In Exodus 17:8-16 God revealed his name as Jehovah-Nissi when the Amalekites begin to attack his people. The Amalekites were predators who would come behind Israel and try to overcome the weak and those who were lagging behind. Joshua fought in the valley, and Moses went up on the mountain and lifted the staff of God. As long as Moses kept his hands up, God won the battle for his people.

Teacher portion, be blessed with the name of Jehovah-Nissi, the Lord your banner. You have authority from God to deal with predatory spirits that are trying to steal, kill, and destroy. Be blessed in the name of the One who teaches your hands to war and fights your battles for you. Be blessed to teach your children to stand firm against the power of darkness and the enemy, so that you will raise up a generation who are strong in the Lord and in the power of his might.

You are blessed because you have a strong and available heavenly Father who does not tolerate the spiritual bullies that try to prey on you. Be blessed with believing your Father's word that he has an endless hatred of the predator spirit that would try to assail you. Be blessed with his protection against being victimized and exploited by spiritual strongmen. Be blessed with freedom in your spirit from the presence of unusual or persistent opposition and harassment. Be blessed with victory of the Lord as you lift up your hands to the throne of God. Be blessed with being set free to worship on a new level as Jehovah-Nissi clears the air of your enemies in testimony of his glory.

Teacher, be blessed with the Lord your banner camping around you at all times and protecting you physically. Be blessed that when the enemy comes in like a flood, your God will raise up a standard against him. Be blessed with becoming a safe place for others, a shelter and a refuge.

Be blessed in the name of Jesus, your Jehovah-Nissi
who fights your battles for you (Exo. 17:15).

95 Jehovah-Shalom — Exhorter Portion — Judges 6:24

Spirit, listen to the Word of God for you in Judges 6:24. "Gideon built an altar to the LORD there and called it The LORD is Peace. To this day it stands..."

Exhorter spirit, be blessed with the birthright of peace in all circumstances. I bless you with your Father's peace saturating you even in the most distressing circumstances. God revealed his nature to Gideon as Jehovah-Shalom. God had gone before him and made a way. Gideon's men blew the trumpets, they broke the pitchers. All the pain, brokenness, sorrow, destruction that you have been through has been in preparation so that your pitcher could be broken and your spirit could begin to shine forth. God's light in you will come out of you and begin to defeat your enemies.

Everything Gideon had been through was preparation for the day that his spirit would come alive, and he would defeat the Midianites, and they would no longer steal the harvest. That's Jehovah-Shalom, that's the God of peace. Those who know their God will do great exploits. That's the ability to do great things for God, knowing he is with you.

Exhorter, be blessed with experiencing the presence of the Holy Spirit when you are in trouble. Be blessed with feeling the peace of the presence of your Father with you, even in trouble. Be blessed with knowing that he has not abandoned you to your enemies. Be blessed with peace and calmness of spirit and soul, in spite of inconvenience or loss, because you know that your Father is very near. Be blessed with the perspective of your Father who knows the end from the beginning. Be blessed with not magnifying the presence of your enemies or trials or problems to seem bigger than the sovereign Lord of the universe. Be blessed with gazing at your Father and glancing at your problems.

Exhorter, be blessed in your ability to reach out and know God. Be blessed with knowing that your Father is available to help you at all times in all that you need. Be blessed with a river of peace flowing over you and permeating everything you are and everything you do. Be blessed with a river of peace that flows out from your spirit and washes over those around you. Be blessed in the Lord of peace in whose name you can find fulfillment in everything God has called you to do as you do great exploits for him.

Be blessed in the name of your Jehovah-Shalom, your peace (Jdg. 6:24).

96 Jehovah-Rohi — Giver portion — Psalm 23:1

God revealed himself as Jehovah-Rohi in Psalm 23:1. "The Lord is my Shepherd." Giver portion, God called you a sheep. Without a shepherd, sheep are useless. It's not your responsibility to find where you are supposed to be or to find food and water or to protect yourself from predators that try to kill you. The shepherd determines the well-being of the sheep, not their ability. That's why Jesus said in John 10, "I am the good Shepherd. I am the door to the sheep. Nobody comes in unless they come through me." You can lie down at night and know that Jesus is your Shepherd. Be blessed to know that he is in charge of your provision, your well-being, your welfare, and your destiny.

Giver portion, be blessed with knowing the goodness of the Shepherd. The devil comes to steal, kill, and destroy, but your Shepherd gives you life and more abundantly. The name of Jehovah-Rohi represents the gift of security given to the sheep by the shepherd. Sheep do not lie down unless they feel secure. The environment must communicate safety to them. Sheep require green pasture with an abundance of food and still water from which to drink, because sheep do not drink from rushing waters.

Giver, be blessed with a sense of safety and security in your world provided by the protecting presence, power, wisdom, and love of your Shepherd. Be blessed with resting in green pastures and knowing he is leading you by peaceful streams. Be blessed with knowing that he is renewing your strength and your spirit day by day. Be blessed with his guidance along right paths, bringing honor to his name. Be blessed that you do not go through life alone, because the Holy Spirit guides you in the way that you should go and leads you in the way of truth. Rejoice that he stakes his own reputation on leading you in righteous paths.

Be blessed with being unafraid because your Shepherd is close beside you. Even when you go through the shadows of dark valleys, you can praise God for the order of the universe which he holds together so that nothing takes him by surprise. Be blessed with habitual confidence in that. Rejoice that death has no power over you, and be released from the spirit of fear in Jesus' name. Be blessed with knowing the protecting rod and staff of your Shepherd.

Be blessed, giver, with the feast of your Father's presence in the presence of your enemies. Be blessed with anointing oil for your head with a cup that overflows with blessing. Be blessed with experiencing his goodness and unfailing love which pursues you all the days of your life. Be blessed with knowing you have a secure place in your Father's house forever.

Be blessed in the name of Jehovah-Rohi, the Lord your great Shepherd who promises you will never lack in him (Ps. 23:1).

97 Jehovah-Tsidkenu — Ruler Portion — Jeremiah 23:6

God revealed himself as Jehovah-Tsidkenu in Jeremiah 23:5-6. Israel's leaders were going astray and were leading unrighteously and corruptly. God came on the scene, and he said, "I will raise up new leadership, and I will lead you in righteousness."

Ruler, God revealed himself as the Lord your righteous leader. You have been affected by unrighteous leadership. Your Father promises to re-parent you, heal you, nurture you, and bring you back to enjoying righteous leadership from him. Be blessed with knowing that your righteousness was positionally secured in Jesus, but be blessed also with putting a high value on pursuing a godly life. Be blessed with focusing on the wellspring of your heart out of which you live and make choices. Be blessed with a lifestyle that is uncompromising, based on what Jesus would do, because he is living in you to do your Father's good will.

Ruler, be blessed with being a righteous leader. Be blessed with taking his righteousness and building righteousness into your life, so that you can be a life-giving leader among your peers. Be blessed in your community with the moral authority of your righteousness having direct implications for the safety and security of others.

Be blessed with a heart that fights for and shepherds the hearts of others, particularly those in your family. Be blessed with looking beyond their outward behavior to their hearts to heal, to restore, to affirm, and to validate them. Be blessed to lead your family with a heart that does not condemn, but continually validates and heals and restores.

Be blessed with obedience to pray for and bless all in authority, so that you and others may live a quiet and peaceful life in all godliness and holiness. Be blessed with favor with righteous civil government, church leadership, and leadership in the marketplace. Be blessed as the Righteous One in you enables you to live righteously without compromise and lead righteously.

Be blessed in the name of Jehovah-Tsidkenu, your righteousness (Jer. 23:6).

98 Jehovah-Shammah — Mercy Portion — Ezekiel 48:35

God revealed himself as Jehovah-Shammah in Ezekiel 48. God promised his people that he would be Jehovah-Shammah, "THE LORD IS THERE."

Mercy, God blesses you with his presence that goes with you everywhere you go. You have access to his presence 365 days a year, 7 days a week, 24 hours a day, and you bring his presence to earth. You have the ability to erase the line between the sacred and the secular. Be blessed with knowing your Father is there for you at all times. God intended this reality from the time of the garden. Adam and Eve experienced his presence as he enjoyed their company. Religion has been trying to get to God with religious days, ceremonies, books, buildings, programs, and songs. God wants you to rediscover the simplicity of the garden where you enjoy his presence as his child.

Mercy, be blessed with knowing deeply that you were made for your Father. Be blessed with knowing how he designed you and what he designed you to contribute. Be blessed with pursuing the pleasure of your Father more than the comforts of life. His presence is indispensable to your having fulfillment, joy, and peace. Be blessed to know that he is there as Abba Father when you need a father. He is there as the answer for your uncertainty and questions. He is there for you as your defender and deliverer when you feel attacked. He is there as your faithful friend when you feel alone. He is there as the God of love when you feel unloved and need a hug. He is there for you as mercy and grace when you're too hard on yourself. He is there for you with hope when you're discouraged and want to quit. He is there for you never failing, always the same, even when you are fickle and faithless. He is there as a quieter of the storm for conflicts and fears within your soul. He is there with true satisfaction when you've tried everything but him. He is there as true riches when you are tempted by the world's allure. He is there as a way-maker when there seems to be no way out.

Be blessed with the fatherness of God. Be blessed with never living a minute without knowing that your Father is there and that no need or desire of yours can strain his resources or his willingness to give you his very best. Be blessed with proving him true over and over again. Mercy, see what your Abba is like, as you see his compassion, his grace, his healing, his goodness, his covenant mercy, and his provision. Be blessed to live as a legitimate son or daughter in the earth, knowing that you are loved beyond anything you could dream, imagine, or comprehend. Your heavenly Father gives good things to those who ask him. Be blessed with every good thing that your Father has provided for you, for he is a shield for you, your glory and the One who lifts your head (Ps. 3:3).

Be blessed in the name of Jehovah-Shammah,
the Lord who promises to be present with you always (Eze. 48:35).

The Seven Portions Of The Human Spirit

99 Blessing The Prophet Portion Of The Human Spirit — Hebrews 12:14; Matthew 5:8

Spirit, hear God's Word for you in Hebrews 12:14. "Without holiness no one will see the Lord." And in Matthew 5:8. "Blessed are the pure in heart, for they will see God."

Prophet portion, come to be nurtured and blessed. You are always first, found in the tabernacle at the brazen altar where atonement was made for sin, as the priests offered sacrifices for the sins of the people. They dealt with sin at the brazen altar before carrying the names of the people on the ephod into the presence of holy God. You can't get into the holy place until you've done business with God about sin at the brazen altar. God gave you a keen sense of right and wrong and placed within you his holy response to sin by repentance. As the innate moral compass that discerns right from wrong, your place is vital. Be blessed as you understand sin and righteousness and respond with conviction and repentance. You want a lifestyle of holiness because of the Holy One who lives in you, breathing his holiness into your being.

Be blessed, prophet, as you find closure from the past, knowing that all your sin is under the blood of Jesus Christ. Repentance brings cleansing, refreshing, and joy, because sin has been totally paid for. Be blessed as you know that God remembers your sins no more, and the debt has been paid in full. Be blessed as you forgive others and release them.

Prophet, as you deal with your own sin, you earn authority to help others deal with their sin. Because you have received God's mercy, you can release his love, goodness, and no condemnation that leads to repentance and the holiness of God in others, so that they can come into God's fullest design for them. God placed in you the gift and mission to bring others to recognize when they are not right with him in small ways and large. Be blessed to lead others to know the freedom of bringing their sins to Jesus and leaving them there.

You see brokenness and stand in the gap to repair and restore broken lives. Many people have not forgiven themselves, and they think that their past disqualifies or hinders them. Sin was totally cancelled at the brazen altar, as fire consumed the sin offering completely, which foreshadowed the final payment of Jesus for the guilt of sin. You represent Jesus, the sinless sacrifice for sin, the atonement for sin at the brazen altar where God brought final closure. First John 1:9 says, "If we confess our sins, he is faithful and just to forgive our sin and cleanse us of all unrighteousness."

Prophet, your Father's purpose is to reconcile men and women to himself. You are surrounded with people whose names and faces he knows, because he created them. He is already at work drawing them, and his Son has already paid the full price to redeem them out of sin's slave market. Be blessed as you let him bring truth and love for them out of the well of the Holy Spirit in you. This is your message: "You will know the truth, and the truth will set you free. And if the Son sets you free, you will be free indeed." Be blessed in leading the way in truth and freedom.

Be blessed in the name of the Son who gave his life as the sin-bearing Sacrifice for all who receive him (1 John 2:2).

100 Blessing The Servant Portion Of The Human Spirit — John 13:3-5

Spirit, listen to the Word of God for you in John 13:3-5. "Jesus knew that the Father had put all things under his power, and that he had come from God and was returning to God; so he got up from the meal, took off his outer clothing, and wrapped a towel around his waist. After that, he poured water into a basin and began to wash his disciples' feet, drying them with the towel that was wrapped around him."

Beloved, listen with your spirit to receive special honor. Be blessed, child of God, treasure of the Almighty, most precious to your Abba. Be blessed with the security in his identity and the honor that Jesus had as one who serves. You have been given everything you need for life and godliness, and you have his nature as you serve (2 Pet. 1:3).

Servant, be blessed in your role of cleansing for leaders. You are pictured in the tabernacle as the laver of cleansing for washing away sin, conflict, brokenness, and distortion. You know how to serve leaders as you bear their burdens for a time by coming alongside them. Be blessed as you powerfully lift their load of criticism, opposition, trial, hardships, pressures, schedules, demands, expectations, and dealing with infirmity and death. Be blessed as you transfer it to the Father so that they can breathe more freely. Be blessed to be the Elisha who washes "Elijah's" hands, so that he can enter the presence of God and do the work of God. Every leader needs an Elisha. Be blessed as you serve with a great anointing to wash those whom God causes you to come alongside.

Everybody is a leader to somebody, so be blessed with effectively transferring to the cross of Jesus the toxicity of everybody's problems, situations, and discouragement that they are eager to dump on you. Let your burden-bearing heart represent the Burden-bearer, so that others can be washed in your cleansing words and the prayers of your listening heart.

Servant, God has blessed you with the mission and authority to wash your soul from its wounded past in a broken world and to remove all traces of being a victim. You are needed to bring unity and harmony, as you demonstrate the servant heart of Jesus when you take a towel and "wash the feet" of all the portions of the spirit. You cleanse the interior atmosphere of the seven-fold gifts in you, so that as a unity you can thrive in the purity of the presence of God. You wash, cleanse, and lift the load, but the soul's domain is to hinder that with discouragement and negativity. "I'm too this, I'm too that" (too old, too young, too late, too... etc.). Be blessed to cleanse all the "too's" that the soul rehearses and replays. At God's holy laver, cleanse the soul of the toxic emotions of unworthiness and inadequacy and shame. Cleanse the defilement of all sin, negative words spoken, comparisons made, lies of the enemy, vows and judgments, etc., so that the purity of God's beautiful spirit design shines through. Be blessed to fulfill his glorious purpose in cleansing the soul and bringing it to the honor, dignity, and authority of your standing as a beloved covenant son/daughter of the King.

Servant, receive the download from the Holy Spirit of power for cleansing in your own sense of being. Cleanse the body memories of everything that it is oppressing and warped and twisted. In the soul and the body, replace all defilement with knowledge of the glory of holy God. You have an anointing for cleansing from sin, conflict, brokenness, and distortion.

Be blessed to continually create a clean life-giving atmosphere, as you, in the spirit realm, unstop plugged ears, wash the scales from veiled eyes, and rub weary backs, figuratively speaking, as you honor and serve your own being as well as your brothers and sisters in Christ.

Servant, the whole earth is groaning, waiting for the manifestation of sons and daughters of God like you (Rom. 8:22), waiting for you to speak his healing for poverty, disease, addictions, and natural catastrophe. When you do that, the environment, land, the weather, leadership, families, infirmity, and premature death feel and demonstrate your great authority for cleansing through prayer and blessing.

Christ elevated you to a position of greatness when he said that the servant of all is the greatest in his economy. In his name that is above all names, you are highly favored, you are the head, not the tail; you are above, not below. Servant, be blessed with great honor from Jesus when he says, "Well done, good and faithful servant." Be blessed in Jesus' name and receive honor as a powerful and precious priestly servant of the Most High God, so that you show forth the glory of him who called you out of darkness into his marvelous light.

Be blessed in the name of the Holy Servant of all,
through whom is healing (Acts 4:30).

101 Blessing The Teacher Portion Of The Human Spirit — Isaiah 30:20-21; 1 John 2:20,27

Spirit, listen to God's Word in Isaiah 30:20-21. "Your teachers will be hidden no more; with your own eyes you will see them. Whether you turn to the right or to the left, your ears will hear a voice behind you, saying, 'This is the way; walk in it.' " And in 1 John 2:20,27. "But you have an anointing from the Holy One, and all of you know the truth. As for you, the anointing you received from him remains in you, and you do not need anyone to teach you. But as his anointing teaches you about all things and as that anointing is real, not counterfeit — just as it has taught you, remain in him."

Teacher portion, I invite you to be blessed as you see God's picture of you in the tabernacle. On the table of showbread the priests placed fresh bread every day. This is a picture of you, teacher. As you speak what God has said to you from his Word, you show forth the Bread of life. You have the anointing of the Holy Spirit to teach you all things. As you continue listening to him, you will feed others and mature in your authority to speak for God in the world. People don't want to hear you say what somebody else said. They want to hear what God has said to you, as you receive and understand from him. Get a revelation of who you are, get hold of the Word of God, who he is, and stand with his authority for his kingdom to come on earth as his will is being done in heaven. Be blessed to receive the truth of Jesus the Word of God and get the Holy Spirit's revelation of him and let him have full expression in your life.

Teacher, be blessed to let Jesus your Teacher fill you without mixture, for he is pure. Receive the work of the Holy Spirit and the word of wisdom for your prophet, servant, exhorter, giver, ruler, and mercy portions. Your Father is building a fortress of wisdom and righteousness.

Teacher, you exercise a profound effect on those around you by taking God's truth, not man's opinion, and sowing it into them. His Word will not return to him void. Jesus taught as he was going from place to place. In the normal course of life, you selectively scatter seeds of wisdom. Be blessed to see the multiplication factor in the seeds you plant. In the natural, you plant a seed and reap a plant that bears seeds. You are responsible for planting the seeds God assigns to you. He'll take care of the harvest.

Be blessed with encouragement, teacher. Be blessed to see the potential in you God has sown for years to multiply the fruitfulness of your life to this point. Give the Gardener his crop this year with no mental or spiritual fallow ground. Be blessed in his timing in his appointed season. Be blessed with perception to see, and receive, and bring forth God's appointed multiplication in Jesus' name. You don't have to do the producing, any more than an oak tree strives to produce acorns. Be the oak of righteousness that God planted you to be, and let God give the increase.

Be blessed in the name of the Lord of the harvest (Mat. 9:38).

102 Blessing The Exhorter Portion Of The Human Spirit — Isaiah 60:1

Spirit, listen to the Word of God for you today in Isaiah 60:1 "Arise, shine, for your light has come, and the glory of the LORD rises upon you."

Exhorter portion, come to the front to be blessed. You know God uniquely, and you have been making him known as you function dynamically in your ministry of interpreting him with practical wisdom. God celebrates how you express him with clarity that others can understand. That's God's good gift for your spirit as a whole and for others.

Your strength is knowing God and shining him forth like the sun, moon, and stars. Like the limitless stars in the sky, you will make God known to many in the multiplication of generations to come. As the heavens declare the glory of God, your light will shine. The Bible says that "The LORD rises upon you and his glory appears over you" (Isa. 60:2). Others will see and hear how you know God and see the glory of God that's in you. Get excited about this. God has made you for this. "For God, who said, 'Let light shine out of darkness,' made his light shine in our hearts to give us the light of the knowledge of the glory of God in the face of Christ" (2 Cor. 4:6).

Exhorter, you are pictured in the lampstand in the tabernacle. You are vital to the mission of making God famous, as you shine your light on the other portions of the spirit and on your world as only you can, to engage them and transition them to interacting with God's truth. Be blessed to come to your full place of mission and destiny.

You can know God and bring his light to all the human spirit. That is represented by the seven candles of the Lord on the lampstand, the seven Spirits of God that burn inside you. The Spirit of the Lord, the Spirit of wisdom and understanding, the Spirit of counsel and power, the Spirit of knowledge and of the fear of the Lord are burning brightly.

Exhorter, like the 7-pronged lampstand, you burn with the light of the entire counsel of God. Be blessed with fresh oil today to burn brightly and shine the deep intimate knowledge of God to all portions of the spirit and to others. Be blessed as you speak God's words that will lift up the spirit of others, and be blessed yourself to be lifted up by God's words, as you speak words of exhortation from the download of his Spirit into you.

Exhorter, be blessed to lead the way in meeting people where they are and light their blindspots, ignorance, and prejudice. Be blessed as you winsomely plead with them past their sin and hang-ups to come to the loving, welcoming Light of the world. God is drawing them, preparing them to be his Friend, because he is the Friend of sinners. Be blessed to be his ambassador of reconciliation. No preparation is too great for that appointment by the King of all kings to increase his fame in all the earth. Say, "Yes, LORD, walking in the way of your laws… your name and renown are the desire of our hearts" (Isa. 26:8).

Be blessed in his name and renown as the Friend of sinners (Mat. 11:19).

103 Blessing The Giver Portion Of The Human Spirit — John 3:16

Spirit, hear God's Word for you in John 3:16. "For God so loved the world that he gave his one and only Son..."

Giver, in Jesus' name be blessed in what you are known for, as you express the nature of God by wanting to nurture and be with family and friends to celebrate them, whether there is an occasion or not. The people are the occasion. Just because. You are willing to sacrifice whatever is necessary to nurture those in your care and see them fulfill all the potential in their spirits. Many times you have sacrificed personal needs to see someone else's needs fulfilled. God counts your resourcefulness and sacrifice to nurture others as sweet incense. God loves all expressions of himself in his children. He is extravagantly generous with himself and his love, not just things. You are alive in every cell when you are participating with God this way. Be blessed as you are strong and fruitful in your giver gift.

Giver, God made you to be rich in intercession and worship to see God's destiny and purposes fulfilled, so that others can experience all God's best. Your essence and work is pictured in the altar of incense where very expensive spices became fragrant smoke to enter before the priest into the presence of God. You have prepared the way of many servants of God into his presence with your intercession and worship, at great cost to your comfort and convenience, but you counted it as a privilege. God sees that and counts it a sacrifice to him, a sweet aroma before him.

The giving and praying of the Gentile Cornelius came up to God as a memorial, a sweet smelling incense before him. He sent an angel to tell Cornelius that he was accepted in his sight. You attract the attention of heaven when you are offering up intercession and worship for those whom God wants to touch. He may give you a special assignment to bring Jews and Gentiles together to the grace and power of the true and living God. Be blessed in breaking down the dividing wall at the altar of intercession and worship. Be blessed to celebrate the engrafting of many others into God's family. Be blessed to bring the gospel and glory of God to nations around the world. There is more to your anointing for the world, as you bear their spirits before God and ask him to show his mercy and faithfulness to them because he so loved the world that he gave his only Son.

Giver, be blessed with holy courage, as all fearful places give way to the faith of the prophet and the vision of the exhorter. No longer ask where you will get the resources for mental, emotional, physical, or financial tasks. As you give, you will never run out of God's resources. Just like the widow whose barrel never ran out of meal and the oil never ran dry (2 Kgs. 4:1-7), God will give back to you again and again. He will open the floodgates of heaven and pour out so much blessing that you will not have room enough for it. God will cause all grace to abound to you, so that you, always having all sufficiency in all things, may abound in every good work (2 Cor. 9:8). Be blessed, giver, as you sacrifice in God's holy temple, to worship and intercede for yourself, your family, those around you, and our world.

Be blessed in the name of God's indescribable Gift (2 Cor. 9:15).

104 Blessing The Ruler Portion Of The Human Spirit — 1 Chronicles 13:6

Spirit, listen to the Word of God for you in 1 Chronicles 13:6. "…the ark of God the LORD, who is enthroned between the cherubim — the ark that is called by the Name."

Ruler, come to be blessed. You are represented in the tabernacle by the ark of the covenant which held the Ten Commandments, the manna, and the rod of Aaron. The ark represented the name of God among his people, and he made his dwelling place there. For maximum good of your whole being, attend to the three items in the ark: the law, manna, and the rod that budded.

The ark contained the law, representing submission to God's Word and his ways. As you submit to his Word and his ways, you show faith, and it puts you in the place for God to work. Take your example from the Roman centurion who had a servant who was sick (Mat. 8:5-13). Jesus was on his way to heal his servant, and he told Jesus, "I'm a man under authority. I said to one go and he goes, and to another come and he comes. I understand authority, and I recognize your authority, because I recognize you're a man under authority. So speak the word, and my servant will be healed." Jesus said, "I haven't seen this kind of faith in all of Israel." You have authority that God has placed in you to lead because of submitting to him. When you obey God and submit to his law, this puts you in position to see God's supernatural dealings in your life and household.

Ruler, be blessed with the lesson of the manna. God miraculously provided manna for Israel in the desert. This life-giving provision fed his people for forty years. It foreshadowed the future Bread of life who would come into the world, die, and be raised to live in you. Be blessed in God's life-giving essence in you that nourishes you. Let God father you as his true son/daughter in his love, so that you are a blessing as a fathering leader to the whole of the spirit and to your world. Be blessed as a life-giver, sustained daily in the Word of God, and building up others as you represent the Father to them. Be blessed with bringing sons to maturity.

Be blessed with the rod that budded. It signifies your God-given priesthood. By causing the rod to bud, God validated the priesthood of Aaron. God is with you in your priestly role to your family and your world.

Ruler, God placed specific ruler DNA in you. You have God-given ability and mandate to lead the other portions of your spirit for the good of the goals he set before you. He designed you to lead by his Word and in submission to him with life-giving manna and so fulfill your priestly calling with great authority. Be blessed as you live in dominion in Christ. You make a way in goals, tasks, and order. You know how to be focused and plan for all seven portions of the spirit. You may not have been nurtured and invited to take your full place, but be blessed as you live in God's design for you.

Ruler, you bring synergy and forward momentum to the other gifts of the spirit. Prophet is about congruency, and mercy is about alignment; ruler, you are about synergy, investments with high yield, the whole being greater than the sum of the parts. Be blessed to assign tasks for each of the other six portions of the spirit, as you lead in harmony with the other six gifts to accomplish God's agenda that makes him smile.

Be blessed to know God's assignment for you in nature. On the sixth day Genesis 1:28,31 says, "God blessed them (Adam and Eve) and said to them, 'Be fruitful and increase in number; fill the earth and subdue it. Rule over the fish of the sea and the birds of the air and over every living creature that moves on the ground.' " God called your mandate to subdue the earth "very good." Be blessed to build and to lead in maximum harmony with nature, because it was God's idea.

Ruler, be blessed to live in God's priorities and in a timely way in step with him. Be blessed to live in his order and authority with those around you, to prioritize and organize in the ordinary things of life. Be blessed with being at the right place at the right time, being fruitful and having dominion that the totality of your spirit and the world needs.

Be blessed in the name of the Ruler and Shepherd of God's people (Mat. 2:6).

105 Blessing The Mercy Portion Of The Human Spirit — Genesis 2:2-3

Spirit, listen to God's Word for you in Genesis 2:2-3. "By the seventh day God had finished the work he had been doing; so on the seventh day he rested from all his work. And God blessed the seventh day and made it holy, because on it he rested from all the work of creating that he had done."

Mercy, celebrate God who is with you today. Celebrate how he sees you, pure and holy and chosen and set apart to him. The ever-changing kaleidoscope of beauty in motion is a picture of you. Think about a kaleidoscope with all the delights to the eyes of color, motion, creativity, originality, and grace. That is the result of strict compliance to God's laws of the physics of reflected light. You represent total harmony of beauty and science that he placed in the universe. You take ordinary lines, colors, and forms that are lifeless in the hands of somebody else, and you make them into a lavish feast for the senses.

On your day God rested and celebrated what he had made. There was no production on the seventh day, but there was enormous motion in the spirit, when the previous six days came together in integration of God's manifest purpose of rest in the earth. And God called it complete and blessed.

Mercy, be blessed to step back and smell the roses, to enjoy and admire. You can savor what God has done and is doing in such a way that it comes to a higher place. You feel the presence of God and don't have to understand what it's about. You celebrate him as his Spirit embraces you, and he brings great rest and blessedness to your life. You love divine alignment and harmony. By the blessing of your presence with God's presence entwined, you bring all the other gifts into alignment. Know today that you are a work in progress. At the same time, you are a finished work in God's mind, because he stands out of time and he knows the end from the beginning. Be blessed to see that his design makes a thing of beauty in the earth through you.

Mercy, be blessed even when you sense that things aren't lined up, because that validates that alignment is God's birthright for you. You will see the full picture of seemingly contradictory alignments like mercy and judgment, love and retribution, grace and truth, holy and secular. That is no contradiction to you, as God's mercy, love, and grace simultaneously endure with his holiness, judgment, and righteousness. You can receive that, because you bear the imprint of heaven. At that moment he placed you in your mother's womb and formed your earthly existence, God already knew that you would understand the full scope of his unlimited being, beyond expressing him in words. God wants you to be nurtured according to his words "It's very good," as you live in divine order with his purposes and plans for all the gifts inside. He is nurturing you to the full completion in all his things which your eye has not seen, your ear has not heard, and your imagination has not conceived.

Mercy, you're designed by the infinite creativity of your Father to fulfill your specific unique design. Don't let anybody try to force you into their "box" for you. Be blessed as you lead the spirit in appreciating your originality, for you are one-of-a-kind and extremely valued. This day was created specially for you and you specially for this day. Enjoy a magnificent sense of being on earth today in harmony and alignment with God's design, and live the beautiful kaleidoscope in motion that you are. Enjoy being you in full freedom and new wholeness because of who you are in God. Be blessed to see what he is always seeing and hear what he is always saying for you.

Be blessed in the name of Jesus the LORD, who is always with you (Mat. 28:20).

106 Be Blessed In Your Whole Being — Be Who God Made You To Be — Genesis 1:27; Isaiah 43:6-7

Spirit, listen to God's Word for you in Genesis 1:27. "So God created man in his own image, in the image of God he created him." And in Isaiah 43:6-7. "Bring my sons from afar and my daughters from the ends of the earth — everyone who is called by my name, whom I created for my glory, whom I formed and made."

Spirit, your heavenly Father created you, formed you, and molded you specially for this day. You are made to look like him. You are unique and priceless to him. As your physical fingerprints don't match anybody else's, neither your physical DNA nor your spiritual DNA matches anybody else's. You are an original son/daughter of Most High God, not a cheap copy. He called you by name and created you for his glory. You're specifically designed by the poly-variegated wisdom of your Creator God to fulfill your special purpose in him.

In your whole being, be blessed today. Stand tall and recognize that you are a spiritual being, made in God's image. You live in a human body and have human experiences, but your identity is spiritual. Spirit, tell your soul to come behind you, and tell your body to get behind your soul. Be intentional in asking for divine alignment to come into your spirit, soul, and body in total congruency with the unique design of God for each moment, as you look into his face and see yourself as he sees you.

Spirit, be true to the masterpiece of God's design that you are. You are one of God's best designs, an ever-changing life-mobile — a unique living, breathing set of his best designs in all seven rainbow colors. A rainbow isn't a rainbow if even one of the colors is missing. As light is reflected in a prism, it must show forth all seven colors. It's a principle that God put into the physics of light. He wants you to show forth all seven colors of himself in you. He adds wonderful depth and color of his light to bring out his richest design in your life, as prophet, servant, teacher, exhorter, giver, ruler, and mercy begin to flourish as never before in total integration and harmony for his glory. God is so big that one color inside of you is not enough. God is not monochromatic. Revelation describes all the colors of the gemstones, the gold, the crystal water, the light, and the color that is present around God. Be blessed in all seven facets of your spirit to reflect his glory.

Spirit, be blessed as the perfecting work of Jesus Christ takes place in your life. Be blessed to live as a beautiful son/daughter of God as you enjoy all the blessings of our triune God and his 7-fold Holy Spirit whose lamp blazes in the throneroom day and night. Look up at him and catch a spark from his 7-fold light (Rev. 1:4, 3:1, 4:5). Enjoy being you and living in full freedom and new wholeness. Be blessed in the fullness of the divine birthright that God created in you to flourish in his kingdom today. Be blessed in him as you grab hold of all your birthright. You were born with it. It is yours. Claim it.

Be blessed as you enjoy a sense of being on earth in harmony with God's design and live with the divine sense of destiny like never before. Be blessed in God's joy and pleasure as you embrace life with irrepressible zest for being who he made you to be.

Be blessed in the name of the Lord your Maker who crowns you with glory and honor (Isa. 54:5; Ps. 8:5).

Looking Unto Jesus

107 Looking Unto Jesus I — Hebrews 12:2

Spirit, hear Hebrews 12:2 NKJV. "... looking unto Jesus, the author and finisher of our faith..." Look to Jesus. Turn your face heavenward and fix your eyes on him to hear these three words that hold the secret of life... looking unto Jesus.

Be blessed, looking unto Jesus the Living Word –
... to learn who he is and what he has done and what he does even now
... to learn what he gives, what he wants
... to find in his character your pattern and in his Spirit your power
... to find in his person the ultimate satisfaction of your being.

Be blessed, looking unto Jesus the crucified One –
... to find in him your pardon and peace. "Look to Me, and be saved, all you ends of the earth! For I am God, and there is no other" (Isa. 45:22)
... to receive in him the finished work of his lovingkindness in his sacrifice for your sin
... to receive the cleansing of his blood to wash white as snow your sin-stained heart.

Be blessed, looking unto Jesus the risen One –
... to find in him power over the grave and hell itself
... to receive from him the signature on your life that you have been with him in his resurrection life.

Be blessed, looking unto Jesus the Ascended One –
... to find in him your heavenly Advocate, who is now appearing for you before the face of your Father
... to receive the ministry of his heavenly priesthood continually interceding for you.

Be blessed, looking unto Jesus the living Lord –
... to receive from him the grace of keeping short accounts for sin, as you bow before his Kingship to recognize, to hate, to confess and forsake your sins
... to receive the transformation of your rebel will by him who was spared no temptation, yet yielded to none.

Be blessed, looking unto Jesus your strength –
... to be made perfect in your weakness and frailty, when you waver in your commitment
... to be rekindled from within when you have stumbled over his command to love him only with all your heart, and mind, and soul, and strength
... not looking at your strength or your weakness, so that his strength may be perfected in you.

Be blessed, looking unto Jesus the Way –
... that your life may be hidden with him in God in everything that comes your way today
... to live in the way of his grace for each moment, living not at all outside the consciousness of his presence
... to receive from him your assignment to the Father's business for the day and the grace sufficient to do it with joy in his love and patience.

Based on the booklet "Looking Unto Jesus" by Theodore Monod, 1874, published in France. Translated from French by Helen Willis.

108 Looking Unto Jesus II — Hebrews 12:2

Spirit, hear God's Word for you in Hebrews 12:2 NKJV. "... looking unto Jesus, the author and finisher of our faith..." Look unto Jesus. Turn your face heavenward and fix your eyes on Jesus to hear these three words that hold the secret of life... looking unto Jesus.

Be blessed, looking unto Jesus who conquered death —
... to live in the Father's house in his presence far from fear of death (John 14:3)
... for the blessed hope of your sure reward when he is revealed in glory.

Be blessed, looking unto Jesus your author and perfecter —
... to fix your gaze on him and on nothing else
... as the Finisher of faith encourages, sustains, and sums up your faith in himself
... as the source of your faith, its object and its perfection.

Be blessed, looking unto Jesus your Mighty Warrior —
... and not at the schemes of the enemy
... renouncing the thoughts, reasoning, imagination, inclinations, wants, and plans of the flesh
... choosing against the customs, example, rules, and judgments of the world
... with certainty that the battle is the Lord's.

Be blessed to look unto Jesus your life —
... and not to your best and holiest efforts and observances to earn God's favor
... and not to any person, for in following Jesus alone you will never lose your way
... saying to him, "Wherever you lead, I'll go"
... keeping to the way that his light illuminates, because in him is life, and that life is the light of men (John 1:4).

Be blessed to look to Jesus whose name is Jealous —
... and not at your position, your family, your credentials, your doctrine, your sincere intentions, the good opinion of others, or your own opinion of yourself
... not putting any other person or thing between you and him
... to know Jesus as your closest friend and highest loyalty
... to receive his pleasure in your plea that you are his alone, and you have given him your heart in unrivaled affection and complete devotion.

Be blessed to look to Jesus your joy —
... and not at earthly joy to find in it your identity or legitimacy
... to receive from him good things made more precious because they come as gifts from his loving hand and point to his goodness
... to enjoy his good gifts in communion with him and use them for his glory
... to make his glory the single object of your life and receive his grace for everything that glorifies him.

Based on the booklet "Looking Unto Jesus" by Theodore Monod, 1874, published in France. Translated from French by Helen Willis.

109 Looking Unto Jesus III — Hebrews 12:2

Spirit, hear God's Word for you in Hebrews 12:2 NKJV. "... looking unto Jesus, the author and finisher of our faith..." Look unto Jesus. Turn your face heavenward and fix your eyes on Jesus to hear these three words that hold the secret of life... looking unto Jesus.

Be blessed to look to Jesus the Lamb of God –
... and not at our sins any longer than to confess them and let him deliver you from them and receive his full pardon
... and not the unworthiness of your own life, for you will become like that upon which you fix your attention
... and not at the past from which you have come, tho' rescued and healed by God's grace
... looking at yourself only in the presence of the cross, only through Jesus who gives life
... forgiving yourself, lest you fall into the pride of "How could I have done such a thing?"
... praising God for the greatness of the sacrifice which atoned for sin and of the grace which pardoned it
... knowing that the blood of the Lamb is the only all-sufficient remedy.

Be blessed to look to Jesus, for from him and through him and to him are all things (Rom. 11:36) –
... and not at his enemies or your own to magnify their offenses or to fear them
... to receive from Jesus the power to love them and to overcome evil with good
... as the first cause of everything in your life, so that you can show the same gratitude for those who do not do you good as those who do
... receiving everything as Father-filtered, trusting that you can hear Jesus say, "You do not realize now what I am doing, but later you will understand" (John 13:7).

Be blessed to look to Jesus who comes walking on the storm –
... and not at the terrifying storm-tossed waves of circumstance or your own sinking feet
... to know that the One who breathed the storm can also still it with a breath or hold you up across it to meet his loving hands.

Be blessed to look to Jesus who made the bitter water sweet –
... and not at your troubles to count them, or magnify them, or compare them, or find some satisfaction in tasting their bitterness and fall into self-pity
... for him to sanctify your troubles, for in them he will produce patience, joy, sympathy, hope, and strength
... to accept them from his hand, to bear them with love, with gratitude, with joy and find in them for yourself and for others a source of blessing.

Be blessed to look to Jesus your Friend –
... to be blessed with friendships that draw you nearer to the Friend who sticks closer than a brother
... to know his faithfulness when others are unfaithful.

Based on the booklet "Looking Unto Jesus" by Theodore Monod, 1874, published in France. Translated from French by Helen Willis.

110 Looking Unto Jesus IV — Hebrews 12:2

Spirit, hear God's Word for you in Hebrews 12:2 NKJV. "... looking unto Jesus, the author and finisher of our faith..." Look unto Jesus. Turn your face heavenward and fix your eyes on Jesus to hear these three words that hold the secret of life... looking unto Jesus.

Be blessed to look to Jesus the fulfillment of the law –
... and not at any pretense of righteousness in your spiritual attainment
... and not at the law that gives commands and gives no strength to carry them out, that always condemns and never pardons.
... and not to be so foolish to start with the Spirit and try to obey in the flesh to attain your goals, for Jesus is the end of the law for righteousness (Rom. 10:4)
... to know that what he requires he also inspires and is the means for doing it as a free gift of grace (Phil. 2:13)
... to obey with your whole heart and most secret thoughts with delight and joy to please him.

Be blessed to look to Jesus the One who came to serve –
... and not at what you are doing for him and not to your success
... to make no idol of ministry or fruitfulness or success as the world measures success
... to be a faithful steward
... to give account of your stewardship of his commands and promptings from a heart that is filled with his love from which service is the overflow.

Be blessed to look to Jesus the Giver of spiritual gifts –
... and not at the gifts of yesterday's grace, although for them you are grateful
... and not to today's gifts given for today's work, except to use them for his glory.

Be blessed to look to Jesus who is faithful –
... and not at the height of your joy, the strength of your assurance, or the warmth of your love
... and not at your ever-changing heart, but looking steadily at Jesus, who is always the same. When feelings fade or fail, his faith with its strength remains with you.

Be blessed to look to Jesus your victory –
... and not at your holiness, for holiness is the fruit of your redemption, not the root. It is the work of Jesus Christ for you; it is the work of the Holy Spirit in you which renews you in His likeness.
... and not to your doubts, for if you look away from them to your Lord Jesus, who is the Truth (John 14:6), the doubts will scatter in the light of his presence.
... and not at your defeats or victories, to be neither cast down nor puffed up
... fighting the good fight of faith from victory in Jesus, which is the gift of God through him.

Be blessed to look to Jesus –
... and not at your faith. The adversary turns your eyes from your Savior to discourage you if your faith is weak or to fill you with pride if it is strong, and either way to weaken you
... to receive power that comes from your Savior by faith
... and it is from him and in him that you know what it is good for you to know about the world and about yourself, your sorrows and your dangers, your resources and your victories
... in him to see everything in its true light, because he shows it to you. All that you do not learn from him, it is better for you not to know.

Be blessed to look to Jesus –
… from moment to moment
… without allowing yourself to be distracted by memories of a past which you should leave behind you or by occupation with a future of which you know nothing.
Unto Jesus now if we have never looked unto him –
Unto Jesus afresh, if we have ceased doing so –
Unto Jesus only,
Unto Jesus still.

Be blessed to look to Jesus always –
… with a heart more constant, more confident, "changed into the same image from glory to glory" (2 Cor. 3:18), for you will be like him; for "you shall see him as he is" (1 John 3:2).

Based on the booklet "Looking Unto Jesus" by Theodore Monod, 1874, published in France. Translated from the French by Helen Willis. Published by Bible Light Publishers Ltd, P. O. Box 442, Fo Tan, New Territories, Hong Kong. http://www.biblelight.com, fax 852-2604-3253, email info2@biblelight.com. There is no copyright on my copy of the little booklet. The text can be downloaded at http://gracenotebook.biblemessages.com/pub/26

Epilogue

111 You Are A Priest — Isaiah 61:6

Spirit, hear the Word of the Lord for you. Isaiah 61:6 promises, "You will be called priests of the LORD and ministers of your God." And in Revelation 1:6. "[Jesus] has made us to be a kingdom and priests to serve his God and Father — to him be glory and power for ever and ever! Amen."

Spirit, when Jesus died on the cross, the veil of the holy of holies was torn from top to bottom. Now the privilege of access to the inner court belongs to all believers. What an awesome privilege! You may boldly come into the holy of holies to praise, worship, adore, and glorify your Father. The essence of New Testament priesthood is access to God based on your redemption in Jesus Christ. Be blessed with knowing the power and joy of your free access to him. You are a kingdom of priests under the ministry of Jesus your High Priest. Receive the words of 1 Peter 2:5 and 9. "You also, like living stones, are being built into a spiritual house to be a holy priesthood, offering spiritual sacrifices acceptable to God through Jesus Christ. But you are a chosen people, a royal priesthood, a holy nation, a people belonging to God, that you may declare the praises of him who called you out of darkness into his wonderful light." You are a priest and minister to God. The priestly functions are your privilege as a member of the royal priesthood (1 Pet. 2:9). This is your true spiritual inheritance. Be blessed in drawing near to him, abiding in his presence, and dwelling in him, and he in you, as you offer spiritual sacrifices of praise and prayer.

Peter had in mind the three functions of priests in the Old Testament: to go into the tabernacle or temple and minister to God, to represent the people to God and to represent his words to the people, and bless the people in his name. Spirit, be blessed as you minister to God in the secret place where he releases his heart to you. Be blessed as you seek to know him intimately and experience all of who he is. Be blessed to be in love with him and to want to please your beloved more than anything else. Worship and adore him, being joyfully, willingly submitted to the One you love. Be blessed to meet him in worship in complete surrender of all you are. Be blessed to draw near as the Spirit of the Lord abides in you, indwells you, rests on you, and anoints you.

Spirit, be blessed as you represent God to others by releasing his heart of blessing to your world. By standing in the gap in prayer, faith, intercessory living, and blessing, you open the door for restoration for yourself and your family. You are an instrument of renewal and rebuilding of generations of desolation and ruin. As God moves upon you, you can bless and minister to others, so that God can convict, woo, love, and reconcile them. He will make all things new and glorify himself as he ministers through you, and the glory of the throneroom puts its stamp on all you are and do in his name

Spirit, you are blessed to be a blessing. Be blessed to speak deeply personal words of acceptance, identity, meaning, affirmation, and legitimacy. Be blessed to envision God's special future for others as they come into the fullness of all he made them to be. Be blessed to let God's presence and blessing flow through you to his glory and praise. Be blessed as you sow to the Spirit, and you will reap the things of the Spirit, for the one who sows to the Spirit reaps life. Be blessed in the Spirit of life (Rom. 8:2).

Be blessed in the name of Jesus, your High Priest (Heb 3:1; 9:11).

112 You Display His Splendor — Isaiah 61:3

Spirit, listen to the Word of God for you in Isaiah 61:3. "They will be called … a planting of the LORD for the display of his splendor."

Jesus quoted Isaiah 61:1-2 as he announced his purpose statement in Luke 4. He said, "The Spirit of the Lord is on me to preach the gospel to the poor, heal the broken-hearted, to set captives free, to open blind eyes, to open prison doors, and to proclaim the favorable year of the Lord." That's not the end of the sentence in Isaiah 61. Isaiah continues that he wants to make a holy exchange with you: his comfort for grief, his crown instead of ashes, his gladness for mourning, and his praise instead of despair. It continues, "You will be an oak of righteousness, a planting of the Lord" — and the weight of the entire passage of Isaiah 61:1-3 falls on the next word — "**for** the display of his splendor."

Spirit, Jesus came to earth for you — to heal you, set you free, and restore you for a purpose: so that you will display his splendor. This is the fulfillment of every word that has been spoken over you. This defines you. You live to show forth his glory; you are called to this. This is what God gets you up in the morning to be. Be blessed in your calling, for it is God's bottom-line appointment of you. His purpose in you is that people see and feel and respond to the weight and strength of your life, the glory of his life lived through you as you live in the splendor, strength, and weight of the glory of Jesus.

Isaiah 62:3 says that you will be a crown of splendor in the Lord's hand. Don't pray toward that; receive it as a gift. This is the true meaning of your life in your essence. God sees you as a splendid, glorious crown in his hand. Jesus said to his Father in John 17:22, "I have given them the glory that you gave me." Spirit, you have the glory of Jesus. He has given it to you, and it's the unique glory of your life. That glory of Jesus is who you are, and that is God's final word on who you are.

Your life is shining his light, the seven prismatic colors of God in you, the manifold wisdom of God. You are on a journey further into that identity, legitimacy, freedom, and confident hope. It is true of you now, and it is becoming more true of you.

Spirit, God says in Psalm 8:5 that he crowned you with glory (that's the word splendor) and honor and majesty that is unique to you. Be blessed as you shine your unique testimony to the greatness of God. Christ came, lived, and died to bring out the richness, the riches, of your life as you show forth his radiance all day long. 2 Corinthians 3:18 says, "We, who with unveiled faces all reflect the Lord's glory, are being transformed into his likeness with ever-increasing glory, which comes from the Lord, who is the Spirit." That is your birthright. You are blessed as you receive the light of Jesus shining in you to shine out of you. God wants to display his Spirit in you to display his Spirit through you, so that his beauty and truth will touch and warm the spirit of others.

But you have an enemy who wants to get you and others to turn your glory into shame. Paul says in 2 Corinthians 4:4 that the god of this age has a strategy: to blind your mind to keep you from seeing the light of the glory of Christ. Spirit, speak to the mind that Satan has blinded to keep you from seeing the light of the glory of Christ in you. Satan is trying to put out your light. He knows who you are, and he fears who you are becoming. He knows the significance of your life, and he battles to stop you from displaying Jesus in all his glory.

Lies will come at you to shut down or destroy the calling and splendor of your life from the inside or the outside. Your enemy works to cause you to disdain your glory or feel disqualified, through words that inflame old wounds, old judgments and vows, old tapes that he is good at playing. "Old" is his stock in trade, and he will use others to accomplish his purposes. Don't remember the former things. Don't settle for the lies. He can't put out the light. He can't keep you from living that light, being that light. You do not have to live in the story that Satan has written for you.

God, who said, "Let light shine out of darkness," made his light shine in you, spirit, to give you the light of knowledge of the glory of God in the face of Christ (2 Cor. 4:6). Truth lives in you to reveal, develop, and display the glory and splendor of your life. Where sin and lies abound, grace and truth do much more abound. God in you is bigger than Satan's assault to deaden you, your heart, and your desire, to shut down the glory in your life, to keep you from affirming the splendor that is your inheritance. You are right in the middle of God's good and perfect truth for you. Jesus can live his life through you.

Whether your soul feels like this is true or not, you are living the story that God birthed you for. Your splendor is seen in a hug, a smile, a card you write, a phone call, a kindness. Your splendor is seen in the small "never-mind" details of your life. God is deeply involved in your every breath to reveal his splendor. He put you right where you are, in the family, in the marriage, in the valley of decision where you are. He placed you there for the specific purpose of letting his splendor be seen, letting his light shine in your spirit to shine the light of his glory through you.

Spirit, be blessed with seeing the greatest splendor in the area of your greatest wounding. The enemy's wounds are inflicted in the place of your truest strength, as an effort to take you out. The wounds are markers for your greatest strength, the truest gifts of God in you. In your Father you have something deep, substantial, beautiful, authentic, and powerful to offer yourself and others, as you begin to display the nature of the Man Christ Jesus. God created you for this very time in your life. He knows exactly what is happening in your family, in your world, and he knows the impact you will have. It is never too late to accomplish the purpose for which God created you. Be blessed as you live into the purpose for which he created you. Your times are in God's hands. Tomorrow you won't wake up with all of it. But tomorrow you will be closer than you are today.

Spirit, live with his glory and your splendor on display through you. Live in the glory of your full command presence. That's not arrogance, that's God in you. Your calling is to be his intimate friend and discover "Who am I really? How do I become? How do I shine Jesus forth?" Spirit, in his book God wrote for you freedom, dominion, hope, and holy-what-is-it yet to be revealed. Your "why" is that God is working in you what will give him the most pleasure and display the most of him. God is at work in you causing you to fill your place in pleasing his heart and to fill the place in the world he designed for you to display him. He is pleased that your life offers others the blessing of his presence and strength.

Spirit, be blessed, because you hold the key. Take this adventure with God. He will confide in you his way chosen for you. He is doing something of himself in you that is wonderful and unique, something that bonds you to him with everlasting cords of love.

Be blessed in the name of Jesus who is the Splendor revealed in you (Ps. 145:5).

Staying In Your Spirit

Calling our spirit to come, to wake up and take its proper place of leadership over soul and body is the easy part. The hard part is staying in our spirit. Paul weighs in on the subject in Galatians 5:25. "Since we live by the Spirit, let us keep in step with the Spirit." Furthermore, he says that that is the identifying mark of those who are sons of God. "Those who are led by the Spirit of God are sons of God" (Rom. 8:14).

The first part of John 15 is dedicated to staying in our spirit. Jesus says, "Remain in me, and I will remain in you" (John 15:4). Ten times in one chapter Jesus used the word remain. It takes discipline and pure hard work. There is no silver bullet or impartation anybody can give us nor any magic wand that they can wave over us. It is an inside job. It is crucially important, because with our spirits we relate to God. Jesus said, "Stay with me," or more importantly "Stay connected to me," or "Stay in me." Of course, we are saved. This is not about salvation. It is about living in him. Jesus came and died and was resurrected to give us the abundant life he promises. John 15:4 says, "No branch can bear fruit by itself; it must remain in the vine. Neither can you bear fruit unless you remain in me."

Remaining in our Father's love at times takes our fullest choice, intention, and effort. We choose to receive what he says about us, rather than what our soul defaults to. Are we feeling unfulfilled, unimportant, insignificant? Jesus snaps us back to the basics. "As the Father has loved me, so have I loved you. Now remain in my love" (John 15:9). Do you hear what he said? "As my Father in heaven, the God of the universe, loves me (his Son), that's how I love you." We are there, but we must choose to stay in this awareness.

How To Stay In Your Spirit

1. Seek the wisdom of God in his Word and by prayer (Prov. 2:1-8; Jam. 1:5).

When you want to know what God says, read where he speaks the most — his Word. Read the scriptures about the spirit in the back of this book. As you read your Bible, intentionally read with your spirit. Meditate on the Word in your spirit and let the Word make its home in you (Col. 3:16). Read it as God's letter to you. Ask questions with your spirit. "How does this relate to me? Is God telling me something about himself? Is he telling me something about me?" God invites you to come and taste and see that he is good. Let his Word become a part of you. Pray it back to God. Take the scriptures through your spirit, not just your head. Did you argue with what you read? If so, you were in your soul. Did you try to change what it said or justify how you feel, which is different from what it said? Did you dismiss what it said or slough over it and say, "That doesn't pertain to me"? Was your experience that an hour later you couldn't remember what you read? Then you read it in your soul, and God did not write it on your spirit. Your spirit houses the homing device that knows how to draw near to God, so your spirit needs to be in the forefront when you are reading the Word.

2. Let the Word transform your mind (Rom. 12:1-2).

Not all reading is transformational. Most of it is informational. To be transformational, call your spirit to the front, and read from your spirit to be life-giving. Philippians 4:8 is a start: "Whatever is true, whatever is noble, whatever is right, whatever is pure, whatever is lovely, whatever is admirable — if anything is excellent or praiseworthy — think about such things." Engage your spirit with each of these qualities, not just think about them with your mind, and then pass everything through that eight-fold test of transformation.

3. Hear and obey.

We need to work on our communication skills with God and practice active listening. Often we do all the talking. We dump our problems on him and tell him how we want him to fix it. We listen to him with one ear and half attention. Hearing is not complete without obedience. Jesus said this is how I live my life as man on earth: "I do exactly what my Father has commanded me" (John 14:31). Jesus connected obeying with remaining in his Father. "If you obey my commands, you will remain in my love, just as I have obeyed my Father's commands and remain in his love" (John 15:10). We want our spirit and our soul to be present to God, but it starts with our spirit being willing not to go our own way. From John 7:17 comes a personal prayer: "I am willing to be made willing." Then we are clear to hear from God with our spirit and lead our soul to submit its will to him. Sometimes it is a struggle to tune out competing desires, but when our heart is single, when we are not double-minded and unstable in all our ways, the unity of spirit with Spirit is a beautiful place to remain.

4. Be intentional.

Be aware of the difference between your spirit and your soul. The soul wants to be in charge and take the place of the spirit, and most people cannot distinguish between the two. The Bible says there will be a tug-of-war between spirit and soul. Make the choice not to let your soul rule to follow its desires. Stop feeding the soul. The soul is the flesh, and we cannot please God when we are in the flesh. We are to put on Christ and make no provision for the flesh. You may have to turn off TV or talk radio. Don't listen to gossip or questionable music. Be intentional to seek God's best. Choose to look with your spirit to the Holy Spirit as the Source of control. We cannot talk about our spirit apart from Christ in us.

5. Get healing for soul wounds.

In the absence of real diligence, our selfish, wounded soul will want its own way, and the enemy will do everything he can to aid and abet it. Our soul and body may respond out of past wounds with a tone of voice, a shrug, a stare, or rolling the eyes. We need healing to be complete spirit, soul, and body, so that the spirit can speak loudly enough to be heard and engage the soul and body in a righteous way. That's the secret to righteous living.

6. Emphasize cooperation between soul and spirit.

Our soul is not bad, because God made it. When our spirit engages our soul in loving others or serving God, there is a big difference in how we feel and the life-giving quality of our actions. Our ultimate goal today is to please God, to show Christlikeness in our life. We can't do that alone. We need to be complete spirit, soul, and body for others to see Christ in us. To do that, we can't give in to the unholy demands of soul and body. Are all their demands unholy? Of course not. Our desire for a bowl of ice cream may make our Father smile, but it might not. That's why we keep our face turned to him for his approval. We want our soul to be in righteous relationship with our spirit. When our spirit is in right relationship with God and takes righteous leadership, our soul is more receptive to following for its own good. But it is pesky and wants its own way.

To live a spirit-led life, we choose to let Christ live through us through the power of the Holy Spirit. Does my spirit direct my life, or does Christ live through me, or do I live by the Spirit? The answer is "yes." This is not a "religious" answer. It is the key to understanding the growth of our spirit. We have tried to live in the Spirit with our soul, and the result is living like a yo-yo, up and down, moving in and out of our spirit being in leadership. Consistent success is possible when our spirit rises up and takes it righteous place.

7. Make **Blessing A Lifestyle.**

God has been preparing us with a huge deep deposit from which to overflow to others. It is wonderful to be enlarged by large-spirited people. We are also enlarged by ministering to others whose spirits are eager to grow and thrive. A seminary professor had a bicycle accident, in which he was seriously injured. After months of rehabilitation and various medications, he still felt such severe pain that it hindered his studying and teaching. An $80 massage three times a week was the only means of keeping his pain under control. But how to afford it? He decided to take massage therapy lessons. In class as they were practicing giving a massage to each other, he discovered that giving a massage alleviated his pain as much as receiving one. So he gave three massages a week, and his pain problem was solved.

So it is with blessing. We are blessed every time we bless others. God told Abraham he was blessed to be a blessing. It's a circle. We can't out-give God's blessings. The more blessings we give, the more return to us. Read the piece by Jill Carattini on page 18 about our call to scatter blessings. We have authority in Jesus as a priest to bless.

You might ask, "Why don't you just pray for people?" Blessing does not replace praying. It is a totally different investment in our lives. Blessing is speaking on behalf of God the desires of his heart for another person. Blessing requires active listening to God's heart for others. If we are to live from the Spirit where Jesus dwells in us, our spirits must be enlarged to experience more of him, in listening, in loving, and in obeying. We have real intimacy with God in the deepest place of who we are from our spirits, because God is spirit. Blessing someone's spirit benefits the person in a different way than praying for them. Truth is already revealed in Scripture, such as the truth that we are the beloved of God in Christ Jesus. It is more powerful to speak that truth to the person's spirit, "I bless you as the beloved of God," rather than asking God to show his love to the person. It speaks with more power, precision, and clarity and leaves less room for the person's soul or mind to doubt that God loves them when you say, "You are the beloved," instead of "God, please show them that you love them."

You might wonder, "I read my Bible and pray, so why do I need to do this?" Often we read and pray with our minds, and our spirit is not engaged. God by his Spirit wants to minister truth to our human spirit. God designed for the spirit to be in control and guide us under his lordship. Listen to God in his Word and by his Spirit for his purposes for his children. Seek his heart for the needs of the specific person. You might start with one of your favorite promises or a verse that God highlights that speaks of his intentions for abundant life. Wait and listen to what God is saying about his design and purposes for the person, in the person, and through the person.

Think blessing. Think being a blessing and giving a blessing. Incorporate blessing into your way of life. Pass it on. So many weary people need the refreshment of a simple blessing. Bless them with the fullness of God's love and grace.

Getting Started Developing A Lifestyle Of Blessing

Begin your journey of blessing others with your own blessings. The Bible is your best source of blessings.

1. Read a verse or passage with your spirit (see page 89). Maybe read from more than one translation. The process starts with engaging your spirit in reading, asking questions, and listening. Let's use 2 Corinthians 9:8 as an example. "God is able to make all grace abound to you, so that in all things at all times, having all that you need, you will abound in every good work."

2. Make the verse personal first. Think about who God is for you... able, gracious, available, giving. Engage your spirit in processing what that means to you. Ask God questions, "What does this mean? What do you want to show me? What do you want to reveal about yourself?" You might think about these personal applications: I have everything I need for every circumstance. I have it when I need it. I am blessed by God's graciousness which he gives me all the time.

3. Let God lead you in forming a blessing. Ask, "How do you want me to apply what you are saying as a blessing for my friend who has a need today?" Invite their spirit to hear the verse. Then start with God, what he says about himself in the verse. Then expand it to what he promises for the person because of who he is for them, in them, and through them, if applicable. This might be your blessing from 2 Corinthians 9:8.

Listen, spirit, to the Word of God for you in 2 Corinthians 9:8. "God is able to make all grace abound to you, so that in all things at all times, having all that you need, you will abound in every good work." Spirit, your Father is the God of all grace which he gives to you in unlimited supply. Be blessed today to know that he provides for you generously from the fullness of himself. Out of his gracious provision, he will give you everything you need when you need it for every circumstance you are facing today. Be blessed to rest assured that he is watching out for you at all times in every way. Be blessed to know that you will lack nothing in him. Be blessed as he works in you the peace and certainty that everything he ordains for you he abundantly provides. No need of yours strains his resources. You don't depend on yourself or others, because God gives you all his abundant grace. Your dependency is on his loving favor. You are blessed with his grace in every aspect of your life at all times. Be blessed with freely having all that you need for everything God calls you to do. Be blessed in the name of the all-sufficient One.

On the following pages, write blessings God gives you, and pass them on! As you bless, you will see that spirits are awakened, nurtured, encouraged, and strengthened. And blessing others will do for you what it does for them!

Blessings

Blessings

Blessings

Scriptures And Resources

Scriptural Foundation For The Human Spirit

For God, who said, "Let light shine out of darkness,"
made his light shine in our hearts
to give us the light of the knowledge of the glory of God in the face of Christ.
But we have this treasure in jars of clay
to show that this all-surpassing power is from God and not from us.
2 Corinthians 4:6-7

God Is Spirit

John 4:24 God is spirit, and those who worship Him must worship in spirit and truth.

One Of The Names Of God Is God Of The Spirits Of All Mankind.
Numbers 16:22 Moses and Aaron fell facedown and cried out, "O God, God of the spirits of all mankind, will you be angry with the entire assembly when only one man sins?"
Numbers 27:16 May the LORD, the God of the spirits of all mankind, appoint a man over this community.

He Is Also Called Father Of Our Spirits.
Hebrews 12:9 How much more should we submit to the Father of our spirits and live!

Christ Became A Life-Giving Spirit.
1 Corinthians 15:45 "The first man Adam became a living being." The last Adam became a life-giving spirit.
Romans 8:10 But if Christ is in you, your body is dead because of sin, yet your spirit is alive because of righteousness.
Mark 2:8 Immediately Jesus knew in his spirit that this was what they were thinking in their hearts…
Luke 23:46 Jesus called out with a loud voice, "Father, into your hands I commit my spirit."

The Holy Spirit, The Third Person Of The Trinity, Gives Life.
Genesis 1:2 AMP ... the Spirit of God was moving (hovering, brooding) over the face of the waters.
Job 33:4 The Spirit of God has made me; the breath of the Almighty gives me life.
John 6:63 The Spirit gives life… The words I have spoken to you are spirit and they are life.
Romans 8:15-16 For you did not receive a spirit that makes you a slave again to fear, but you received the Spirit of sonship. And by him we cry, "*Abba,* Father." The Spirit himself testifies with our spirit that we are God's children.

What Is The Human Spirit?
The Origin And Nature Of The Human Spirit

We have a human spirit.
Ecclesiastes 12:7 The spirit returns to God who gave it.

God formed our spirit.
Genesis 1:26 Then God said, "Let us make man in our image, in our likeness..."
Genesis 2:7 The LORD God formed the man from the dust of the ground and breathed into his nostrils the breath of life, and the man became a living being.
Psalm 139:13 You created my inmost being; you knit me together in my mother's womb.
Zechariah 12:1 The LORD... who forms the spirit of man within him...
Ecclesiastes 11:5 KJV As thou knowest not what is the way of the spirit, nor how the bones do grow in the womb of her that is with child: even so thou knowest not the works of God who maketh all.

The human spirit receives the life of God.
1 Corinthians 6:17 But he who unites himself with the Lord is one with him in spirit.
Job 34:14-15 If it were his intention and he withdrew his spirit and breath,
all mankind would perish together and man would return to the dust.

God's spirit reveals who we really are in our inmost being.
Proverbs 20:27 The lamp of the LORD searches the spirit of a man; it searches out his inmost being.

Our spirit serves God.
Romans 1:9 NKJV God is my witness, whom I serve with my spirit in the gospel of His Son...

God's Spirit marks our spirit as his.
Romans 8:16 The Spirit himself testifies with our spirit that we are God's children.

Our spirit knows us.
1 Corinthians 2:11 Who among men knows the thoughts of a man except the man's spirit within him? In the same way no one knows the thoughts of God except the Spirit of God.

Our spirit sustains our life.
Proverbs 18:14 A man's spirit sustains him in sickness, but a crushed spirit who can bear?
James 2:26 ... the body without the spirit is dead...

We glorify God with our body and spirit.
1 Corinthians 6:20 NKJV For you were bought at a price; therefore glorify God in your body and in your spirit, which are God's.

We worship with our spirit.
John 4:24 God is spirit, and his worshipers must worship in spirit and in truth.
1 Corinthians 14:16 If you are praising God with your spirit...

The Scriptures Confirm That We Have An Inner Being

Psalm 51:6 Surely you desire truth in the inner parts; you teach me wisdom in the inmost place.

Psalm 103:1 Praise the LORD, O my soul; all my inmost being, praise his holy name.

Psalm 139:13 You created my inmost being…

Proverbs 23:16 My inmost being will rejoice when your lips speak what is right.

Proverbs 26:22 The words of a gossip are like choice morsels; they go down to a man's inmost parts.

Proverbs 20:27 The lamp of the LORD searches the spirit of a man; it searches out his inmost being.

Luke 1:51 He has scattered those who are proud in their inmost thoughts.

1 Peter 3:4 Instead, it should be that of your inner self, the unfading beauty of a gentle and quiet spirit, which is of great worth in God's sight.

Romans 7:22 For in my inner being I delight in God's law;

2 Corinthians 4:16 NKJV Therefore we do not lose heart. Even though our outward man is perishing, yet the inward man is being renewed day by day.

Ephesians 3:16 I pray that out of his glorious riches he may strengthen you with power through his Spirit in your inner being…

Is There A Difference Between Soul And Spirit?

The Bible recognizes three separate entities in one person.
I Thessalonians 5:23 May the God himself, the God of peace, sanctify you through and through. May your whole spirit, soul and body be kept blameless at the coming of the Lord Jesus Christ.

Spirit can be distinguished from soul.
Hebrews 4:12 For the word of God is living and active. Sharper than any double-edged sword, it penetrates even to dividing soul and spirit, joints and marrow; it judges the thoughts and attitudes of the heart.

The soul is not bad, because God has a soul.
Jeremiah 32:36,41 This is what the LORD, the God of Israel, says… I will rejoice in doing them good and will assuredly plant them in this land with all my heart and soul.

Jesus had a soul.
Matthew 26:38 Then he said to them, "My soul is overwhelmed with sorrow to the point of death. Stay here and keep watch with me."

Traits And Characteristics Of The Spirit And Soul

Alive
Romans 8:10 But if Christ is in you … your spirit is alive because of righteousness.

Anger
Ecclesiastes 7:9 NKJV Do not hasten in your spirit to be angry, for anger rests in the bosom of fools.
Ezekiel 3:14 The Spirit then lifted me up and took me away, and I went in bitterness and in the anger of my spirit, with the strong hand of the LORD upon me.

In Anguish
Job 7:11 Therefore I will not keep silent; I will speak out in the anguish of my spirit, I will complain in the bitterness of my soul.
1 Samuel 1:10 NKJV And she was in bitterness of soul, and prayed to the LORD and wept in anguish.
Genesis 42:21 NKJV "We are truly guilty concerning our brother, for we saw the anguish of his soul when he pleaded with us, and we would not hear; therefore this distress has come upon us."
Exodus 6:9 NKJV Moses spoke thus to the children of Israel; but they did not heed Moses, because of anguish of spirit and cruel bondage.

Answers
Job 20:3 NKJV I have heard the rebuke that reproaches me, and the spirit of my understanding causes me to answer.

Anxious
Daniel 2:3 NKJV And the king said to them, "I have had a dream, and my spirit is anxious to know the dream."

Become strong
Luke 1:80 And the child grew and became strong in spirit; and he lived in the desert until he appeared publicly to Israel.
Luke 2:40 NKJV And the Child grew and became strong in spirit, filled with wisdom; and the grace of God was upon Him.

Bitterness
1 Samuel 1:10 NKJV And she was in bitterness of soul, and prayed to the LORD and wept in anguish.
1 Samuel 30:6 David was greatly distressed because the men were talking of stoning him; each one was bitter in spirit because of his sons and daughters. But David found strength in the LORD his God.

Blessing
1 Corinthians 14:16 NKJV Otherwise, if you bless with the spirit, how will he who occupies the place of the uninformed say "Amen" at your giving of thanks, since he does not understand what you say?
Genesis 27:4 NKJV "And make me savory food, such as I love, and bring it to me that I may eat, that my soul may bless you before I die."
Psalms 103:2 NKJV Bless the LORD, O my soul, and forget not all his benefits…

Broken

Psalms 51:17 The sacrifices of God are a broken spirit; a broken and a contrite heart, O God, you will not despise.

Job 17:1 My spirit is broken, my days are cut short, the grave awaits me.

Proverbs 17:22 NKJV A merry heart does good, like medicine, but a broken spirit dries the bones.

Isaiah 65:14 My servants will sing out of the joy of their hearts, but you will cry out from anguish of heart and wail in brokenness of spirit.

Psalm 76:12 He breaks the spirit of rulers; he is feared by the kings of the earth.

Calm

Proverbs 17:27 NKJV A man of understanding is of a calm spirit.

Committed to God

Psalm 31:5 Into your hands I commit my spirit; redeem me, O LORD, the God of truth.

Luke 23:46 Jesus called out with a loud voice, "Father, into your hands I commit my spirit." Then he had said this, he breathed his last.

Compels

Job 32:18 I am full of words, and the spirit within me compels me.

Contaminated

2 Corinthians 7:1 Since we have these promises, dear friends, let us purify ourselves from everything that contaminates body and spirit, perfecting holiness out of reverence for God.

Contrite

Psalm 34:18 NKJV The LORD is near to those who have a broken heart, and saves such as have a contrite spirit.

Isaiah 66:2 "This is the one I esteem: he who is humble and contrite in spirit, and trembles at my word."

Isaiah 57:15 NKJV For thus says the High and Lofty One who inhabits eternity, whose name is Holy: "I dwell in the high and holy place, with him who has a contrite and humble spirit, to revive the spirit of the humble, and to revive the heart of the contrite ones."

Created by God

Psalm 139:13 You created my inmost being; you knit me together in my mother's womb.

Crushed

Psalm 34:18 The LORD is close to the brokenhearted and saves those who are crushed in spirit.

Proverbs 15:4 The tongue that brings healing is a tree of life, but a deceitful tongue crushes the spirit.

Proverbs 15:13 A happy heart makes the face cheerful, but heartache crushes the spirit.

Proverbs 17:22 A cheerful heart is good medicine, but a crushed spirit dries up the bones.

Defiled by gossip

Proverbs 18:8 The words of a gossip are like choice morsels; they go down to a man's inmost parts.

Delights in God's law

Romans 7:22 For in my inner being I delight in God's law.

Despairing
Isaiah 61:3 … for those who grieve in Zion— to bestow on them a crown of beauty instead of ashes, the oil of gladness instead of mourning, and a garment of praise instead of a spirit of despair.

Devoted to the Lord
1 Corinthians 7:34 An unmarried woman or virgin is … to be devoted to the Lord in both body and spirit.

Different
Numbers 14:24 Because my servant Caleb has a different spirit and follows me wholeheartedly, I will bring him into the land he went to, and his descendants will inherit it.

Distinguished from soul
Hebrews 4:12 For the word of God is living and active. Sharper than any double-edged sword, it penetrates even to dividing soul and spirit, joints and marrow; it judges the thoughts and attitudes of the heart.

Distressed
Isaiah 54:6 "The LORD will call you back as if you were a wife deserted and distressed in spirit— a wife who married young, only to be rejected," says your God.

An example
1 Timothy 4:12 NKJV Let no one despise your youth, but be an example to the believers in word, in conduct, in love, in spirit, in faith, in purity.

Excellent
Daniel 5:12 NKJV Inasmuch as an excellent spirit, knowledge, understanding, interpreting dreams, solving riddles, and explaining enigmas were found in this Daniel …
Daniel 6:3 NKJV Daniel distinguished himself above the governors and satraps, because an excellent spirit was in him…

Fails
Psalm 143:7 Answer me quickly, O LORD; my spirit fails.

Faints
Ezekiel 21:7 "Every heart will melt and every hand go limp; every spirit will become faint and every knee become as weak as water."
Psalm 77:3 I remembered you, O God, and I groaned; I mused, and my spirit grew faint.
Psalm 142:3 When my spirit grows faint within me, it is you who know my way.
Psalm 143:4 So my spirit grows faint within me; my heart within me is dismayed.
Isaiah 57:16 I will not accuse forever, nor will I always be angry, for then the spirit of man would grow faint before me— the breath of man that I have created.

Faithful
Proverbs 11:13 NKJV He who is of a faithful spirit conceals a matter.

False
Micah 2:11 NKJV If a man should walk in a false spirit and speak a lie, saying, 'I will prophesy to you of wine and drink,' even he would be the prattler of this people.

Fearful
2 Tim. 1:7 NKJV God has not given us a spirit of fear, but of power and of love and of a sound mind.
Acts 2:43 NKJV Then fear came upon every soul, and many wonders and signs were done through the apostles.

Fervent
Acts 18:25 NKJV This man had been instructed in the way of the Lord; and being fervent in spirit, he spoke and taught accurately the things of the Lord, though he knew only the baptism of John.
Romans 12:11 NKJV ... Not lagging in diligence, fervent in spirit, serving the Lord...

Finds life
Isaiah 38:16 Lord, by such things men live; and my spirit finds life in them too.
You restored me to health and let me live.

Follow their own spirit
Ezekiel 13:3 This is what the Sovereign LORD says: "Woe to the foolish prophets who follow their own spirit and have seen nothing!"

Formed by God
Zechariah 12:1 The LORD, who stretches out the heavens, who lays the foundation of the earth, and who forms the spirit of man within him, declares…

Gentle
1 Corinthians 4:21 Shall I come to you with a whip, or in love and with a gentle spirit?
Galatians 6:1 Brethren, if a man is overtaken in any trespass, you who are spiritual restore such a one in a spirit of gentleness, considering yourself lest you also be tempted.

Gentle And Quiet
1 Peter 3:4 Instead, it should be that of your inner self, the unfading beauty of a gentle and quiet spirit, which is of great worth in God's sight.
1 Peter 3:4 NKJV … rather let it be the hidden person of the heart, with the incorruptible beauty of a gentle and quiet spirit…

Give understanding
Job 32:8 It is the spirit in a man, the breath of the Almighty, that gives him understanding.

Given up
Matthew 27:50 And when Jesus had cried out again in a loud voice, he gave up his spirit.
John 19:30 When he had received the drink, Jesus said, "It is finished." With that, he bowed his head and gave up his spirit.

Glorify God
1 Corinthians 6:20 NKJV For you were bought at a price; therefore glorify God in your body and in your spirit, which are God's.

Grieved
Daniel 7:15 I, Daniel, was grieved in my spirit within my body, and the visions of my head troubled me.
Isaiah 54:6 NKJV "For the LORD has called you like a woman forsaken and grieved in spirit, like a youthful wife when you were refused," says your God.

Isaiah 65:14 NKJV Behold, My servants shall sing for joy of heart, but you shall cry for sorrow of heart, and wail for grief of spirit.
1 Samuel 30:6 NKJV David was greatly distressed, for the people spoke of stoning him, because the soul of all the people was grieved, every man for his sons and his daughters.

Groans
John 11:33 NKJV When Jesus saw her weeping, and the Jews who came with her weeping, He groaned in the spirit and was troubled.

Guarded
Malachi 2:15 Has not the LORD made them one? In flesh and spirit they are his. And why one? Because he was seeking godly offspring. So guard yourself in your spirit, and do not break faith with the wife of your youth.

Hardened
Deuteronomy 2:30 "Sihon king of Heshbon would not let us pass through, for the LORD your God hardened his spirit and made his heart obstinate…"
Daniel 5:20 NKJV But when his heart was lifted up, and his spirit was hardened in pride, he was deposed from his kingly throne, and they took his glory from him.

Haughty
Proverbs 16:18 Pride goes before destruction, a haughty spirit before a fall.

Heavy
Isaiah 61:3 NKJV To console those who mourn in Zion, to give them beauty for ashes, the oil of joy for mourning, the garment of praise for the spirit of heaviness; That they may be called trees of righteousness, the planting of the LORD, that He may be glorified.
Psalm 119:28 NKJV My soul melts from heaviness; Strengthen me according to Your word.

Humble
Proverbs 16:19 NKJV Better to be of a humble spirit with the lowly, than to divide the spoil with the proud.
Proverbs 29:23 NKJV The humble in spirit will retain honor.
Psalm 35:13 NASB I humbled my soul with fasting…

Inquiring
Psalm 77:6 I remembered my songs in the night. My heart mused and my spirit inquired…

Joyful
Colossians 2:5 NKJV … I [am] with you in the spirit, rejoicing to see your good order and the steadfastness of your faith in Christ.
Psalm 35:9 Then my soul will rejoice in the LORD and delight in his salvation.

Kept blameless
1 Thessalonians 5:23 May God himself, the God of peace, sanctify you through and through. May your whole spirit, soul and body be kept blameless at the coming of our Lord Jesus Christ.

Knows the thoughts of a man
Mark 2:8 Immediately Jesus knew in his spirit that this was what they were thinking in their hearts, and he said to them, "Why are you thinking these things?
1 Corinthians 2:11 For who among men knows the thoughts of a man except the man's spirit within him? In the same way no one knows the thoughts of God except the Spirit of God.

Knows we are fearfully and wonderfully made
Psalm 139:14 NKJV I will praise You, for I am fearfully and wonderfully made; Marvelous are Your works, and that my soul knows very well.

Laments
Isaiah 16:11 My heart laments for Moab like a harp, my inmost being for Kir Hareseth.

Life-giving
1 Corinthians 15:45 So it is written: "The first man Adam became a living being"; the last Adam, a life-giving spirit.

Longs for God
Isaiah 26:9 My soul yearns for you in the night; in the morning my spirit longs for you. When your judgments come upon the earth, the people of the world learn righteousness.

Loves
2 Timothy 1:7 For God did not give us a spirit of timidity, but a spirit of power, of love and of self-discipline.
Deuteronomy 6:5 Love the LORD your God with all your heart and with all your soul and with all your strength.

Lowly
Proverbs 16:19 Better to be lowly in spirit and among the oppressed than to share plunder with the proud.
Proverbs 29:23 A man's pride brings him low, but a man of lowly spirit gains honor.
Isaiah 57:15 For this is what the high and lofty One says— he who lives forever, whose name is holy: "I live in a high and holy place, but also with him who is contrite and lowly in spirit, to revive the spirit of the lowly and to revive the heart of the contrite."

Made perfect
Hebrews 12:23 You have come to God, the judge of all men, to the spirits of righteous men made perfect…

Moved
Ezra 1:5 … with all whose spirits God had moved, arose to go up and build the house of the Lord which is in Jerusalem.
John 11:33 When Jesus saw her weeping, and the Jews who had come along with her also weeping, he was deeply moved in spirit and troubled.

New
Ezekiel 11:19 I will give them an undivided heart and put a new spirit in them; I will remove from them their heart of stone and give them a heart of flesh.
Ezekiel 18:31 Rid yourselves of all the offenses you have committed, and get a new heart and a new spirit. Why will you die, O house of Israel?
Ezekiel 36:26 I will give you a new heart and put a new spirit in you… I will remove from you your heart of stone and give you a heart of flesh.

No deceit
Psalm 32:2 Blessed is the man whose sin the LORD does not count against him and in whose spirit is no deceit.

No rest
2 Corinthians 2:13 NKJV I had no rest in my spirit, because I did not find Titus my brother; but taking my leave of them, I departed for Macedonia.

Not exploitive
2 Corinthians 12:18 I urged Titus to go to you and I sent our brother with him. Titus did not exploit you, did he? Did we not act in the same spirit and follow the same course?

One with the Lord
1 Corinthians 6:17 But he who unites himself with the Lord is one with him in spirit.

Overwhelmed
Psalm 77:3 NKJV I remembered God, and was troubled; I complained, and my spirit was overwhelmed.
Psalm 142:3 NKJV When my spirit was overwhelmed within me, then You knew my path. Therefore my spirit is overwhelmed within me; My heart within me is distressed.
Psalm 143:4 NKJV Then the waters had overwhelmed us, the stream had gone over our soul.
Matthew 26:38 Then [Jesus] said to them, "My soul is overwhelmed with sorrow to the point of death. Stay here and keep watch with me."

Passed to someone else
2 Kings 2:9 When they had crossed, Elijah said to Elisha, "Tell me, what can I do for you before I am taken from you?" "Let me inherit a double portion of your spirit," Elisha replied.
2 Kings 2:15 The company of the prophets from Jericho, who were watching, said, "The spirit of Elijah is resting on Elisha." And they went to meet him and bowed to the ground before him.

Patient
Ecclesiastes 7:8 NKJV The patient in spirit is better than the proud in spirit.

Poisoned
Job 6:4 The arrows of the Almighty are in me, my spirit drinks in their poison.

Poor
Matthew 5:3 Blessed are the poor in spirit, for theirs is the kingdom of heaven.

Praises God
Psalm 103:1 Praise the LORD, O my soul; all my inmost being, praise his holy name.
Psalm 146:1 Praise the LORD. Praise the LORD, O my soul.
1 Corinthians 14:16 If you are praising God with your spirit…

Pray and sing
1 Corinthians 14:14 For if I pray in a tongue, my spirit prays, but my mind is unfruitful.
1 Corinthians 14:15 I will pray with my spirit, but I will also pray with my mind; I will sing with my spirit, but I will also sing with my mind.

Present in spirit
1 Corinthians 5:3-4 Even though I am not physically present, I am with you in spirit. And I have already passed judgment on the one who did this, just as if I were present. When you are assembled in the name of our Lord Jesus and I am with you in spirit, and the power of our Lord Jesus is present…
Colossians 2:5 For though I am absent from you in body, I am present with you in spirit and delight to see how orderly you are and how firm your faith in Christ is.

Proud
Luke 1:51 He has scattered those who are proud in their inmost thoughts.
Ecclesiastes 7:8 NKJV The patient in spirit is better than the proud in spirit.

Provoked
Ecclesiastes 7:9 Do not be quickly provoked in your spirit, for anger resides in the lap of fools.
Acts 17:16 NKJV While Paul waited for them at Athens, his spirit was provoked within him when he saw that the city was given over to idols.

Refreshed
Proverbs 25:13 Like the coolness of snow at harvest time is a trustworthy messenger to those who send him; he refreshes the spirit of his masters.
1 Corinthians 16:18 They refreshed my spirit and yours also. Such men deserve recognition.
2 Corinthians 7:13 By all this we are encouraged. In addition to our own encouragement, we were especially delighted to see how happy Titus was, because his spirit has been refreshed by all of you.

Receive truth and wisdom
Psalm 51:6 Surely you desire truth in the inner parts; you teach me wisdom in the inmost place.

Received by God
Acts 7:59 While they were stoning him, Stephen prayed, "Lord Jesus, receive my spirit."

Rejoices
Proverbs 23:16 My inmost being will rejoice when your lips speak what is right.
Luke 1:46-47 Mary said: "My soul glorifies the Lord and my spirit rejoices in God my Savior."

Renewed
Ephesians 4:23 NKJV Be renewed in the spirit of your mind...
2 Corinthians 4:16 NKJV Therefore we do not lose heart. Even though our outward man is perishing, yet the inward man is being renewed day by day.

Return
Luke 8:55 Her spirit returned, and at once she stood up.

Revived
Genesis 45:27 When they told him everything Joseph had said to them, and when he saw the carts Joseph had sent to carry him back, the spirit of their father Jacob revived.
Isaiah 57:15 "I live in a high and holy place, but also with him who is contrite and lowly in spirit, to revive the spirit of the lowly and to revive the heart of the contrite."

Rises against you
Ecclesiastes 10:4 NKJV If the spirit of the ruler rises against you, do not leave your post; for conciliation pacifies great offenses.

Ruled
Proverbs 16:32 NKJV He who is slow to anger is better than the mighty, and he who rules his spirit than he who takes a city.

Sanctified
1 Thessalonians 5:23 NKJV Now may the God of peace Himself sanctify you completely; and may your whole spirit, soul, and body be preserved blameless at the coming of our Lord Jesus Christ.

Saved
1 Corinthians 5:5 Hand this man over to Satan, so that the sinful nature may be destroyed and his spirit saved on the day of the Lord.
James 5:20 NKJV Let him know that he who turns a sinner from the error of his way will save a soul from death and cover a multitude of sins.

Searched by the Lord
Proverbs 20:27 The lamp of the LORD searches the spirit of a man; it searches out his inmost being.

Serve
Romans 1:9 NKJV God is my witness, whom I serve with my spirit in the gospel of His Son, that without ceasing I make mention of you always in my prayers…

Sighs deeply
Mark 8:12 NKJV He sighed deeply in His spirit, and said, "Why does this generation seek a sign? Assuredly, I say to you, no sign shall be given to this generation."

Sorrowful
1 Samuel 1:15 NKJV Hannah answered and said, "No, my lord, I am a woman of sorrowful spirit. I … have poured out my soul before the LORD."
Jeremiah 31:25 NKJV I have satiated the weary soul, and I have replenished every sorrowful soul.
Matthew 26:38 Then he said to them, "My soul is overwhelmed with sorrow to the point of death. Stay here and keep watch with me."

Steadfast
Psalm 51:10 Create in me a pure heart, O God, and renew a steadfast spirit within me.

Strengthened
Ephesians 3:16 I pray that out of his glorious riches he may strengthen you with power through his Spirit in your inner being…

Stirred up
1 Chronicles 5:26 So the God of Israel stirred up the spirit of Pul king of Assyria…
2 Chronicles 21:16 NKJV Moreover the Lord stirred up against Jehoram the spirit of the Philistines and the Arabians who were near the Ethiopians.
Ezra 1:1 Now in the first year of Cyrus king of Persia, that the word of the Lord by the mouth of Jeremiah might be fulfilled, the Lord stirred up the spirit of Cyrus king of Persia…

Stubborn
Deuteronomy 2:30 For the LORD your God had made his spirit stubborn and his heart obstinate in order to give him into your hands, as he has now done.

Stuporous
Romans 11:8 As it is written: "God gave them a spirit of stupor, eyes so that they could not see and ears so that they could not hear, to this very day."

Subject to the prophets
1 Corinthians 14:32 The spirits of prophets are subject to the control of prophets.

Sullen
1 Kings 21:5 NKJV Jezebel his wife and said to him, "Why is your spirit so sullen that you eat no food?"

Sustains him
Proverbs 18:14 A man's spirit sustains him in sickness, but a crushed spirit who can bear?

Timid, or powerful, loving and self-disciplined
2 Timothy 1:7 For God did not give us a spirit of timidity, but a spirit of power, of love and of self-discipline.

Troubled
John 12:27 NKJV "Now is my soul troubled; and what shall I say?"
John 13:21 After he had said this, Jesus was troubled in spirit and testified, "I tell you the truth, one of you is going to betray me."
Genesis 41:8 NKJV Now it came to pass in the morning that his spirit was troubled, and he sent and called for all the magicians of Egypt and all its wise men.
Daniel 2:1 NKJV Now in the second year of Nebuchadnezzar's reign, Nebuchadnezzar had dreams; and his spirit was so troubled that his sleep left him.

Turned against God
Job 15:13 NKJV … You turn your spirit against God, and let such words go out of your mouth…

Unfaithful
Psalm 78:8 They would not be like their forefathers— a stubborn and rebellious generation, whose hearts were not loyal to God, whose spirits were not faithful to him.

United
Philippians 1:27 Whatever happens, conduct yourselves in a manner worthy of the gospel of Christ. Then, whether I come and see you or only hear about you in my absence, I will know that you stand firm in one spirit, contending as one man for the faith of the gospel

Unruled
Proverbs 25:28 NKJV Whoever has no rule over his own spirit is like a city broken down, without walls.

Utters mysteries
1 Corinthians 14:2 For anyone who speaks in a tongue does not speak to men but to God. Indeed, no one understands him; he utters mysteries with his spirit.

Watched over
Job 10:12 You gave me life and showed me kindness, and in your providence watched over my spirit.

Wayward
Isaiah 29:24 Those who are wayward in spirit will gain understanding.

Weighed by the Lord
Proverbs 16:2 NKJV All the ways of a man are pure in his own eyes, but the Lord weighs the spirits.

Willing
Psalm 51:12 Restore to me the joy of your salvation and grant me a willing spirit, to sustain me.
Matthew 26:41 Watch and pray, lest you enter into temptation. The spirit indeed is willing, but the flesh is weak.
Exodus 35:21 NKJV Then everyone came whose heart was stirred, and everyone whose spirit was willing, and they brought the LORD's offering for the work of the tabernacle of meeting, for all its service, and for the holy garments.

Worships
John 4:23 Yet a time is coming and has now come when the true worshipers will worship the Father in spirit and truth, for they are the kind of worshipers the Father seeks.
John 4:24 God is spirit, and his worshipers must worship in spirit and in truth.

Benedictions

The Lord be with your spirit. Grace be with you. 2 Timothy 4:22
The grace of the Lord Jesus Christ be with your spirit. Philemon 25
The grace of our Lord Jesus Christ be with your spirit, brothers. Amen.
Galatians 6:18
The grace of the Lord Jesus be with your spirit. Philippians 4:23

New from The Father's Business

13 week video based study for groups and individuals

RUACH JOURNEY

Ruach Journey is a chance for men and women to engage with scripture in order to understand how God created us to live with our spirit, soul, and body aligned with Father, Son, and Holy Spirit. This 13 week video based study will explore what has hindered us from living from the abundance that Jesus promised each of us as believers.

Ruach Journey includes practical ways to bless and nourish our spirits and also how to recognize when we are living in less than God designed. Ruach Journey is an invitation to discover the richness of the treasure He has placed in you - spirit, soul, and body. In this study, Sylvia Gunter and Elizabeth Gunter will take you deeper into the themes and concepts of You Are Blessed In The Names of God and Free To Be You.

Resources Available

Leader's Kit -
Contains one Study Guide, one Leader's Guide, Free To Be You, and a set of 8 DVDs.

Ruach Journey Study Guide -
13 weeks of interactive study including listening guides, discussion questions, and between session activities.

Blessings for Life

What may seem like a few simple words can bring hope and healing to very dry ground in yourself and others. That is what blessing the spirit is all about. As you bless your spirit and the spirit of others, you are nourishing what God has already planted deep inside.

This books contains a short teaching on the biblical foundation for blessing your spirit, soul, and body and 50 blessings of hope and healing for all of life. Some of the titles are:

Identity | Belonging | Worth | Peace | Ministry of Jesus

Physical Healing | Hope In Disappointment | Forgiveness

Healing From Trauma | Direction | Favor

What People Are Saying About Blessings For Life

"I love the Blessings for Life book!! It's a wonderful resource full of beautiful blessings for a variety of needs all perfectly ordered in one place. The teachings on spirit, soul and body make it a perfect way to share with others! LOVE!!"

"I lost my precious husband on Good Friday. In my grief I have been reading Blessings For Life. It helped me to realize the power of God's blessings and the meaning of these as well as how they apply to me personally. The book has helped me to focus on the positive aspects of my faith instead of the pain of my grief. It has led me to the Word and helped me to journal with a focus on a future with a purpose even though I have no idea what it is. Thank you!"

Also From The Father's Business...

* ***Prayer Portions***—360-page intercessory prayer manual with sections on praise, repentance, warfare, personal devotional life, and intercession. Practical resources to use in leading groups as well as challenge and encouragement in developing a well-rounded prayer life with your Father in heaven who delights to answer the prayer of his children.

* ***Daily Study Guide for Prayer Portions***— *The Daily Study Guide* directs you through *Prayer Portions* in 12 weeks of five days of assignments for each week. It is a companion study tool for *Prayer Portions.* Each day's assignment is in two parts: a minimum requirement and an optional Going Further section. It builds a solid foundation for a lifetime of prayer. Your journey of communicating with your Father is lifelong. *The Daily Study Guide* will point you to him as the first option of your heart, not your last resort. You may study it personally or with a group.

* ***For The Family and Por La Familia*** (Spanish)— a collection of vital prayer tools for husbands and wives, dads and moms, who want to know God's Word, obey His will, pray His heart, and see Him glorified in their families.

* ***Prayer Essentials For Living in His Presence, Vol. I***— 306 pages on worship, repentance, and spiritual warfare. Takes up where *Prayer Portions* leaves off, with deeper and more detailed understanding and tools on these foundational subjects. Provokes us to keep company with God, to hunger to become a house of prayer, to pray with a keen sense of His power and presence.

* ***Prayer Essentials For Living in His Presence, Vol. II***—344 pages on intimacy with God, intercession, and the Word of God as prerequisites for a life lived in His presence. Takes up where *Prayer Portions* leaves off with more encouragement and resources on these subjects. Encourages us into new intimacy with the Lord Jesus, stimulates us to live an intercessory life, sharpens our ears to hear Him in His living, active Word.

* ***Who I Am In Christ***— a 12-page booklet on who you are, what you have, and what you can do through your inheritance in your identity in Christ. The church today urgently needs to know two key foundational truths: who God is and who we are in Him.

* ***He Is The I AM***— a 12-page booklet with 365 names of God, featuring a teaching on praying the names of God and an application. The two most foundational truths the church needs to know today are who God is and who we are in Him.

* ***Praying Like Jabez***— a life-changing 31-day devotional guide to praying the five index prayers of 1 Chronicles 4:10 and applying their truth to growing in our life with God and in community with our families, our church, our neighbors, and our world.

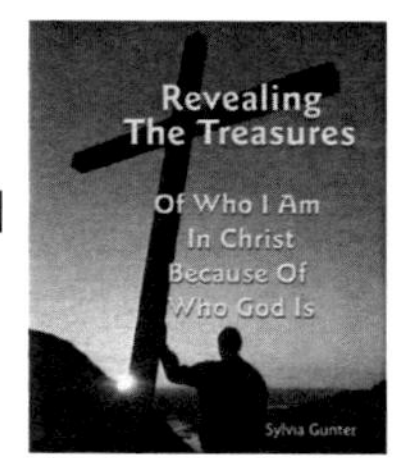

* ***Revealing The Treasures***— an A-to-Z alphabet of 445 truths of who God is and who we are in Him because of who He is with scriptures expressing these truths. For years people have been transformed through the truth in the booklets *Who I Am In Christ* and *He Is The I Am. Revealing The Treasures* blends these truths into a greatly expanded message. The unique format of this book allows you to study from the perspective of who God is or who you are in Christ.

* ***Nuggets Of The Treasures***— a 20-page excerpt from *Revealing The Treasures. Nuggets* is an introductory sampler of those truths about the wealth of your true identity as a beloved child of God.

* ***Daily Spirit Blessings***— a 20-page excerpt from *Blessing Your Spirit.* This booklet is an abbreviated sampler of all 61 blessings. This is a taste of the spirit to Spirit communion God has for us, as He settles our identity and legitimacy in Himself.

* ***Free To Be You***— God desires for you to discover the joy of living out of everything He has put in you for life and godliness. This journey will require peeling back some layers to get beyond what you do to why you do what you do. True freedom is waiting when you cease striving to fit in everyone else's box and become exactly who God designed you to be. This study of the gifts of Romans 12 includes profiles of each gift, Biblical character studies, interviews with each gift, and a blessing for each gift.

* ***Living In The Fullness Of The Trinity***— contains 175 prayer triplets that invite you deeper into the heart of God. Enrich your relationship with each Person of the Trinity and savor the richness of the Three in relationship with one another. Trinity praying is an invitation to enjoy talking to God in His completeness—Father, Son, and Holy Spirit.

* ***Safe In The Father's Heart: Finding The Father's Love You Have Always Wanted***— is an invitation to wholeness, peace, and joy as you live in God's delight in you as His child. This book is Sylvia's story of discovering and experiencing the Father heart of God. Her prayer is that God may speak to the hearts of many. God is powerful enough to create the universe and personal enough to delight in holding you in His Father heart. He is waiting to show you the depths of His love for you.

* ***Soldier's Psalm Card***— The text of Psalm 91 and the story of its use in World War I is printed on these laminated cards. It fits easily into a shirt pocket or helmet liner. This has become very dear to men and women in the military, law enforcement officers, and those who love them and pray for them. Units in the Middle East are praying this together daily, with 21st century proof of God's protecting hand in charge of precious lives in harm's way.

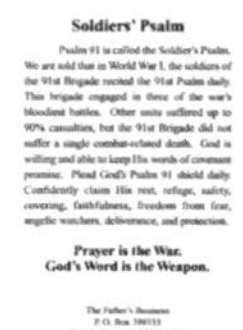
Soldiers' Psalm

Prayer is the War.
God's Word is the Weapon.

Get prices and order online on our website www.thefathersbusiness.com

The Father's Business • P.O. Box 380333 • Birmingham, AL 35238-0333

Email info@thefathersbusiness.com

